A NATURALIST'
BIR
OF
SINGAPORE

Text: **Yong Ding Li and Lim Kim Chuah**
Photography: **Lee Tiah Khee**
with contributions by Francis Yap and Con Foley

JOHN BEAUFOY PUBLISHING

Reprinted in 2023

This edition first published in the United Kingdom in 2017 by John Beaufoy Publishing
11 Blenheim Court, 316 Woodstock Road, Oxford OX2 7NS, England
www.johnbeaufoy.com

10 9 8 7 6 5

Photo Credits
Front cover: main Crimson Sunbird – National bird of Singapore (Lee Tiah Khee), *bottom left* Straw-headed Bulbul
(Lee Tiah Khee), *bottom centre* Red-legged Crake (Lee Tiah Khee), *bottom right* Violet Cuckoo (Francis Yap).
Inside back cover: top row, left to right: Yellow-crowned Bishop, Southern Red Bishop, Common Waxbill, Red
Avadavat, Orange-cheeked Waxbill (all Francis Yap); bottom row, left to right: Blue-winged Pitta (Con Foley),
Black Bittern, Chestnut-winged Cuckoo (Lee Tiah Khee)
Back cover: Stork-billed Kingfisher (Lee Tiah Khee)
Title page: Buffy Fish Owl (Lee Tiah Khee). **Contents page:** Olive-backed Sunbird (Lee Tiah Khee).
Main descriptions: All photos by Lee Tiah Khee except as detailed below. Photos are denoted by a page number
followed by t (top), b (bottom), l (left), r (right) or c (centre). **Shahril Ahmad** 114b; **Wang Bin** 35t; **Abdelhamid
Bizid** 45t, 88br, 136t, 139br, 144br, 157bl; **Cheng Heng Yee and Quek Oon Hong** 21c, 21b, 46b, 81b, 104b 122b,
154b; **Frankie Cheong** 31t, 56b, 144t, 144c; **Choy Wai Mun** 144bl; **Con Foley** 23b, 40b, 71b, 72tl, 72tr, 88tl,
90b, 108b, 119b, 131b, 140tl, 146tl, 146tr, 149bl, 150tr, 151tl, 152b; **John and Jemi Holmes** 94t, 123b; **Raphaël
Jordan** 126t; **Jennifer Leung** 109bl; **Lim Kim Chuah** 88tr, 115b; **Lim Kim Seng** 72br; **Yann Muzika** 37t; **Alan
OwYong** 15; **Ronald Orenstein** 152t; **Seetoh Yew Wai** 147b; **Andrew Tan** 72bl; **Tan Gim Cheong** 61t; **Myron Tay**
158b; **Michelle and Peter Wong** 37bl, 85bl; **Francis Yap** 12, 13, 20t, 22t, 24t, 26bl, 28t, 33bl, 36t, 38tr, 39tl, 39b,
40t, 41tl, 41b, 54t, 55t, 58b, 66b, 69t, 73bl, 76b, 77b, 78t, 79b, 80b, 81t, 82t, 83b, 86bl, 86br, 88b, 91b, 93t, 95b,
99b, 101t, 103bl, 106t, 109br, 111b, 114tl, 114tr, 121t, 123t, 124t, 125t, 131t, 135bl, 137b, 139t, 139bl, 140b,
143b, 145tr, 145bl, 145br; **Yong Ding Li** 7, 26br, 28b, 92t, 121bl, 134b; **Mohamad Zahidi** 73br, 78b, 80tr, 129tr,
140tr, 143tl, 148br, 150br, 156t

ISBN 978-1-912081-65-3

Edited by Krystyna Mayer
Designed by Gulmohur Press
Printed and bound in Malaysia by Times Offset (M) Sdn. Bhd.

·CONTENTS·

Introduction

Located at the tip of the Thai-Malay Peninsula, the Republic of Singapore consists of a group of about 64 low-lying islands no more than 140km north of the equator. Covered with lush lowland tropical forests, freshwater swamp forests and mangrove swamps at the time of Singapore's founding in 1819 by Sir Stamford Raffles, an avid naturalist himself, the environment has undergone tremendous change in the past two centuries. Much of the original forest cover is now gone, replaced by large expanses of urban areas and well-manicured parks. On the other hand, old fruit orchards and relict rubber plantations have been left to regenerate into patches of secondary forest which now attract many bird species. A number of excellently managed nature reserves and a network of public parks protect the remaining birdlife, which exceeds 390 species and continues to grow annually. Although many of Singapore's hornbills, barbets and trogons are now locally extinct, the remaining patches of woodland nonetheless support a surprising diversity of resident and migratory birds, and Singapore is probably the easiest place in Southeast Asia to see a number of specialities such as Spotted Wood Owl, Straw-headed Bulbul, Red-legged Crake, Copper-throated Sunbird and the elusive Jambu Fruit Dove. Numerous visiting birdwatchers take advantage of these opportunities and regularly visit Singapore's nature reserves whenever they are passing through the region. Surely, few can resist the opportunity to track down three species of pittas, all within easy reach of the airport! The easy availability of birdwatching equipment and books means that the country sees an ever-increasing number of keen birdwatchers, conservationists, ecologists and general nature lovers.

This book aims to introduce the birdwatcher and nature photographer to some of the most exciting birds to be encountered in the country. The photographs are all of wild birds, and were mostly taken (>90%) locally. The book's pages feature most regular occurring migratory species and nearly all of Singapore's resident birds. For the keen birdwatcher, ecologist or nature lover, it is hoped that this book will provide a comprehensive introduction to Singapore's diverse avifauna, and a handy guide to the many birdwatching opportunities available in the country.

Geography and Climate

The Republic of Singapore is bounded by the low-lying state of Johor at the southern tip of Peninsular Malaysia to the north and the islands of Indonesia's Riau Islands Province to the south and southwest. Singapore island (Pulau Ujong), at 650km^2, is the largest of the 64 islands in the Republic of Singapore, stretching approximately 49km east–west and 25km north–south. The island's land area continues to increase with ongoing land reclamation, mainly on the eastern and western coastlines. Generally topographically flat, the island reaches its maximum elevation at Bukit Timah, a granitic hill rising to 164m above sea-level. A number of low hills and ridges carved out of sedimentary rocks fringe the southern and western coasts. Kent Ridge, for example, runs along Singapore's southwestern coast, peaking at Mount Faber (105m) and Telok Blangah Hill at its southernmost terminus.

Singapore island is drained by a number of small rivers that radiate from the centre of the island to the coast, the longest being the Kranji and Kallang rivers. Most, if not all, major rivers, most recently the Serangoon and Punggol rivers, are now dammed to create reservoirs. Along the coast there are also numerous small tidal creeks, many of which are lined with remnant patches of mangroves. Some of the best examples can be found within Sungei Buloh Wetland Reserve.

Of Singapore's satellite islands, the largest are Pulau Tekong and Pulau Ubin. Both lie off the north-eastern corner of Singapore island and are drained by a number of streams and tidal creeks. Most of the remaining islands do not exceed 1km^2 in area. Some are steep outcrops with a low-lying fringe (e.g. Pulau Jong), while others consist entirely of low sandy ground with small areas of coral reefs, seagrass meadows or mangroves (e.g. Pulau Hantu, Cyrene Reef). The rocky outcrop of Pedra Branca is Singapore's easternmost point; it is located more than 40km from the main island at the entrance to the South China Sea.

Singapore's climate typifies the humid tropics, being consistently hot and wet throughout the year. Rainfall is high, with an annual average of 2,358mm, but it may reach 2,650mm locally, especially around the island's central reservoirs. There is a significant increase in rainfall between November and January due to the northeast monsoon, which brings abundant moisture from the South China Sea. December is usually the wettest month, receiving well over 300mm of rainfall and registering the highest number of rain days of any month. The southwest monsoon that blows from June to September usually coincides with the driest time of the year, with September receiving the lowest rainfall of any month. The El Niño Southern Oscillation (ENSO) drives aberrant climatic patterns across the Asia–Pacific region and has been linked to unusually dry or wet years.

The mean daily temperature is about 27°C, and this varies little throughout the year. The hottest days are usually in May, when the temperature may reach as high as 31–33°C even in the shade. December, on the other hand, sees the coolest days, given the effects of rain. Mean daily temperature in December hovers around 26.5°C, and may dip to 22°C. Cloud cover usually forms towards the afternoon, and daily sunshine varies from 4.5 hours to as high as 9 hours during drier months. Humidity is high throughout the year, averaging 83.5%, and becomes most apparent from April to September when there is little wind.

Mangroves at Sungei Buloh Wetland Reserve.

HABITATS AND BIRD COMMUNITIES

During the last glacial period about 11,000 years ago, global sea-levels were much lower and Singapore was part of the exposed Sunda shelf, which included the Thai–Malay Peninsula and the islands of Borneo, Sumatra, Java, Bali and Palawan. Collectively, the region is known to biogeographers as Sundaland. The bird fauna of Sundaland differs from surrounding regions in mainland Southeast Asia, the Philippine archipelago or the islands of Wallacea to the east. Sundaland's forests support diverse assemblages of woodpeckers, trogons, babblers and many widespread forest species shared with mainland Southeast Asia and the Indian subcontinent (e.g. woodshrikes, leafbirds). By contrast, the islands of the Wallacean region and New Guinea to the east support many honeyeaters, whistlers, whistlers and fruit doves, Australasian groups which are either poorly represented or absent from Sundaland. The geographic isolation of well-forested Sundaland drove evolution of a highly endemic bird fauna, with a large proportion of resident species (c.20–25%) unique to this region, termed 'Sundaic endemics'. The ancient land connections between the Thai-Malay Peninsula and the Greater Sunda Islands gave rise to fairly uniform assemblages of birds in the lowlands, including pheasants, hornbills, trogons, broadbills, pittas, bulbuls, babblers and sunbirds. Since no part of Singapore's relief is truly montane, none of the birds typical of mountains in Southeast Asia, such as shrike-babblers, leaf warblers, laughingthrushes and *Arborophila* partridges, ever occurred here.

Drastic alterations in Singapore's vegetation as a result of land use change have driven many forest birds to local extinction. Parkland, urban green spaces and secondary scrub replaced lowland rainforest and became the dominant habitat types, eventually attracting a number of open-country bird species. Some, such as the Sunda Pygmy Woodpecker, have expanded beyond their original niche in the mangroves to take advantage of widespread parkland and are now amongst Singapore's commonest birds. Other species have colonised Singapore from Malaysia and Indonesia, where similar scrubby habitats occur. For instance, the Savanna Nightjar, a recent colonist from Sumatra, started showing up in open barren scrubland in Singapore in the late 1980s and is now one of the commonest nightjars. The same can be said of species like the Red-wattled Lapwing, a formerly rare species that colonised Singapore from cultivated land in Malaysia.

Primary Vegetation

Given its equatorial climate, Singapore and much of Southeast Asia support tropical evergreen rainforests rich in plant and animal species. Ecologists classify Singapore's original vegetation into three main types: lowland rainforests, freshwater swamp forests and mangrove forests. Each of these supports characteristic communities of birds, with some overlap.

Lowland rainforests or 'primary dryland forest' formed the largest component of Singapore's pre-settlement vegetation cover. Primary lowland rainforests are recognised by their complex three-dimensional structure with distinct layering: shrub layer, middle storey, canopy and the crowns of the tallest trees forming the emergent layer. Floristically, Southeast Asian lowland rainforests are dominated by trees of the dipterocarp family (notable genera include *Shorea*, *Dipterocarpus*, *Hopea*), hence the frequently used term, lowland dipterocarp forest. Here, dipterocarps not only account for the greatest proportion of large trees, but also attain their

Primary lowland rainforest in the Central Catchment Nature Reserve.

greatest diversity globally. On the whole, floral diversity is very high in Singapore's rainforests. Researchers sampling plots in the Bukit Timah Nature Reserve found over 300 tree species within a few hectares. Historical clearance means very little of this remains (c. 118.3ha, less than 1% of original extent), all of which is now protected in nature reserves. Tropical rainforests were the richest habitats for birds in Singapore, supporting pheasants, trogons, hornbills, broadbills and many more babbler species than today.

Freshwater swamp forests historically occurred along Singapore's low-lying river valleys. They are usually waterlogged, therefore supporting distinct plant communities although many plant genera are shared with rainforests. Currently, freshwater swamp forest is largely confined to the north-eastern part of Singapore's Central Catchment Nature Reserve (c.87ha), with smaller patches elsewhere (e.g. Pulau Tekong). Freshwater swamp forest can be distinguished by plants such as Swamp Pandan (*Pandanus atrocarpus*) and numerous palms (e.g. *Oncospermum* sp.). Many swamp forest trees have stilt roots or pneumatophores as adaptations to regular inundation. Ornithologically, swamp forests share most species with lowland rainforests, although some, such as White-chested Babbler, are more common in swamp forests.

Mangroves (c. 662.4ha) line much of Singapore's coasts and historically extended further inland along some of the major rivers, growing within the zone regularly inundated by brackish water. Mangroves support lower floral diversity than freshwater swamp forest or lowland rainforest, but play host to a distinctive plant community with diverse adaptations to saline and anoxic conditions. In response to frequent inundation and low oxygen, mangrove trees have evolved a myriad of root structures, including knee (*Bruguiera*), pencil-like (*Avicennia*) and stilt (*Rhizophora*) root structures. Singapore's mangrove bird communities are poor in species, but contain a few species nearly exclusive to this habitat, notably Mangrove Pitta, Mangrove Blue Flycatcher and Copper-throated Sunbird.

Secondary Vegetation and Other Human-modified Habitats

Most of Singapore's remaining forests can be described as 'secondary', since they have been disturbed at some point in time either by exploitation (e.g. logging) or agriculture. As there are many types of secondary forests, defined by their distinctive plant communities and at varying stages of succession, we broadly classify them here as 'mature secondary forest' and 'young secondary forest' for convenience.

Mature or tall secondary forest is confined to the Central Catchment Nature Reserve and is similar to primary lowland rainforest in terms of its plant communities. Studies have found tall secondary forest to have markedly lower plant diversity than primary forest, and to show lowered representation by certain families, especially dipterocarps and orchids. However, most forest birds also occur in mature secondary forest, including many barbets, bulbuls, babblers and leafbirds.

Young secondary forest refers to a number of distinct plant communities. In Singapore, many abandoned fruit orchards and rubber plantations are invaded by fast-growing trees such as *Macaranga*, *Rhodamnia* and *Ficus*, as well as invasives such as Albizia (*Falcataria moluccana*), Earleaf Acacia (*Acacia auriculiformes*) and African Tulip (*Spathodea campanulata*). Many abandoned areas of agricultural land eventually succeed into woodland dominated by Albizia and Earleaf Acacia trees. Where the soil is nutrient-poor, forest dominated by stands of Tiup-tiup (*Adinandra dumosa*) develops. Some of the best examples of young secondary forest can be found along the Kent Ridge, the Railway Corridor and in the Western Catchment. These forests are used by a handful of adaptable forest birds including Banded Woodpecker, Greater Racket-tailed Drongo and many nesting raptors. Typically, birdlife in young secondary forest tends to include species from open habitats (e.g. Oriental Dollarbird, Yellow-vented Bulbul), as well as a number of established aliens such as Red-breasted Parakeet, Lineated Barbet and White-crested Laughingthrush.

Urban parkland is no doubt the most extensive habitat type in Singapore. Thanks to the government's 'garden city' policies, numerous exotic ornamentals such as the Rain Tree (*Albizzia saman*), Trumpet Tree (*Tabebuia rosea*) and Senegal Mahogany (*Khaya senegalensis*) were planted along road dividers, beside car parks and in public parks all over the country. While these manicured patches are of little value to forest birds, a number of open-country and mangrove species have expanded beyond their niches to utilise these habitats. Typical birds include the abundant Pink-necked Green Pigeon, Pied Triller, Sunda Pygmy Woodpecker, Golden-bellied Gerygone, Common Iora, Common Tailorbird, Olive-backed and Brown-throated Sunbirds and, in recent years, the Blue-crowned Hanging Parrot.

Land reclamation continually creates new habitats, and some of the best examples can be found on Singapore's easternmost and westernmost coasts, and Pulau Tekong. Recently reclaimed land is usually invaded by various species of grass and vine such as Beach Morning Glory (*Ipomaea pes-caprae*) and subsequently by Giant Mimosa (*Mimosa pigra*), *Casuarina* and *Acacia* trees. Such habitats are favoured by munias, shrikes, Paddyfield Pipit and Zitting Cisticola. Where grassy scrub becomes waterlogged, freshwater marshes may form, attracting waterbirds such as crakes, bitterns and even ducks. Unfortunately, such habitats are usually ephemeral and are eventually cleared to make way for planned development.

Breeding Season and Nesting

Of nearly 150 species resident in Singapore, about 126 are known to have bred, with the remainder assumed to have bred without their nests being discovered. Most species, notably passerines, breed between March and July, after which breeding activity gradually declines, possibly coinciding with a reduction of food resources. However, some waterbirds and raptors such as the Grey-headed Fish Eagle may breed during the wetter, monsoon months. Prior to nesting, many birds engage in courtship displays, or become more vocal to attract mates and defend territory, and this is arguably the easiest time to observe many species.

Many birds, especially smaller passerines such as white-eyes, fantails and babblers, construct small inconspicuous cup-shaped nests that are not easily seen by potential predators. Larger species (e.g. herons) gather in colonies of tens to a few hundred and build their stick nests in relatively exposed spots. Large raptors such as the Changeable Hawk-Eagle and White-bellied Sea Eagle usually construct massive stick-piled nests on the tallest trees, which are often very conspicuous. Hole-nesters such as woodpeckers and barbets are able to excavate cavities in trees, but others, including mynas and parakeets, rely on holes left by woodpeckers, or natural cavities formed in rotten tree trunks. Clutch sizes vary from one in some raptors to as many as four in many passerines, but by and large are lower than those of temperate birds.

Bird Migration

The shift in the seasons has a major influence on the many birds breeding across much of Eurasia. Many ducks, shorebirds, raptors, cuckoos and passerine species breed in the deciduous and Taiga forests, and tundra that cover much of temperate, boreal and Arctic Asia in spring. The end of summer drives one of nature's great phenomena: billions of birds depart their increasingly food-scarce breeding grounds and head south into warmer parts of Africa, Asia, Australia and the Pacific islands on a number of different migratory routes. Many migratory raptors, shorebirds and waterfowl use the East Asian-Australasian Flyway, which takes them through Korea, eastern China and into continental Southeast Asia and the Thai–Malay Peninsula, including Singapore. Many species, and the bulk of the wintering populations of some, termed 'passage migrants' (e.g. Oriental Pratincole, Asian Dowitcher, Japanese Sparrowhawk), continue to head towards the Indonesian archipelago, Australia and the South Pacific. On the other hand, a number of species stay over in Singapore from November to March (e.g. Whimbrel, Asian Brown Flycatcher, Brown Shrike) and are termed as 'winter visitors'.

The arrival of different groups of birds peaks at different times, and this depends on the departure times from their breeding areas, the migratory routes taken, the number of stopovers, weather conditions and various other environmental factors. By mid-August many shorebirds are already in Singapore while there are few migratory passerines. By mid-October, migratory passerines such as shrikes, flycatchers and warblers peak in their arrivals and become very common in parks and forests, while raptor movement over Singapore tends to peak between early to mid-November. Many of these migratory birds wintering in Singapore have flown thousands of kilometres from their breeding ranges in the coniferous and mixed deciduous forests of north-east China, Mongolia, eastern Russia, Korea and Japan. A few, including the Pacific Golden Plover, possibly Singapore's most numerous nonpasserine migrant, occupy the coastal tundra of northernmost Russia and Alaska in spring. Although many of these migrants have fairly large breeding ranges, some, such as the localised Green-backed Flycatcher and the Brown-chested Jungle Flycatcher, occur in only small parts of China and winter exclusively in Sundaic Southeast Asia. One species, the Horsfield's Bronze Cuckoo, is unusual among migrants in Singapore. It is the only species breeding in continental Australia that arrives in Singapore from late May onwards, and occuring through September, during the austral winter.

Conservation Issues
Some of Singapore's most abundant birds, notably Javan Myna and House Crow, are not native to the country. These two examples represent the tip of the iceberg, and a closer scrutiny of Singapore's bird list reveals many more species with foreign origins (e.g. Coconut Lorikeet, Sooty-headed Bulbul). The pet bird trade and an established songbird-keeping tradition among some locals set the stage for many escaped, non-native birds. This problem is further accentuated by religious practices that encourage the intentional release of captive animals, particular small birds (see back cover). While the Javan Myna and House Crow appear to have been deliberately introduced, others, such as the two cockatoo species, Red-breasted Parakeet and White-crested Laughingthrush, may have originated from escaped birds which have since established breeding populations. The White-crested Laughingthrush used to be confined to one or two locations in western Singapore, but has since spread widely and is now found across much of the country. The Javan Myna was scarce when first documented a few decades ago, but is now Singapore's most abundant bird. Their large noisy roosts, even in busy Orchard Road, have invoked disdain from residents and tourists. Whether these invasive birds pose a serious threat to native species remains a matter of informed speculation, but case studies from elsewhere show that many native birds are eventually out-competed and pushed towards extinction.

Much of Singapore's original lowland rainforests, freshwater swamp forests and mangroves had been lost to development before the end of the 19th century. In fact, forest clearance by gambier planters started even before British colonisation. Based on comparisons with historical records compiled by colonial-era ornithologists Frederick Nutter Chasen and Carl Gibson-Hill, about 70 bird species, the majority dependent on forests, are now extinct in the country. Many mangrove species such as the Mangrove Whistler have suffered significant decline, with small, possibly non-viable populations persisting on some of the wooded offshore islands. The majority of forest birds are listed in Singapore's Red Data Book, the foremost publication on local biodiversity conservation (see p.172), and some, including the iconic but critically endangered White-bellied Woodpecker, may have already been extirpated. Of persisting forest species like the Short-tailed Babbler, recent studies have found low levels of genetic diversity in subpopulations in the Central Catchment, thus underscoring the effects of habitat fragmentation on bird populations.

Research from Southeast Asia and other tropical regions shows that forest birds, notably large-bodied and specialist insectivorous species, are most prone to extinction. Only four of thirteen species of babblers are still found in Singapore, the other nine having gone extinct in the past century. None of the trogons or broadbills has survived such a drastic loss of habitat.

Young secondary forest dominated by Albizia trees in Central Catchment Nature Reserve.

While it is hard to pinpoint when exactly these species disappeared, it is clear that the past 200 years of forest loss and fragmentation pushed most of Singapore's forest birds towards extinction. Fortunately, the authorities have taken heed. Besides protecting and managing all of Singapore's last rainforests in nature reserves, much effort has been made to rehabilitate forests through widespread reforestation of degraded areas. Furthermore, a major ecological corridor, the 'Ecolink' bridge, was completed in 2013 to connect forests in the Bukit Timah and Central Catchment Nature Reserve to enhance movement of wildlife. Relevant laws (e.g. the Wild Animal and Bird Act, Parks and Trees Act) and their active enforcement offer protection from poaching and mean that many highly sought-after species in the pet trade, such as the Straw-headed Bulbul and Common Hill Myna, are more abundant in Singapore than in much of their Southeast Asian ranges.

Migratory birds have received less attention from conservationists, but have suffered steep declines. The loss of intertidal mudflats (e.g. Serangoon Estuary) to reclamation and other forms of development have constantly reduced the amount of wintering habitat for migratory waterbirds. The fact that annual censuses have registered lower numbers of many migratory shorebirds year after year is not surprising, and some formerly abundant waders such as Curlew Sandpiper and Red-necked Stint are now scarce. Even less is known about migratory passerines and cuckoos, but the continuing loss of forests must have significantly reduced wintering habitat for many species in Singapore and across Southeast Asia. Mortalities suffered by migratory birds passing through Singapore as a result of disorientation from city lights are regularly reported. During migration passage months like October, members of the public regularly retrieve injured or dead Black Bitterns, pittas, Oriental Dwarf Kingfishers and even thrushes. The impacts of city lighting on migrating bird populations remain poorly known and is now part of a long-term study led by the Nature Society (Singapore).

To better document the conservation status of birdlife in Singapore, the National Parks Board, the chief government agency tasked with the responsibility for conserving biodiversity, has carried out regular bird ringing exercises at the nature reserves, and in collaboration with the National University of Singapore's Lee Kong Chian Museum of Natural History has spearheaded a number of long-term biodiversity surveys, species reintroduction programmes and conservation-specific citizen-science initiatives. Efforts to monitor and reintroduce the formerly extinct Oriental Pied Hornbill on mainland Singapore are beginning to bear fruit. Such efforts complement the work of the country's largest non-government nature conservation organisation, the Nature Society (Singapore). The society maintains Singapore's national bird list and coordinates routine national bird censuses as well as specific annual surveys targeting raptors, waterbirds and urban parrots. The annual bird census initiated by the society in 1986 is no doubt the longest-running attempt to monitor the abundance of Singapore's avifauna and has generated considerable data to inform conservation initiatives.

Much remains to be learned about the distribution of nightbirds in Singapore. The Barred Eagle Owl has only been seen a handful of times in recent years, mostly in the nature reserves.

Where to Watch Birds

The opportunities for birdwatching in Singapore are endless, and made easy by an excellent transport network. It is possible to see over 150 species on a 3 to 4 day trip covering the major habitats from late September to October. While it is convenient to explore these areas alone, it is worth noting that the Nature Society (Singapore), National Parks Board and the Lee Kong Chian Museum of Natural History regularly conduct guided birdwatching trips and general nature walks. Their contact details can be found at the end of the book. Here we describe some of the best birdwatching spots in Singapore, the key species found, and potential means of access (*see also* map on inside front cover).

Primary and Secondary Forest

Central Catchment Nature Reserve Arguably the best site for forest birds in Singapore; accessed from the HSBC TreeTop Walk at Venus Drive, the Upper and Lower Peirce Reservoir Park or MacRitchie Nature Trail near Lornie Road, all which can be reached by public transport. All three species of leafbirds, Red-crowned Barbet, Blue-rumped Parrot, Long-tailed Parakeet, Chestnut-bellied Malkoha, Asian Drongo-Cuckoo, Short-tailed Babbler, Asian Fairy-bluebird and Grey-headed Fish Eagle can be regularly found here. Early October to mid-December is the best time to see migrants, and most walks produce a good selection of flycatchers, warblers and cuckoos. The globally threatened Brown-chested Jungle Flycatcher occurs here in good numbers annually. Climbing up the 22m tall Jelutong Tower is a must to observe canopy-dwelling species such as leafbirds, bulbuls, sunbirds and flowerpeckers. In all, over 180 species have been recorded in this nature reserve, including the recently rediscovered Buff-rumped Woodpecker and Black-and-white Bulbul.

Bukit Timah Nature Reserve Another excellent site for forest birds, best visited on weekdays when there are fewer people. The birdlife is similar to the Central Catchment Nature Reserve, but its main attraction is the fig tree (*Ficus benjamina*) at the summit, which attracts anything from Red-crowned Barbets and Cinereous Bulbuls to wintering flycatchers, thrushes and warblers when in fruit. A good time to visit is a mid-October morning, just after a night of rainy weather, which can bring large numbers of migratory passerines. The summit is excellent for observing swifts, including wintering needletails. Hindhede and Dairy Farm nature parks at the fringes of the reserve are excellent for finding Straw-headed Bulbul, Red-legged Crake and Grey-headed Fish Eagle, as well as cuckoos and flycatchers in winter. When the fig trees by the Wallace Education Centre are in fruit, green pigeons, leafbirds, Asian Fairy-bluebird and Eyebrowed Thrush can also be encountered. Access to Bukit Timah Nature Reserve is through Hindhede Drive, near a bus-stop served by many services along Upper Bukit Timah Road, and the Beauty World and Hillview MRT stations.

Brown-backed Needletails are regularly observed over the summit of Bukit Timah hill during the migration period.

Singapore Zoological Gardens A most unlikely place to go for a birdwatching trip, the Singapore Zoo is surprisingly rich in wild birds and sports a list of over 100 species, including the rare Crested Goshawk, Grey-headed Fish Eagle and globally threatened Straw-headed Bulbul. The stretch of woodland immediately after the Treetops Trail is particularly good for Straw-headed Bulbul, while some of the less-used trails are excellent for resident Red-legged Crakes. A number of forest birds such as Asian Fairy-bluebird, Thick-billed Green Pigeon, Black-headed and Asian Red-eyed Bulbul are possible here. The heronry just by the reptile house is now the easiest place to see good numbers of both Grey and Purple Heron, the latter in steep decline. The rare Masked Finfoot has been seen in the reservoir inlets along the road (Mandai Lake Road) to the zoo. Access is by public bus services 138, 926 and 927.

Parkland and Secondary Scrub
Singapore Botanic Gardens The nearest important birdwatching site to the city centre and accessible by many public buses and the Botanic Gardens MRT station, this site offers an excellent introduction to parkland birds in Singapore. Specialities here include Changeable Hawk-Eagle, Buffy Fish Owl, Brown Hawk-Owl, Red-legged Crake, Long-tailed Parakeet,

Grey-rumped Treeswift, Common Hill Myna and many sunbirds. In winter, Rufous-bellied Eagle, Watercock, Yellow-rumped Flycatcher, Malayan Night Heron, Blue-winged Pitta, Hooded Pitta and Orange-headed Thrush have all been seen, the last three fairly regularly. A scrutiny of the dense shrubs in the Ginger Gardens in December–January usually reveals hidden pittas, rails and thrushes. Altogether, more than 130 species have been recorded from the gardens. The Singapore Botanic Gardens was declared a UNESCO World Heritage Site in 2015 in recognition of its outstanding historical and scientific importance.

Chinese and Japanese Gardens   These two manicured thematic gardens were 'discovered' a few years ago by bird photographers, and have proved to be excellent sites to observe a number of interesting species. Both gardens can be easily accessed from the nearby Lakeside MRT station. Besides the usual complement of open-country species such as Common Flameback, Coppersmith Barbet and even the locally rare Crested Goshawk, the gardens come alive in October–January with many flycatchers, warblers and kingfishers. In recent years Grey Nightjar, Malayan Night Heron, Ruddy Kingfisher, Hodgson's Hawk-Cuckoo and Band-bellied Crake have all been seen here. Both sites are also good for observing migrating raptors in early November, with many Black Bazas and Crested Honey Buzzards passing through.

Pasir Ris Park   About 10 minutes' walk from the Pasir Ris MRT station, this well-wooded park has become increasingly popular for birdwatching. Besides the remnant mangroves, the park contains some secondary woodland which in recent years has regularly hosted Red Junglefowl, Buffy Fish Owl, Spotted Wood Owl, Crested Goshawk and many species of migratory cuckoos. The mangrove patches are where herons, Ashy Tailorbird, Copper-throated Sunbird, and very rarely, Mangrove Pitta, can be seen. At low tide, the mudflats fringing the mangroves also support some shorebirds and occasionally Pacific Reef Heron and Chinese Egret. It is possible to see over 30 species in a morning, including many common parkland birds.

Pulau Ubin   Accessed by regular ferries ($3/person/trip) from the jetty at Changi village, Pulau Ubin supports an interesting mix of open-country, secondary-forest and mangrove species, and is undoubtedly the best place to see Mangrove Pitta (a small population continues to persist on the island's western and northern mangroves), Cinnamon-headed Green Pigeon, Mangrove Blue Flycatcher and wintering Chinese Egret. A number of species that are scarce on mainland Singapore can be easily found here, including genuinely wild Red Junglefowl, Great-billed Heron, White-rumped Shama, Green Imperial Pigeon and Oriental Pied Hornbill. Straw-headed Bulbuls remain common on the island, along with a long list of other open-country species including Long-tailed Parakeet, Common Flameback and Rufous Woodpecker. All of Singapore's resident owls including the recently discovered Brown Wood Owl can also be found here. Additionally, a number of very rare species like Oriental Darter, Black-and-red Broadbill and Black-winged Flycatcher-shrike have been reported in recent years, and are probably dispersants from nearby Malaysia. With more than 200 species recorded to date, the island deserves at least a full-day excursion.

Bukit Batok Nature Park   This 32ha patch of secondary forest and abandoned rubber estates is within walking distance of the Bukit Timah Nature Reserve, besides being served by many bus services along Bukit Batok East Avenue 6. The park has a bird list in excess of 150 species and is the most accessible site for the Straw-headed Bulbul. The woodland along the trails leading to the war memorial site at the summit should be checked for woodpeckers, bulbuls, flowerpeckers and sunbirds, and it was here that the Thick-billed Flowerpecker was rediscovered a few years ago. Other specialities include Blue-eared Kingfisher, Banded Bay Cuckoo, Grey-rumped Treeswift, Yellow-vented Flowerpecker, Red-legged Crake and breeding White-bellied Sea Eagle.

Mangroves, Mudflats and Open Country
Sungei Buloh Wetland Reserve   The approximately 200ha of mangrove forest, mudflats and brackish ponds that make up this reserve constitute Singapore's best known birdwatching spot, and boasts an impressive list of over 200 species. The period from September–November is the best time to visit as this coincides with the arrival of large numbers of migrant shorebirds and egrets. Besides Terek, Curlew and Wood Sandpipers, the Endangered Nordmann's Greenshank has shown up here in the past, on top of a long list of locally rare waders ranging from Great Knot to Grey-headed Lapwing. Migratory flycatchers and warblers can also be encountered in winter. Visits to the reserve in the middle of the year tend to be quieter, but this is nevertheless a good time to see residents such as the ever-present Copper-throated Sunbird, Ashy Tailorbird, Stork-billed Kingfisher and, with luck, the Great-billed Heron. Access is from Kranji MRT station, which is served by bus service 925 and the Kranji Countryside Express Bus ($3/person/round-trip).

Kranji marshes and grasslands   Although somewhat off the beaten track, this site can be accessed by the Kranji Express Shuttle from the Kranji MRT station. Those who make it here

Freshwater marshland habitat by the Kranji Reservoir.

can see a rural side of Singapore that used to be widespread 30–40 years ago. At the end of Neo Tiew Lane 2 is a pond surrounded by reedy marshland that is home to herons, Black-backed Swamphen, Common Moorhen, Ruddy-breasted and White-browed Crakes, and in winter a host of warblers such as Oriental Reed, Black-browed and Pallas's Grasshopper Warblers, Black-capped Kingfisher and various bitterns. The woodland that lines this road is excellent for shrikes, weavers, parakeets, cuckoos and Black-winged Kite, and both Grey-headed Fish Eagle and Changeable Hawk-Eagle are known to nest here. About 80 species have been recorded. A large part of the marshes has been zoned as a conservation area and can only be accessed with permission from the National Parks Board.

Lorong Halus Wetlands   Formerly a dumping ground, parts of Lorong Halus have now been landscaped into a wetland park. This site adjoins the Serangoon reservoir and is a good place to be introduced to open country birds like Yellow-bellied Prinia, Baya Weaver, Large-tailed and Savanna Nightjar, Lesser Coucal and Barred Buttonquail. A couple of freshwater ponds opposite the wetlands park are where Little Grebe, as well as various bitterns and rails occur. Shorebirds, egrets and herons can also be seen on the reservoir banks. In recent years, rarities like Booted Eagle and Pheasant-tailed Jacana have also been reported. In all, over 100 species have been recorded. Best accessed by taxi via Pasir Ris Farmway.

Pelagic Birdwatching
Finding seabirds has always posed a logistical challenge to birdwatchers, given the inevitable yet expensive need to charter a boat. Recent interest by the Nature Society (Singapore)'s Bird Group and the National Parks Board has spawned regular offshore boat trips to survey Singapore's surrounding seas for terns, petrels, shearwaters and skuas. These trips usually traverse the Singapore Straits, a major shipping lane to Singapore's southeast, and head towards the international waters south of Johor's southeastern tip. Occasionally, these pelagic trips have gone as far as Singapore's easternmost lighthouse island of Pedra Branca.

These pelagic excursions have shed much light on the diversity of seabirds wintering in or passing through Singapore's territorial waters. For instance, surveys have uncovered small numbers of Aleutian Terns regularly wintering in Singapore waters, and the presence of three skua species, two of which (Pomarine Skua and Long-tailed Jaeger) were previously unknown. These surveys also recently discovered a passage of Short-tailed Shearwaters through Singapore waters, and yielded the first national records of Lesser Black-backed Gull, Red-footed Booby and potentially, Bulwer's Petrel. Flocks of swiftlets, bee-eaters and Pied Imperial Pigeons have also been sighted on these trips. Anyone with an interest in observing seabirds should contact the Nature Society (Singapore) or the National Parks Board.

Opportunities for Naturalists

Although Singapore's avifauna has been more thoroughly studied than most other parts of Southeast Asia, much remains to be learnt. Birdwatchers will be able to make significant contributions to our understanding of the ecology of many species if they make a conscious effort to keep detailed records of their observations.

One area which birdwatchers can contribute to concerns the breeding biology of many of our resident forest species. The nests of many forest birds, including all three leafbird species and even the common Short-tailed Babbler, have never been found in Singapore, while breeding details for many are lacking. Birdwatchers should keep an eye out for breeding birds by taking hints from their behaviour. Should active nests be found, detailed notes should be taken on location, date, calls, nest structure, type of food items, frequency of parental attendance and development of the chicks, while maintaining minimal disturbance to the breeding birds. Investing in a directional microphone, a digital sound recorder and compatible sound analysis software will also prove invaluable in documenting the associated bird vocalisations. With climate change known to be a key threat to biodiversity, well-kept records have great scientific value in revealing changes in the breeding ecology of many species.

Birdwatchers and naturalists can also play an important role in documenting potentially important ecological interactions between birds. Competition from two or more species targeting similar food or nest resources can lead to the decline of the weaker competitor. Observed declines of the Oriental Magpie-Robin in the 1980s, for example, were anecdotally linked to population expansion of the non-native Javan Myna, although there was limited observational evidence. Another interesting interaction worthy of documentation is that between cuckoos and their hosts. Many cuckoos parasitise a number of smaller passerines, but many aspects of these interactions remain poorly understood, including the host species and their responses to nest parasitism.

The phenomenon of bird migration is yet another area where much remains to be learnt. We do not know the wintering abundances of many of our migratory birds here, whether they are declining, how they interact with resident birds, and their flight paths through Singapore. While birdwatchers and amateur naturalists may lack access to specialised equipment such as mist-nets and transmitting units, keeping detailed notes could reveal much on the timing of migration and associated ecological changes, some of which may be scientifically significant. The more adventurous ones can even attempt moon-watching with a telescope, on moonlit nights in the migration period (September–October), to monitor the movement of night-flying migrants.

Bird Photography
Given the easy access of both birdwatching sites and premier photography equipment, interest in bird photography in Singapore has swelled tremendously. It is possible to collect a decent haul of photographs at many of the sites, although densely forested sites tend to prove more challenging, given less than optimal light conditions. Furthermore, most birds are very active and do not remain in one position long enough to be easily captured on screen. One solution is to position oneself at a fixed location, preferably concealed in a hide, and wait for birds to show up. Fruiting and flowering trees attract many species and are good places to practise bird photography.

To be an effective photographer, one needs to be equipped with the right tools, which should include a good DSLR (digital single-lens reflex) camera, a sufficiently long telephoto lens of at least 400mm to provide sufficient reach (or an extender) and a sturdy tripod. External flash units can be used to compensate for poor lighting conditions, but should be used with discretion to prevent possible injury to birds' eyes. Equally critical are loads of patience and a good knowledge of bird behaviour and habitats.

Playback of bird sounds using digital recorders and amplifiers is increasingly being used to lure birds into better viewing positions, but needs to be carried out with discretion. If playback is to be used, it should be done in short snippets and with long pauses in between since it otherwise disrupts a bird's activities and renders it vulnerable to predators. We also strongly discourage the use of playback on birds that are known to be actively nesting.

As bird photography and birdwatching have grown very popular in recent years, we urge all in the field to observe appropriate codes of conduct (see also nss.org.sg/documents/NSSEthics. pdf) and exercise common sense to ensure minimal disturbance to wildlife, while setting good examples for beginners to the hobby.

Bird Identification

Bird identification is often not as easy as it seems, involving more than simply matching a bird seen against a photograph in a book. The challenges faced by a birdwatcher in the field are diverse, not least that one often has to cope with less-than-optimal conditions for identifying birds quickly. Birds are usually seen very briefly – in flight, at poor angles or in poor light conditions. Species with distinct patterns, proportion or coloration may be easy to identify, but you are eventually faced with similar-looking species, unfamiliar geographical races or birds at various ages and levels of plumage moult.

In spite of these difficulties, it is possible to identify birds through a series of steps. This starts from being able to pick out the key features and 'jizz' of the bird before going back to a field guide. Knowing the different species that can occur in any given habitat goes a long way towards narrowing the possibilities. Having a pair of good binoculars (8–10 × 42) and knowledge of calls will also help greatly. A good view gives one a clear idea of body and tail shape, size and key plumage features, and helps in further narrowing the possibilities to a few species of the same genus or family. The next step is usually to look out for specific combinations of identification features, such as facial pattern, bill structure, leg colour, wing and tail patterning. The figure opposite shows the general topography of a bird and the features that are useful in identification. Knowing the names of these parts of the birds will also help you to write meaningful and specific descriptions that will be useful for identification.

Submission of Rare Records

The Records Committee of the Nature Society (Singapore)'s Bird Group compiles Singapore's national list and regularly convenes meetings to review records of rarities and species new to the country. These transactions are published in the Nature Society's newsletter and the group's bulletin *Singapore Avifauna*. Records of rare species or species deemed unusual should be submitted to the Records Committee with accompanying details on locality, weather and a detailed description of the bird.

Taxonomy and Nomenclature

We have adopted the sequence, nomenclature and taxonomy of the World Bird List version 7.2, published by the International Ornithologist's Union. This list captures most of the recent taxonomic changes, which have resulted in revisions of many English and scientific names. For example, evidence from genetic analysis has resulted in the Asian Paradise Flycatcher being split into multiple species. Singapore supports at least two of these splits, including the Blyth's and Amur Paradise Flycatchers. At the higher taxonomic level, the falcons are now known to be closely related to parrots and passerines, and thus their position in taxonomic listings have been re-ordered accordingly. More such revisions are expected to follow in the coming years. Simplified Chinese names listed after the scientific names follow the standard bird names used in mainland China (available at www.cnbird.org.cn), while Malay names follow that adopted in the Nature Society (Singapore)'s checklist with some revisions.

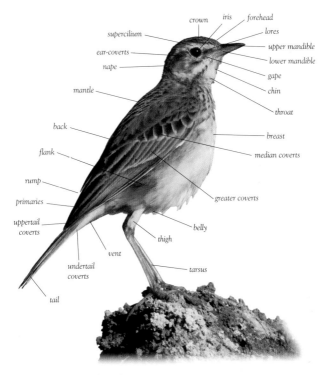

Topography of a bird (Paddyfield Pipit).

King Quail ▪ *Excalfactoria chinensis* 蓝胸鹑 Pikau 14cm

DESCRIPTION ssp. *chinensis*. A small quail that may be confused with the similar-sized but unrelated Barred Buttonquail (see p.48). Male has a well-marked white malar stripe against a black throat patch that contrasts with bluish-grey underparts, breast and flanks. Female

is mostly buffy-brown, with a buff-coloured crown and barring on breast and flanks. **DISTRIBUTION** S China, Taiwan, Indian sub-continent and much of Southeast Asia, east to New Guinea, Australia and the Bismarck Islands. Widely introduced elsewhere. **HABITS AND HABITATS** Uncommon resident of open scrub and grassland, including wet areas. Often colonises recently reclaimed land. Difficult to see well due to habit of keeping to thick grass, usually only seen when flushed. **SITES** Open grassy and scrubby areas across Singapore (e.g. Tuas coast, Kranji marshes). **CONSERVATION** With extensive clearance of grasslands, may be threatened in future.

LEFT: *Male.* RIGHT: *Female*

Red Junglefowl ▪ *Gallus gallus* 原鸡 Ayam Hutan 78cm (M), 43cm (F)

DESCRIPTION ssp. *spadiceus*. The only pheasant in Singapore. Resembles the domestic chicken, and care is needed to distinguish wild birds from these and hybrids. Genuinely wild birds have grey feet and legs, richer plumage, and tend to be shyer. Male (shown) has rich orange hackles, a green tail and a conspicuous white ear patch. Female is smaller, with a smaller ear patch and a much shorter tail, and is drab brown with

extensive vermiculation and streaking. **DISTRIBUTION** Much of Indian sub-continent, S China and mainland Southeast Asia, east to Sumatra, Java and Philippines. Widely introduced. **HABITS AND HABITATS** Uncommon resident of secondary forests, forest edge, scrub and old plantations. Usually seen in small groups consisting of a number of females and one dominant male. Call similar to domestic fowl but the last syllable ends abruptly. **SITES** Pulau Ubin, Western Catchment area. **CONSERVATION** Nationally endangered. Populations threatened by hybridisation with domestic fowl. Recently has colonised secondary woodland on mainland Singapore.

Lesser Whistling Duck
■ *Dendrocygna javanica* 栗树鸭 Belibis Kembang 40cm

DESCRIPTION Dainty-looking duck with a contrasting dusky-brown crown and nape. Much of face, neck and breast light brown, while upperparts rich dark brown with rufous fringes, giving a scaly appearance to the back. Flight feathers are black; flanks are marginally fringed white. Similar to Wandering Whistling Duck *D. arcuata*, which is larger and has more extensive white plumes on flanks. **DISTRIBUTION** Much of Indian sub-continent, S China and Southeast Asia, east to Greater and Lesser Sundas. **HABITS AND HABITATS** Uncommon resident of marshes and lakes with reedy fringes. Has also been observed in small ponds in parks and secondary scrub. Shy, flushes easily when approached. Birds seen at the Botanic Gardens are of unknown origin and there is evidence of hybridisation with Wandering Whistling Duck. Nests in tree-holes. Call is a shrill disyllabic whistle. **SITES** Lorong Halus wetlands, Kranji marshes. **CONSERVATION** Formerly common; has declined, as much habitat has been lost. Nationally endangered.

Cotton Pygmy Goose ■ *Nettapus coromandelianus* 棉凫 Itik Kapas 36cm

DESCRIPTION ssp. *coromandelianus*. A small, compact-looking waterfowl, largely white and green. Male has a metallic green crown and an iridescent band at the base of the neck, giving a 'necklaced' appearance. In flight, a white band stretching from the primaries to the base of the secondaries is clearly visible. Female is less strongly marked and lacsk the green iridescence of the males. **DISTRIBUTION** S China, Taiwan, much of Indian sub-continent and Southeast Asia, east to Philippines, New Guinea and Australia. **HABITS AND HABITATS** Very rare resident and non-breeding visitor. Marshes and lakes with reedy fringes. Usually seen in small groups of both sexes but tend to be shy. Formerly regular in the Western Catchment. **SITES** Kranji marshes. **CONSERVATION** Nationally critically endangered.

ABOVE: *Female.* BELOW: *Male*

Swinhoe's Storm Petrel ■ *Oceanodroma monorhis* 黑叉尾海燕
Lelayang-Laut Jepun 19–20cm

DESCRIPTION A small, mostly dark brown seabird with a pale band across the upperwing coverts, inconspicuous white shafts on flight feathers, all-dark underwing and forked tail. Care needs to be taken to separate from similar-looking but larger Bulwer's Petrel which may occur. **DISTRIBUTION** Breeds on small islets off Russian Far East, Korea, Japan, NE China and possibly islets in North Atlantic. Migrates to Indian Ocean and Arabian Sea.

HABITS AND HABITATS Fairly common passage migrant in Singapore Straits. Autumn passage September–November, peaking in October. Spring passage April–May. Scarcity of records from the Straits of Malacca during migration suggests that birds move south after passing Singapore Straits. Feeds mainly on the wing by dipping onto the water surface. Has a somewhat erratic swooping and bounding flight pattern; rests on water when not foraging. **SITES** Singapore Straits. **CONSERVATION** Globally near threatened. Declines have been detected in breeding colonies in NE Asia, especially S Korea (e.g. Chibaldo).

Little Grebe ■ *Tachybaptus ruficollis* 小鸊鷉 Tetimbul Kecil 28cm

DESCRIPTION ssp. *poggei*. A small, unmistakable duck-like bird with a prominent yellow gape patch. Breeding adults (shown) greyish brown, with a rich rufous patch from cheek to neck sides. Non-breeding birds pale brown, with darker upperparts. **DISTRIBUTION**

Widespread across Eurasia and Africa: Europe, much of Sub-Saharan Africa, Indian sub-continent, east to Southeast Asia, Philippines and New Guinea. **HABITS AND HABITATS** Rare resident of marshes, ponds and lakes with reedy fringes, including abandoned quarries. Nest is a small platform of water plants by the water's edge, with a clutch of about 4. Dives for fish and small invertebrates. Call is a soft, accelerating trill. **SITES** Lorong Halus wetlands. **CONSERVATION** Nationally critically endangered. Present at up to 4 sites, while 2 populations have apparently disappeared (Tampines, Dairy Farm Nature Park) and another is in decline.

Yellow Bittern ■ *Ixobrychus sinensis* 黄斑苇鳽 Pucung Kuning 37cm

DESCRIPTION A small, pale buffy-brown bittern. Male is black-crowned, and black on flight feathers and tail. Juvenile (shown) usually shows heavy dark streaking on back and underparts. Similar-looking Von Schrenck's Bittern (see p.24) has rich chestnut head sides, and chestnut patch on wing bend, both absent in Yellow Bittern. **DISTRIBUTION** Breeds in N Indian sub-continent and much of E Asia to as far north as Russian Far East and Southeast Asia, east to Philippines. Northern populations migrate to winter in S India, Southeast Asia, Wallacea and New Guinea. **HABITS AND HABITAT** Common resident and migrant. Mangroves, freshwater marshes and wet grassland, including small stands of reeds in parkland (e.g. Botanic Gardens Eco Lake). Solitary. Often freezes with neck outstretched when it senses danger. When flushed, utters a coarse, staccato 'kak-kak-kak' as it takes flight. **SITES** Sungei Buloh Wetland Reserve, Kranji marshes, Lorong Halus wetlands. **CONSERVATION** No issues.

Cinnamon Bittern ■ *Ixobrychus cinnamomeus* 栗苇鳽
Pucung Bendang 39cm

DESCRIPTION A small, richly coloured bittern. Male (shown) is uniformly cinnamon-brown on the upperparts, while underparts mostly warm buffish. Female is darker brown on upperparts with fine speckling, and heavily streaked on underparts. In flight, lacks black flight feathers of other *Ixobrychus* bitterns. **DISTRIBUTION** Indian sub-continent and much of E Asia E Asia also Southeast Asia east to Sulawesi. Northern populations winter in Southeast Asia. **HABITS AND HABITATS** Uncommon resident and migrant. Occurs in freshwater marshes, wet grassland, and occasionally scrub and mangroves. Less commonly encountered than Yellow Bittern. Solitary and very secretive, spending much time hidden in dense vegetation. **SITES** Kranji marshes, Lorong Halus wetlands. **CONSERVATION** Loss of freshwater marsh habitats is likely to pose a threat.

LEFT: *Female*. RIGHT: *Male*

Von Schrenck's Bittern ▪ *Ixobrychus eurhythmus* 栗苇鳽
Puchong Gelam 36cm

DESCRIPTION Small, strikingly-coloured bittern with contrasting dark back and pale wings. Adult male (shown) rich chestnut from face, hindneck to lower back, contrasting strongly with buff underparts, shoulder and wing coverts. Female similar but wings entirely chestnut, with bold spotting upperparts and wings. Both sexes crown black. Young birds are heavily spotted on upperparts, and boldly streaked on underparts. **DISTRIBUTION** Breeds S and SE China (rare) to Russian Far East, Korea and Japan. Winters S China

to mainland SE Asia, Thai-Malay Peninsula, Greater Sundas and eastwards to Sulawesi. **HABITS AND HABITATS** Uncommon migrant, occurring along forest streams and swampy forest, very occasionally in scrub and freshwater marshes. Least common of the *Ixobrychus* bitterns. Secretive, spending much time hidden in dense vegetation. Mostly arrives from October, departing by April. Call is a grating 'krkk'. **SITES** Central Catchment Nature Reserve, Kranji marshes, Pasir Ris Park. **CONSERVATION** Forest-dependant species in the wintering range.

Black Bittern ▪ *Dupetor flavicollis* 黑鳽 Pucung Hitam 58cm

DESCRIPTION ssp. *flavicollis*. A large, dark bittern with streaked underparts. Combination of blackish plumage, buffy sides of throat, neck and upper breast and dark bill, legs and feet is diagnostic. First-winter bird (shown) shows pale fringing on upperpart feathers.

DISTRIBUTION Indian sub-continent, S and E China, much of Southeast Asia and Greater Sundas, east to New Guinea and Australia. Northern populations migrate to winter in Southeast Asia. **HABITS AND HABITATS** Uncommon migrant to freshwater marshes, lakes and ponds with well-vegetated fringes and forested streams, occasionally in mangroves. Solitary, foraging in dense cover for frogs and fish. Occurs mostly from October–April, with peak passage migration October–November. **SITES** Kranji marshes, Sungei Buloh Wetland Reserve. **CONSERVATION** Frequent collisions with glass windows suggest high mortality on migration.

Black-crowned Night Heron ■ *Nycticorax nycticorax* 夜鷺
Pucung Kuak 61cm

DESCRIPTION ssp. *nycticorax*. A stocky red-eyed heron with black head, mantle and scapulars, contrasting with mostly pale grey plumage. Bill black and lores greyish blue; feet and legs yellow, becoming reddish during the breeding season. Juvenile brownish overall with white spotting on wings and brown streaking on head and breast. **DISTRIBUTION** Widespread across much of the Americas, Eurasia and Africa. Many northern populations migrate to winter in the tropics. **HABITS AND HABITATS** Uncommon resident of mangroves, ponds, mudflats, canals and well-vegetated reservoir fringes. Crepuscular, often seen dispersing from roost sites to forage in evening. Regularly seen feeding in urban canals at night. Roosts in dense clumps of mangroves and waterside vegetation during the day. Gregarious and nests colonially. A large colony of over 1,000 individuals used to occur in the Khatib Bongsu area. **SITES** Sungei Buloh Wetland Reserve, Lorong Halus wetlands, Singapore Botanic Gardens. **CONSERVATION** Nationally critically endangered due to disturbance of nesting sites.

Malayan Night Heron
■ *Gorsachius melanolophus* 黑冠鳽 Pucung Harimau 50cm

DESCRIPTION A medium-sized, short-necked, rufous heron with contrasting black crown and crest. Bill black, facial skin greenish blue, legs and feet green. Juvenile (shown) is duller with irregular buffish and greyish barring and vermiculations throughout plumage, while throat is pale buffy with dark mesial streak. **DISTRIBUTION** Breeds in SW India, S China, Taiwan, Philippines and Ryukyu Islands. Northern populations migrate to winter in Thai–Malay Peninsula, Sumatra and Borneo. **HABITS AND HABITATS** Rare migrant occurring in primary and secondary forests and old plantations and scrub, usually in the vicinity of small streams. Secretive and shy, taking off when approached and flying to seek refuge on a high perch. Crepuscular, feeding mostly at dusk, hunting for earthworms and other invertebrates. Occurs mostly October–April. **SITES** Central Catchment and Bukit Timah nature reserves, Singapore Botanic Gardens. **CONSERVATION** Forest-dependent in wintering grounds.

Striated Heron ■ *Butorides striata* 小绿鹭 Pucung Keladi 45cm

DESCRIPTION ssp. *javanica*. A small, slate-grey heron with black crown and long nape plumes. Uppersides tinged greenish, with pale fringes to wing feathers. Throat and upper breast white, with prominent black moustachial stripe. Underparts pale grey. Facial skin greenish yellow. Bill black with yellow base to lower mandible. Legs and feet yellowish orange. Juveniles browner. **DISTRIBUTION** Widespread across much of the Americas, Eurasia, Africa and Australia. Some northern populations migrate to winter in the tropics. **HABITS AND HABITATS** Common resident of mangroves, coastal mudflats, canals, rivers, reservoir fringes and even ponds in urban parkland. Solitary, hunts by wading stealthily into shallow water or by waiting motionless beside the water, and sometimes uses small pieces of bread or fish as bait for prey. Gives a loud and harsh 'keyow' when flushed. **SITES** Most suitable habitats across Singapore. **CONSERVATION** No issues.

Chinese Pond Heron ■ *Ardeola bacchus* 池鹭 Pucung-Padi Cina 49cm

DESCRIPTION A small, stocky and short-necked heron. Non-breeding birds, which are most often seen, are streaked brown on head, neck and breast, with brown upperparts and white wings, and are nearly impossible to tell apart from non-breeding Javan and Indian Pond Herons. Early-arriving or late-departing birds may be in diagnostic breeding plumages, chestnut-maroon on head, neck and breast. **DISTRIBUTION** Breeds across much of E Asia to as far north as Russian Far East, NE China and Japan. Northern populations migrate to winter in S China, Southeast Asia and Philippines. **HABITS AND HABITATS** Common

migrant to coastal mudflats, estuaries, freshwater marshes, ponds with reedy fringes and grasslands. Usually seen alone, but up to 25 birds have been seen foraging for invertebrates in open grassy fields at Labrador Park. Arrives September and departs by May. Some begin to moult to breeding plumage as early as mid-March. **SITES** Sungei Buloh Wetland Reserve, Lorong Halus wetlands, Labrador Park. **CONSERVATION** No issues.

LEFT: *Breeding*. RIGHT: *Non-breeding* Ardeola sp.

Javan Pond Heron ▪ *Ardeola speciosa* 爪哇池鷺 Pucung-Padi Emas 45cm

DESCRIPTION ssp. *speciosa*? Not possible to separate from similar-looking Chinese and Indian Pond Herons in non-breeding plumages. Breeding birds (shown) are unmistakable, buff on head and neck with cinnamon-rufous breast, black mantle and scapulars, and rest of body mostly white. **DISTRIBUTION** Parts of mainland Southeast Asia (e.g. C Thailand), Greater and Lesser Sundas, Sulawesi and Mindanao. **HABITS AND HABITATS**

Rare migrant or non-breeding visitor to freshwater marshes, grasslands, ponds with well-vegetated fringes and occasionally coastal mudflats. Previously thought to be a very rare vagrant, but likely overlooked due to difficulty in separating from other pond herons. Increasing frequency of sightings from March to April indicates that it is more regularly occurring than previously thought, possibly dispersing from the large colonies in S Sumatra. **SITES** Lorong Halus wetlands. **CONSERVATION** No issues.

Eastern Cattle Egret ▪ *Bubulcus coromandus* 牛背鷺
Bangau Kerbau 52cm

DESCRIPTION Smaller and stockier than other egrets, with relatively shorter bill and neck, often appearing hunched. Birds in breeding plumage are rufous-orange on head, neck, breast and back; bill reddish with yellow tips, legs pinkish red. Non-breeding birds entirely white with yellow bill and facial skin, and black legs. Recently split from Western Cattle Egret *B. ibis* of Africa and Europe. **DISTRIBUTION** Widespread across Indian sub-continent, E and Southeast Asia, east to Australia. Partly introduced in Singapore.

HABITS AND HABITATS Fairly common migrant, occurring mostly in grasslands, occasionally freshwater marshes; avoids salt water and rarely seen on coastal mudflats. Small free-flying groups from private collections are localised to western Singapore (e.g. Jalan Bahar area). Gregarious and usually in small groups. In the absence of large ungulates in Singapore, Eastern Cattle Egrets are often seen foraging near grass cutters and lawnmowers. **SITES** Suitable habitat throughout Singapore. **CONSERVATION** No issues.

Great-billed Heron ■ *Ardea sumatrana* 大嘴鷺 Pucung Lembu 115cm

DESCRIPTION The largest heron in Singapore. Entirely dusky grey with pale grey plumes on scapulars, lower foreneck and breast. Facial skin dull yellow. In flight, note uniformly

dark underwings, unlike Grey Heron (below), which shows pale grey patch on underwings. **DISTRIBUTION** Much of coastal Southeast Asia from S Myanmar and Greater Sundas to Maluku, New Guinea and N Australia. **HABITS AND HABITATS** Uncommon resident of reefs, rocky stacks, coastal embankments, mangrove-lined creeks and occasionally freshwater bodies (e.g. reservoirs). Never seen too far from the sea, and regularly occurs on the rocky coasts of the small islands S of Singapore. Hunts mainly fish and crustaceans, occasionally wading neck-deep into water. Nests singly in remote mangrove islets; clutch size is 2. **SITES** Tanjong Chek-Jawa, Sungei Buloh Wetland Reserve, St John's Island. **CONSERVATION** Nationally endangered.

Grey Heron ■ *Ardea cinerea* 苍鷺 Pucung Seriap 100cm

DESCRIPTION ssp. *jouyi*. The commonest large heron in Singapore. Head and neck mostly white with diagnostic black cap and nape plumes, and foreneck finely speckled

black. Back and wings grey. Breeding adults develop a bright pinkish-orange bill. Young birds have dark, instead of black, crown and are largely grey on the neck. **DISTRIBUTION** Widespread across Eurasia and Africa, east to East and Southeast Asia. Northern populations migrate to winter in the tropics. **HABITS AND HABITATS** Common resident and probable migrant, occurring in sandy beaches, reefs, mangroves, coastal mudflats, freshwater marshes, wet grassland and canals. Commonest large heron in mangrove and coastal mudflats, sometimes among flocks of waders. Nests communally in tall trees, usually with other herons. Formerly nested at Pulau Ubin. Call is a harsh guttural croak, usually uttered when flushed. **SITES** Sungei Buloh Wetland Reserve, Pulau Ubin, Singapore Zoo. **CONSERVATION** Nationally endangered. The population has steadily grown in recent years.

Purple Heron ■ *Ardea purpurea* 草鷺 Pucung Serandau 90cm

DESCRIPTION ssp. *manilensis*. A large heron with a distinctive chestnut-brown neck, with two black lines running down the neck sides. Cap black, with nape plumes. Upperparts mostly grey, with maroon belly and flanks. In flight, maroon underwings differentiate it from other large herons. Young birds are light brown and lack the neck markings of adults. **DISTRIBUTION** Widespread across Eurasia and Africa, east to much of Southeast Asia, Sulawesi and Lesser Sundas. **HABITS AND HABITATS** Increasingly uncommon resident of mangroves, freshwater marshes, wet grassland, and water bodies with well-vegetated fringes (e.g. reservoirs). The most likely large heron seen inland, especially on flooded playing fields, or fringing vegetation of canals and the central reservoirs. Feeds mostly on fish, frogs and large invertebrates. Nests communally with other heron species. Call is a harsh guttural croak. **SITES** Singapore Zoo, Sungei Buloh Wetland Reserve Kranji marshes. **CONSERVATION** Appears to have declined in recent years. Small nesting groups are known from the Singapore Zoo and Bishan Park.

Great Egret ■ *Ardea alba* 大白鷺 Bangau Besar 91cm

DESCRIPTION ssp. *modesta*. Largest of the white egrets. Longer-necked than all other egrets, and neck distinctly kinked. Non-breeding birds (shown) have yellow bill and facial skin, and black legs. Similar-looking Intermediate Egret is smaller, with a shorter bill and a less distinctively kinked neck. Breeding birds are black-billed with bluish facial skin. **DISTRIBUTION** Widespread across much of the Americas, Eurasia, Africa and Australia. Most northern populations migrate to winter in the tropics. **HABITS AND HABITATS** Fairly common migrant to coastal mudflats, mangroves, estuaries, water bodies with well-vegetated fringes, and occasionally wet grasslands. Tends to occur singly or in small numbers, often mixing with other egrets when foraging. Arrives in September and usually departs by April. **SITES** Sungei Buloh Wetland Reserve, Lorong Halus wetlands. **CONSERVATION** No issues.

Little Egret
■ *Egretta garzetta* 小白鷺 Bangau Kecil 65cm

DESCRIPTION ssp. *garzetta*. A medium-sized egret. All white plumage, with blackish legs contrasting with yellow feet, but black-footed ssp. *nigripes* can also occur. Bill is black and facial skin yellow. Frequently confused with Chinese Egret (see p.31), which has yellowish lower mandible and dark greenish legs. **DISTRIBUTION** Widespread across Eurasia, Africa and Australia. Northern populations migrate to winter in tropics. **HABITS AND HABITATS** Common migrant and non-breeding visitor to mangroves, coastal mudflats, rivers and canals; seldom encountered in marshes and reservoirs. The most numerous egret, often in large flocks and regularly seen even in urban, concretised canals. Spends much of its time stalking for prey, and less active than other egrets. Call is a rough guttural growl, usually uttered when flushed. Some birds seen in Singapore are likely to have dispersed from colonies off S Sumatra or Java. **SITES** Suitable habitat across Singapore (e.g. Sungei Buloh Wetland Reserve, Bukit Timah Canal). **CONSERVATION** No issues.

Intermediate Egret ■ *Egretta intermedia* 中白鷺 Bangau Kendi 69cm

DESCRIPTION ssp. *intermedia*. Superficially resembles Great Egret (see p.29) but much smaller and has a shorter bill, more rounded head, and shorter, less distinctly kinked neck. Bill yellow, often tipped black. Unlike Great Egret, the greenish-yellow gape line does not extend behind the eye. Legs black. **DISTRIBUTION** Widespread across Eurasia, Africa and Australia. Northern populations migrate to winter in the tropics. **HABITS AND HABITATS** Fairly common migrant, occurring mostly in coastal mudflats, mangroves, estuaries, ponds and open wet grassland. Often associates with other egrets, but never in big flocks and usually seen feeding singly. Birds arrive as early as July and depart by May. **SITES** Sungei Buloh Wetland Reserve, Lorong Halus wetlands. **CONSERVATION** No issues.

Chinese Egret ■ *Egretta eulophotes* 黃嘴白鷺 Bangau Cina 68cm

DESCRIPTION A medium-sized egret somewhat similar to Little Egret and Pacific Reef Heron. All-white plumage, with short legs and dagger-shaped bill that tapers near tip. Breeding birds are plumed, with orange bill, blue facial skin, dirty-green legs and yellow feet. Non-breeding birds (shown) have a two-toned bill with pink to yellowish lower mandible, while legs and feet are dirty green. **DISTRIBUTION** Breeds on islets off coast of Russian Far East, E and S China and Korea. Winters mostly in Philippines and Borneo, with small numbers in other parts of Southeast Asia. **HABITS AND HABITATS** Rare migrant to mudflats, sandy beaches and occasionally coastal reefs. A very active feeder often seen walking swiftly (>100 steps per minute) over soft mudflats, before squatting and tilting body forward to stab prey. On sandier substrates runs rapidly in shallow water with neck extended to the side and head tilted until prey is found. Hunting tactics clearly different from other egrets, which tend to be less active feeders. **SITES** Tanjong Chek-Jawa, Sungei Buloh Wetland Reserve. **CONSERVATION** Globally vulnerable.

Pacific Reef Heron ■ *Egretta sacra* 岩鷺 Bangau Batu 58cm

DESCRIPTION ssp. *sacra*. A small, stocky egret. White-morph birds are all white, with dull yellow bill and grey facial skin, with slightly darker upper mandibles and greenish-yellow legs. Dark-morph birds (shown) are entirely slate-grey, and one of two dark herons. Pale-morph birds are similar to Chinese Egret (above), but proportionately shorter-legged, showing little projection of legs beyond tail in flight, and usually with yellowish to pale green bill. **DISTRIBUTION** Much of coastal East Asia and Southeast Asia, east to Australia, New Zealand and the Pacific islands. **HABITS AND HABITATS** Common resident of reefs, rocky stacks, coastal embankments and very occasionally mudflats and canals. Forages by crouching low, suddenly lunging at prey. A much more sluggish hunter than the similar-looking Chinese Egret. Calls include a variety of squawks, growls and guttural grunts. **SITES** West Coast Park, Pulau Ubin, St John's Island. **CONSERVATION** Habitat is increasingly degraded or lost due to coastal development.

Western Osprey ■ *Pandion haliaetus* 鱼鹰 Helang Tiram 50-65cm

DESCRIPTION ssp. *haliaetus*. A familiar long-winged raptor of coasts and large open water bodies nearly worldwide. Upperparts mostly dark brown, contrasting with pale head and underparts. Dark eye-stripe that merges into dark brown of mantle and brown breast band are diagnostic. Unlike male (shown), female has broader breast band, and show dark carpal patch contrasting with pale underwing coverts. Split from Eastern Osprey *P. cristatus* of Australia. **DISTRIBUTION** Widespread across much of the Americas, Eurasia and Africa. Northern populations in Eurasia migrate to winter in Africa, Indian sub-continent, East and Southeast Asia. **HABITS AND HABITATS** Common migrant and non-breeding visitor, occurring in mangroves, coastal mudflats and reservoirs with well-vegetated fringes. Frequently seen resting on man-made structures along the coast. A specialist predator on fish, sighting its prey from afar before plunging feet-first into water to grab prey. Occurs all year-round. **SITES** Kranji marshes, Sungei Buloh Wetland Reserve, Seletar mudflats. **CONSERVATION** No issues.

Jerdon's Baza ■ *Aviceda jerdoni* 褐冠鹃隼 Helang-Baza Perang 40-48cm

DESCRIPTION ssp. *jerdoni*. A small raptor with a long erect crest, sometimes confused with *Accipiter* hawks and hawk-eagles. Adult (shown) head rufous-brown, back and wings dark brown; dark streaks on breast; belly rufous-brown with fine white banding. Young birds are paler and less richly coloured. In flight, note broad subterminal band and three dark bands on tail, and thin white bands on brown underwing coverts. Apparently mimics the plumage of more powerful hawk-eagles. **DISTRIBUTION** Himalayan foothills, S and NE India, S China and parts of mainland Southeast Asia, east to Sulawesi. Some northern populations are apparently migratory, wintering in parts of Southeast Asia. **HABITS AND HABITATS** Uncommon migrant to secondary forest, forest edges, scrub and occasionally parkland. Usually seen in small groups of up to 7 birds. Feeds mostly on snakes, lizards and large insects. First discovered in Singapore in 1996, but subsequently recorded annually. Occurs mostly December–March. **CONSERVATION** Regular occurrence in Singapore is a new phenomenon and could be due to changes in the migratory pathway, or because it was previously overlooked.

Black Baza ■ *Aviceda leuphotes* 黑冠鹃隼 Helang-Baza Hitam 28-35cm

DESCRIPTION ssp. *syama*, *leuphotes*? A small, unmistakable black and white raptor with long erect crest. Head and upperparts mostly black, with prominent white patch on breast and chestnut barring on belly. Undertail coverts black. In flight, wings appear broad, 'rounded' at the end, and narrower at the base. Black undertail and underwing coverts most visible in flight. **DISTRIBUTION** Breeds in Himalayan foothills, S and NE India, S China and parts of mainland Southeast Asia. Some northern populations are migratory, wintering in mainland Southeast Asia, Thai–Malay Peninsula and Sumatra. **HABITS AND HABITATS** Common migrant to secondary forests, forest edge, old plantations, scrub and occasionally parkland. A predator of large insects and lizards, hunting in small groups in the canopy. Flies from tree to tree with a slow flapping flight that is somewhat crow-like. Southbound passage through Singapore is mostly in early November, but small numbers overwinter annually. Usually seen on migration in flocks of up to 100 birds. **SITES** Kent Ridge Park, Kranji marshes, Pasir Ris Park. **CONSERVATION** No issues.

Crested Honey Buzzard ■ *Pernis ptilorhynchus* 凤头蜂鹰
Helang Lebah 53-65 cm

DESCRIPTION ssp. *orientalis*, *ruficollis*, *torquatus*. A medium-sized raptor with variable plumage. Small chicken-like head with slight crest, pale throat, broad wings and longish tail are consistent features. Pale-morph birds largely brown with varying extent of brown barring on underparts. In flight, note black bands across flight feathers. Ssp. *torquatus* is treated as a distinct species (Sunda Honey Buzzard) by some authorities and is similar to the hawk-eagles. Similar to the hawk-eagles. **DISTRIBUTION** Widespread across much of Indian sub-continent, East and Southeast Asia. Northern populations are migratory, wintering in India and Southeast Asia. **HABITS AND HABITATS** Common migrant and rare non-breeding visitor to primary and secondary forests, forest edge, mangroves, old plantations, scrub and parkland. A specialised feeder on bee and hornet larvae, and beeswax obtained by tearing hives. Southbound passage peak in early/mid-November, and flocks totalling a few hundred birds have been seen annually. **SITES** Suitable habitat across Singapore. **CONSERVATION** No issues.

LEFT: *Adult ssp.* torquatus; RIGHT: *Pale morph ssp.* orientalis

Brahminy Kite
■ *Haliastur indus* 栗鸢 Helang-Kembara Merah 44-52cm

DESCRIPTION ssp. *intermedius*. A medium-sized brown and white raptor. Head and breast white with fine streaking, rest of body rich rufous-brown. In flight, note white head, black wing tips and rounded tail base, unlike shallow fork of Black Kite *Milvus migrans*. Young birds are dark brown overall with pale streaks on underparts and, in flight, undersides of flight feathers without streaking. **DISTRIBUTION** Indian sub-continent, S China and much of coastal Southeast Asia, east to New Guinea, Bismarck islands and Australia. **HABITS AND HABITATS** Common resident of secondary forests, scrub, mangroves, old plantations. Frequently seen in flight over urban areas, easily the commonest raptor in Singapore. Large groups are known to gather to roost on some offshore islands (e.g. Coney Island). A scavenger, often seen picking up dead fish. Call is a piercing 'ngeehhh', somewhat like a cat's mew. **SITES** Suitable habitat across Singapore (e.g. Jurong Lake). **CONSERVATION** No issues.

Black-winged Kite ■ *Elanus caeruleus* 黑翅鸢 Helang Tikus 31-36cm

DESCRIPTION ssp. *vociferus*. A small, pale, red-eyed raptor of open country. Head and underparts mostly white while upperparts and wings pale grey, with prominent black wing coverts. Wings extend beyond tail when perched. In flight, black undersides of flight feathers diagnostic. Young birds are browner tinged and have a buff patch on breast. **DISTRIBUTION** Widespread across Eurasia and Africa, from S Europe, Africa

and the Indian sub-continent to S China, Southeast Asia, east to New Guinea. **HABITS AND HABITATS** Uncommon resident of open secondary scrub, grasslands, occasionally freshwater marshes. Preys largely on lizards and small ground rodents. Hovers when hunting, recalling Common Kestrel. Nest is an untidy pile of sticks built in a tree, usually with 3–4 eggs. Call is a high-pitched screech or a piping 'keee'. **SITES** Kranji marshes, Changi coast. **CONSERVATION** As most grasslands are transient habitats poised for future development, more habitat loss is expected.

Grey-headed Fish Eagle ■ *Haliaeetus ichthyaetus* 灰头鱼雕
Helang Kangut Besar 69-74cm

DESCRIPTION A robust-looking raptor with distinct grey head. Grey head intergrades to brown on breast, which is well demarcated from white belly and undertail. Tail white with black terminal band. Young birds less strongly marked and streaked, but lower belly white, unlike juvenile White-bellied Sea Eagle (below). **DISTRIBUTION** Indian sub-continent, S China and much of Southeast Asia, east to Sulawesi. **HABITS AND HABITATS** Common resident of primary and secondary forests, old plantations and scrub adjacent to inland water bodies, less frequently in coastal areas. Feeds mostly on fish but also takes large lizards and terrapins. Unlike White-bellied Sea Eagle, tends not to re-use nests. Nest is a bulky structure of sticks, usually built on tall trees near water (e.g. Albizia). Mostly breeds December–March. Clutch size 2. Call is a harsh, far-carrying 'oooo' or 'aaark'. **SITES** Central Catchment Nature Reserve, Little Guilin, Kranji marshes. **CONSERVATION** Globally near threatened; nationally critically endangered.

White-bellied Sea Eagle
■ *Haliaeetus leucogaster* 白腹海雕 Helang Siput 69-85cm

DESCRIPTION A large, dark-grey and white raptor of sea coasts. Entirely white on head, neck and underparts; back and wings grey with black wing tips. In flight, note white wedge-shaped tail, black flight feathers, and wings held up in a shallow V shape. Juveniles are brownish on the underparts extending to the undertail, while tail shows clear subterminal band. **DISTRIBUTION** Coastal parts of peninsular and E India, S China and much of Southeast Asia, east to Maluku, New Guinea and Australia. **HABITS AND HABITATS** Common resident of primary and secondary forests, old plantations, mangroves and scrub, usually near inland water bodies or the coast; often seen hunting in coastal waters. A specialist predator of fish but also regularly takes sea-snakes. Nest is a large, bulky structure of piled sticks, built on tall trees, and regularly re-used. Clutch size usually 2. Call is a series of monotonous goose-like honking and shrill whistling. **SITES** Central Catchment Nature Reserve, Bukit Batok Nature Park. **CONSERVATION** Competes with Grey-headed Fish Eagle for nesting trees and prey.

Grey-faced Buzzard ■ *Butastur indicus* 灰脸鵟鹰
Helang Kepala Kelabu 46 cm

DESCRIPTION A medium-sized raptor, appearing somewhat like an oversized *Accipiter* hawk. Adult male has a greyish-brown head with prominent white brow, throat and black throat stripe diagnostic. Rest of upperparts and underparts brown, but with white barring on belly. Adult female (shown) whitish on underparts with heavy streaking. In flight, note longish, square-cut tail with three narrow bars, longish wings and fine dark bands on underwings and flight feathers. **DISTRIBUTION** Breeds Russian Far East, NE China, Korea and Japan (excluding Hokkaido). Winters S China and Taiwan, to mainland SE Asia eastwards to the Greater Sundas and Philippines. **HABITS AND HABITATS** Uncommon passage migrant and rare winter visitor to secondary woodland, scrub and open grassland. A predator of small reptiles and frogs. Compared with parts of Peninsular Malaysia, very few birds actually pass Singapore on their southbound passage to Sumatra. **SITES** Changi, Tuas coast. **CONSERVATION** The breeding population in Japan has declined in recent years.

Crested Serpent Eagle
■ *Spilornis cheela* 蛇雕 Helang Kuik 54-68cm

DESCRIPTION ssp. *malayensis*. An unmistakable medium-sized raptor with distinct black crest and yellow face. Plumage dark brown, with spotting on breast and belly, tail black with broad central band. In flight, underwing coverts brown with conspicuous black and white banding on flight feathers and tail. Juveniles are brown, with finely streaked white underparts and two (instead of one) white bands on black tail. **DISTRIBUTION** Indian sub-continent, S China, mainland Southeast Asia, Thai–Malay Peninsula and Greater Sundas. **HABITS AND HABITATS** Very rare resident and non-breeding visitor of primary and secondary forests, and old plantations, occasionally wandering into mangroves and scrub. It is unclear whether the species still breeds in Singapore; some sightings are likely to involve dispersants from Malaysia. A specialist predator of reptiles, particularly tree snakes. Call is an airy whistle, similar to the Changeable Hawk-Eagle (see p.41) but shorter. **SITES** Central Catchment Nature Reserve, Malcolm Park area. **CONSERVATION** Nationally critically endangered. The rarest of the resident raptors, with a known population of 2 birds.

Pied Harrier
■ *Circus melanoleucos* 鹊鹞 Helang Sawah Kelabu 43–50cm

DESCRIPTION A black and white raptor of open country. Male has black head, back, median upperwing coverts and outer flight feathers, with rest of plumage white. Female is dark brown on back and wing coverts, with a pale grey patch on shoulders and whitish thighs. Young birds are mostly rufous-brown on underparts and wing coverts. In flight, note 5 unbroken bars on tail, unlike Eastern Marsh Harrier (below), and pale shoulder patches contrasting with dark brown wing coverts. **DISTRIBUTION** Breeds in NE China, Mongolia and E Russia. Winters in E India, S China and much of Southeast Asia, east to Philippines.

HABITS AND HABITATS Rare migrant to open scrub, grasslands and marshes. Hunts by quartering low in search of ground prey, particularly rodents and frogs. Far less common than Eastern Marsh Harrier, but formerly regular in the Changi area where large expanses of open grassy scrub offered suitable habitat. **SITES** Tuas coast. **CONSERVATION** No issues.

LEFT: *Female*. RIGHT: *Male*

Eastern Marsh Harrier
■ *Circus spilonotus* 白腹鹞 Helang Sawah Besar 43–54cm

DESCRIPTION A large, long-tailed raptor of open country. Male is largely dark brown on the mantle, back and scapulars, heavily streaked on the neck, with streaking extending down to belly. In flight, generally pale below with dark wing tips and streaked underparts. Female is brown, with streaking on neck and underparts and belly and thighs rufous. In flight, note centrally broken thin bars on uppertail. Juveniles are dark brown with pale head. **DISTRIBUTION** Breeds in NE China and much of E Russia. Winters across East Asia (including Japan and Korea) and Southeast Asia, east to Philippines.

HABITS AND HABITATS Uncommon migrant to secondary scrub, open grasslands and marshes. Commonest harrier in Singapore. Hunts by quartering low in search of prey on ground, particularly rodents and frogs. Roosts on the ground at night. Occurs mostly from October–March. **SITES** Kranji marshes, Pulau Semakau. **CONSERVATION** No issues.

LEFT: *Juvenile*; RIGHT: *Adult male*

Chinese Sparrowhawk ■ *Accipiter soloensis* 赤腹鹰
Helang Sewah Cina 25–30cm

DESCRIPTION A small, pale raptor. Adults are entirely grey on the upperparts and white on the underparts, with faint orange barring on breast and a prominent orange cere. In flight, black tips to primaries diagnostic, distinguishing from similar Japanese Sparrowhawk. Young birds are dark brown on upperparts with streaking from throat to breast, while lower belly is barred. **DISTRIBUTION** Breeds in E and NE China, Korea and Russian Far East. Winters across much of Southeast Asia, east to Philippines, Sulawesi and New Guinea. **HABITS AND HABITATS** Uncommon migrant to primary and secondary forests, old plantations, scrub and parkland. Peak passage early November, with small numbers overwintering, including many young birds. Migrates in small flocks, unlike Japanese Sparrowhawk. Preys on small mammals, birds and frogs. Usually silent. **SITES** Parks in the Southern Ridges (Kent Ridge) are good for observing birds on migration. **CONSERVATION** No issues.

LEFT: *Male*. RIGHT: *Female*

Crested Goshawk ■ *Accipiter trivirgatus* 凤头鹰
Helang Sewah Berjambul 40–46cm

DESCRIPTION ssp. *indicus*. A medium-sized, robust-looking raptor with a short crest. Head grey with distinct throat stripe; back and wings dark brown. Breast streaked brown; belly barred rufous. Female (shown) has darker, more spot-like streaks. In flight, note broad rounded wings, black banding across flight feathers, equal-width black and white tail bands and white fluffy vent. Young birds browner with underparts mostly streaked brown. **DISTRIBUTION** Himalayan foothills, E and S India, S China, mainland Southeast Asia, Thai–Malay Peninsula, Greater Sundas, Philippines. **HABITS AND HABITATS** Uncommon resident of primary and secondary forests, mangroves, old plantations, scrub and parkland. A predator of birds and small mammals, taking prey as large as White-breasted Waterhen (see p.44). Formerly rarely seen, a number of recent nest records in parkland, including one in a residential estate in January 2013, suggest it is commoner than thought. Nest is a large bulky cup made of sticks, built high up on a tree. Clutch size is usually 2. Breeds mostly December–March. **SITES** Chinese Gardens, Pasir Ris Park, Pulau Ubin. **CONSERVATION** Nationally critically endangered.

Japanese Sparrowhawk
■ *Accipiter gularis* 日本松雀鷹 Helang Sewah Jepun 23–30cm

DESCRIPTION ssp. *sibiricus, gularis*. A small raptor, similar to Chinese Sparrowhawk. Adult male grey on upperparts and white on underparts with faint orange barring on breast. Adult female has dark barrings on the breast. Young birds have dark brown upperparts with breast streaking and belly barring. In flight, wings lack black tips to primaries, unlike Chinese Sparrowhawk, and tail shows broad dark terminal band. **DISTRIBUTION** Breeds in much of E Russia, China, Mongolia, Japan. Winters across Southeast Asia, east to Sulawesi and Lesser Sundas. **HABITS AND HABITATS** Common migrant to primary and secondary forests, mangroves, old plantations, scrub and parkland. Peak passage is early/mid-November, and migrating birds are usually seen singly. The most commonly encountered *Accipiter* hawk in midwinter. Preys largely on small birds. **SITES** Parks in the Southern Ridges (Kent Ridge) and the hills on Sentosa are good for observing birds on migration. **CONSERVATION** No issues.

LEFT: *Female in flight*; RIGHT: *Juvenile*

Eastern Buzzard ■ *Buteo japonicus* 普通鵟 Helang Gempal Jepun 40–53cm

DESCRIPTION ssp. *japonicus*. A robust raptor with a 'large-headed' appearance. Upperparts mostly dark brown; head and breast paler with fine streaking, contrasting with dark brown on lower flanks, thigh and belly. Juveniles heavily streaked on underparts. In flight, note terminal band on the tail, pale broad wings, and diagnostic black carpal patches, with black tips to flight feathers. Taxonomy confused, formerly considered a race of Common Buzzard *Buteo buteo*, of which ssp. *vulpinus* and *burmanicus* also occur, and tend to be more richly-coloured, with chestnut-brown thighs. **DISTRIBUTION** Breeds E Russia, NE China, Korea and Japan. Winters in E, NE India, mainland Southeast Asia, Thai–Malay Peninsula east to Greater Sundas and Philippines. **HABITS AND HABITATS** Uncommon migrant to secondary scrub and open grasslands. Feeds mostly on lizards and rodents caught from the ground. Small numbers overwinter annually, usually from late October to mid-April; also on passage. Often seen conspicuously perched on bare trees and man-made structures. **SITES** Changi Coastal Road, Tuas West. **CONSERVATION** No issues.

Booted Eagle ▪ *Hieraaetus pennatus* 靴隼雕 Helang Junam 53cm

DESCRIPTION A medium-sized, robust-looking raptor. Pale-morph birds buffy brown on head with dark patch on face; underparts white with faint breast streaking, and buff band on wing coverts contrasting with dark wing feathers. In flight, note nearly black flight feathers contrasting with buff underwings, and pale lower primaries, while tail appears square-ended. Dark-morph birds (shown) largely dark brown, but pale buff on upperwing

coverts. Both morphs show white shoulder patches, often referred to as 'landing lights'. **DISTRIBUTION** Widespread breeder across much of Eurasia, from SW Europe, N Africa and Middle East to E Russia. Winters in Sub-Saharan Africa, Indian sub-continent and parts of Southeast Asia. **HABITS AND HABITATS** Rare migrant, occurring in old plantations, secondary scrub and open grasslands. In recent years, appears to occur more regularly, and a few birds are seen annually in midwinter, especially in Seletar. Makes spectacular dives to catch prey near the ground. **SITES** Seletar West, Lorong Halus wetlands. **CONSERVATION** No issues.

Greater Spotted Eagle ▪ *Clanga clanga* 乌雕 Helang Bintik 60–71cm

DESCRIPTION A large, dark raptor of open country. Adults are dusky brown, with yellow bill and cere. In flight, note broad wings and black flight feathers, with whitish patch to base of primaries. Young birds (shown) have whitish tips to feathers on much of wings and uppertail coverts, giving a spotted appearance,

while belly is streaked buff. Recent genetic analysis has found it to be distinct from the *Aquila* eagles it used to be classified with. **DISTRIBUTION** Widespread across much of Eurasia, from central Europe to E Russia and N China. Winters in Sub-Saharan Africa, Indian sub-continent and parts of Southeast Asia. **HABITS AND HABITATS** Rare (passage?) migrant to open scrub and grasslands. Formerly regular, now rare and only known from 1–2 records annually, although still regular in paddy fields in some parts of Peninsular Malaysia (e.g. Melaka). Mostly hunts ground rodents (e.g. rats), but also known to scavenge. **SITES** Tuas coast, Seletar west. **CONSERVATION** Globally vulnerable.

Changeable Hawk-Eagle
▪ *Nisaetus cirrhatus* 凤头鹰雕　Helang Hindik Biasa 61–75cm

DESCRIPTION ssp. *limnaeetus*. A medium-sized, highly variable raptor, sometimes confused with Crested Honey Buzzard. Pale-morph birds are light brown on the head with a small crest, dark brown on the wings and white on the underparts with bold streaking to the belly. Dark-morph birds are uniformly dusky brown. In flight, note broad wings slightly tapered at base. **DISTRIBUTION** Much of Indian sub-continent, mainland Southeast Asia, Thai–Malay Peninsula, Greater Sundas, S Philippines.

HABITS AND HABITATS Common resident of primary and secondary forests, old plantations. Breeds mostly January–March. Large stick nest built on tall trees, especially Albizias. A generalist predator, taking lizards, birds, rodents and possibly young macaques. Call is a series of shrill, airy whistles. **SITES** Suitable habitat across Singapore, especially Central Catchment Nature Reserve. **CONSERVATION** Nationally endangered. The Singapore population appears to have increased in recent years, with as many as 7 active nests found in a season.

LEFT: *Pale morph juvenile;* RIGHT: *Dark morph adult*

Rufous-bellied Eagle ▪ *Lophotriorchis kienerii* 棕腹隼雕
Helang Perut Merah 53–61cm

DESCRIPTION ssp. *formosus*. A medium-sized raptor with a short crest. Adults have uniformly black upperparts, contrasting with white throat and finely streaked breast. Underwings and belly to undertail coverts rich orange-rufous, with streaks. Young birds (shown) are dark brown on upperparts, white on underparts and show diagnostic black eye-stripe. In flight, note white underwings and finely banded flight feathers. **DISTRIBUTION** Himalayan foothills, NE and S India, Sri Lanka, mainland Southeast Asia, Thai–Malay Peninsula, east to Sulawesi and Maluku. Northern populations are migratory, wintering in many parts of Southeast Asia. **HABITS AND HABITATS** Rare migrant and probable non-breeding visitor, occurring in primary and secondary forest, old plantations, scrub and occasionally parkland. Resident in lowland forests in Malaysia, and hence likely to wander into Singapore. Preys on birds, lizards and small mammals. **SITES** Central Catchment Nature Reserve, Singapore Botanic Gardens. **CONSERVATION** Forest-dependent.

Common Kestrel ■ *Falco tinnunculus* 红隼 Rajawali Padang Biasa 30–34cm

DESCRIPTION ssp. *interstinctus*. A small falcon with a long, round-ended tail. Adult male is grey-headed with black eye and moustachial stripe, contrasting with rufous-brown back and wings, finely spotted black. Female (shown) and young birds have brown head with fine streaking. In flight, note long pointed wings; both sexes show broad subterminal band on tail but female also has 6–7 narrow bars. **DISTRIBUTION** Widespread across Eurasia and Africa, from Europe and Middle East to E Russia and much of East Asia. Northern populations migrate to winter in Africa, Indian sub-continent, E and Southeast Asia. **HABITS AND HABITATS** Rare migrant, occurring in secondary scrub and open grasslands; usually less than 5 records annually. Hovering behaviour during hunting may lead to confusion with unrelated Black-winged Kite(see p.34). Takes mostly small rodents and insects. Occurs mostly November–February. **SITES** Tuas coast. **CONSERVATION** No issues.

Peregrine Falcon ■ *Falco peregrinus* 游隼 Rajawali Kembara 38-51cm

DESCRIPTION ssp. *japonensis* (shown), *ernesti*. A large, unmistakable falcon. Adults are dark grey on the upperparts, with distinct dark moustachial stripe, and white underparts

finely streaked dark grey on breast and barred on belly. Adults of the resident ssp. *ernesti* are rufous-orange on the underparts with fine barring. In flight, note 'triangular-looking' wings, with fairly uniform barring throughout underparts and underwings. Young birds boldly streaked from breast to belly. **DISTRIBUTION** Widespread across much of the Americas, Eurasia, Africa and Australia. Northern populations in Eurasia migrate to winter in Africa, Indian sub-continent, E and Southeast Asia. **HABITS AND HABITATS** Uncommon migrant and possibly resident, based on recent mid-year records, occurring in open secondary scrub, grasslands, urban areas, occasionally wandering into mangroves and parkland. Regularly encountered in the city area, often seen perched on tall transmission towers and ledges of buildings. Has been observed hunting at night using floodlights on buildings. A specialist predator of birds, often taking Rock Dove *Columba livia* and Javan Myna. **SITES** Changi coast, Pulau Ubin, Raffles Place. **CONSERVATION** No issues.

Masked Finfoot ■ *Heliopais personatus* 亚洲鳍趾䴘 Pendendang 54cm

DESCRIPTION Superficially duck-like, but unrelated. Largely dark brown on body, with long greyish neck and bright yellow bill. Unmistakable black mask extends down to throat. Female and non-breeding male have a white throat patch and a more extensive white fringe to the mask. **DISTRIBUTION** Breeds in E India, Bangladesh and parts of mainland Southeast Asia. Apparently winters in Thai–Malay Peninsula and Sumatra. **HABITS AND HABITATS** Very rare migrant to mangroves and secluded, forested inlets

of reservoirs. Secretive, usually seen alone. Feeds on aquatic invertebrates and small animals such as frogs. Most of the world population breeds in mangrove swamps in the Sundarbans, and lowland riverine forests in Kachin, N Myanmar, where habitat loss poses a major threat. Likely to be overlooked, since most of the forested central reservoirs are infrequently surveyed. Usually silent on migration. **SITES** Central Catchment Nature Reserve, Sungei Buloh Wetland Reserve. **CONSERVATION** Globally endangered.

Red-legged Crake ■ *Rallina fasciata* 红腿斑秧鸡 Sintar Api 24cm

DESCRIPTION A chestnut-brown rail with distinct white barring on the lower wings. Plumage largely rich chestnut brown, while lower belly black with fine white banding. The much rarer Slaty-legged Crake *R. eurizonoides* is similar, but has black legs and lacks the white bars on the wings. **DISTRIBUTION** E India, mainland Southeast Asia and Thai–Malay Peninsula, east to Philippines, Sulawesi and Lesser Sundas. Northern populations are migratory, wintering in Southeast Asia.

HABITS AND HABITATS Uncommon resident and migrant, occurring in primary and secondary forests, secondary scrub and occasionally well-wooded parkland, usually near water. Often seen near streams or small drains where birds bathe at dusk. Commonly heard call is a series of nasal 'kek', usually followed by a rattling trill. Other calls include a short monotonous series of 'kok-kok-kok-kok', usually uttered at night. **SITES** Singapore Botanic Gardens, Hindhede Park, Bukit Batok Nature Park. **CONSERVATION** Nationally endangered. Previously thought rare, the bird is now known to be widespread in secondary scrub.

Slaty-breasted Rail ▪ *Gallirallus striatus* 灰胸秧鸡 Sintar Biasa 25cm

DESCRIPTION ssp. *gularis*. The only rail with a long red bill. Crown and nape chestnut-brown, throat to breast bluish-grey. Rest of upperparts including back and wings finely

barred black. Belly and undertail coverts banded dark grey against white. **DISTRIBUTION** S and NE India, much of S China, mainland Southeast Asia and Thai–Malay Peninsula, east to Philippines and Sulawesi. **HABITS AND HABITATS** Common resident of secondary scrub, marshes, wet grasslands and occasionally well-wooded parkland. Generally shy, but occasionally ventures out into the open near the edge of marshes and wet grass. Commonly heard call is a disyllabic 'gelek' or a sudden, raspy 'keek', usually uttered from the safety of dense vegetation. **SITES** Kranji marshes, Lorong Halus wetlands. **CONSERVATION** No issues.

BACK: *Adult*; FRONT: *Juvenile*

White-breasted Waterhen ▪ *Amaurornis phoenicurus* 白胸苦恶鸟 Ruak-ruak Biasa 33cm

DESCRIPTION ssp. *phoenicurus*. A familiar black and white rail with a greenish yellow beak; the commonest rail in Singapore. Upperparts from the crown to the tail and wings entirely black, contrasting sharply with white face and underparts. Undertail coverts chestnut. **DISTRIBUTION** Widespread across much of Indian sub-continent, Southeast

Asia and E China, north to Ryukyus, and east to Sulawesi and Lesser Sundas. **HABITS AND HABITATS** Very common resident and migrant, occurring in mangroves, secondary forests and scrub, marshes, ponds with well-vegetated fringes, wet grasslands and parkland. Bold, often seen venturing into open areas to feed. Breeds all year round, building a shallow pad nest in dense vegetation, with clutch size 3–8. Commonly heard call is a raucous series of 'oo-waks' and a monotonous series of clucks. **SITES** Suitable habitat across Singapore. **CONSERVATION** No issues.

Baillon's Crake ▪ *Porzana pusilla* 小田鸡 Sintar Kecil 20cm

DESCRIPTION ssp. *pusilla*. The smallest rail in Singapore. Upperparts rufous-brown with blackish and white speckling, face to upper belly blue-grey, short yellow bill. Flanks and lower belly to undertail coverts barred black and white. Juvenile (shown) drabber, with a pale brow, lacking the blue-grey of adult, and rufous-buff on breast with faint barring.

DISTRIBUTION Widespread across much of S Europe, Asia, Africa and Australia, from SW Europe discontinuously to E Russia, N China and Japan. Northern populations winter in Indian sub-continent, Southeast Asia and Australia. **HABITS AND HABITATS** Rare migrant to freshwater marshes, wet grasslands and ponds with well-vegetated fringes. Very shy, but occasionally ventures out into the open near the edge of marshes and wet grass, especially in the morning to sunbathe. Otherwise mostly seen when flushed. Usually silent. Occurs mostly November–March. **SITES** Kranji marshes, Lorong Halus wetlands. **CONSERVATION** No issues.

Ruddy-breasted Crake ▪ *Porzana fusca* 红胸田鸡 Sintar Belacan 22cm

DESCRIPTION ssp. *fusca*. A small dark reddish-brown rail. Largely dark brown on upperparts. Underparts rich chestnut to the breast; lower belly and brown black with fine white banding. Legs bright red. Can be confused with Band-bellied Crake *P. paykulli* which is larger, paler, and has more barring on belly. **DISTRIBUTION** Much of E Asia, north to Russian Far East. Also NE India and

much of Southeast Asia, east to Sulawesi. Northern populations migrate to winter in S China and Southeast Asia. **HABITS AND HABITATS** Uncommon resident of secondary scrub, marshes, wet grasslands. Difficult to see well due to habit of keeping to thick vegetation, but occasionally ventures to open edges of marshes and scrub to forage. The nest is a shallow pad of plant matter build on the ground, or in low vegetation. Call is a repeated 'teuk' note, usually ending in a shrill, excited trill. **SITES** Kranji marshes, Lorong Halus Wetlands. **CONSERVATION** Loss of wetland habitats.

White-browed Crake ◾ *Porzana cinerea* 白眉田鸡
Sintar Kening Putih 20cm

DESCRIPTION A small rail with diagnostic facial pattern. Thick black eye-stripe is fringed with white brow and cheek patch while cap is dark grey. Otherwise largely pale grey, nearly white on underparts, with brown back and wings. Bill yellow, orange at the base. **DISTRIBUTION** Mainland Southeast Asia, Thai–Malay Peninsula and Greater Sundas, east to N Australia, New Guinea and islands of the SE Pacific. **HABITS AND HABITATS** Uncommon resident of wet grassland, marshes and ponds with well-vegetated fringes and floating vegetation. Like most other rails, best seen during early mornings when comes out to forage in the open. Call is a series of high-pitched, excited squeaking. **SITES** Lorong Halus wetlands, Sungei Buloh Wetland Reserve. **CONSERVATION** Loss of marshland has reduced available habitat.

Watercock ◾ *Gallicrex cinerea* 董鸡 Ayam-ayam 43cm

DESCRIPTION A large black rail, reminiscent of a Common Moorhen but much larger. Male is entirely black with a long red frontal shield and yellow bill, and red legs. Female and non-breeding male are similar-looking, mostly buff brown with yellow legs. **DISTRIBUTION** Indian sub-continent and much of Southeast Asia, as far north as NE China and Korea, and east to Philippines. Northern populations are migratory, wintering mostly in Southeast Asia. **HABITS AND HABITATS** Uncommon migrant to wet

grassland, marshes and ponds with well-vegetated fringes. Feeds largely on insects, fish and plant matter. Silent in winter. **SITES** Kranji marshes, Lorong Halus wetlands. **CONSERVATION** Loss of marshland has reduced available habitat. Frequently hunted for food in other parts of Southeast Asia.

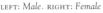

LEFT: *Male*. RIGHT: *Female*

Black-backed Swamphen ■ *Porphyrio indicus* 黑背水鸡
Pangling 42cm

DESCRIPTION ssp. *viridis*. An unmistakable large, dark purplish-blue rail. Red bill, broad red frontal shield and red legs diagnostic.
Plumage mostly dark purplish-blue, with
paler blue head. Recently split from
Purple Swamphen *P. porphyrio* complex.
DISTRIBUTION Mainland Southeast Asia,
Thai-Malay Peninsula east to Sulawesi.
HABITS AND HABITATS Uncommon
resident of freshwater marshes and reedbeds.
Gregarious, often foraging in small parties
for shoots and small invertebrates. Wary,
and quickly takes off into the cover of dense
vegetation at the slightest sign of danger.
Breeding recorded January–March. Call is a
loud, raucous 'gaark'. **SITES** Kranji marshes.
CONSERVATION The only sizeable
populations are in W Singapore in the
Kranji and Western Catchment area.

Common Moorhen ■ *Gallinula chloropus* 黑水鸡 Tiong Air 32cm

DESCRIPTION ssp. *chloropus*. A familiar dark rail with red frontal shield, appearing
somewhat duck-like when swimming. Overall slate-grey plumage with dark brown
back and wings, contrasting with white lining along flanks and white undertail tail
coverts. Diagnostic yellow-tipped red bill and red frontal shield separate it from other
rails. **DISTRIBUTION** Widespread
across much of the Americas, Eurasia
and Africa. Northern populations are
migratory, wintering across the tropics and
subtropics. **HABITS AND HABITATS**
Uncommon resident, and possibly migrant
of freshwater marshes, ponds with fringing
reeds. Usually solitary or in pairs. Forages
on land or in water while swimming,
feeding on a variety of aquatic plants
and invertebrates. Breeding recorded
throughout the year, especially March.
Call is a loud, liquid 'prriok'. **SITES** Kranji
marshes. **CONSERVATION** Resident
populations have declined due to habitat
loss; now largely confined to W Singapore.

Barred Buttonquail ▪ *Turnix suscitator* 棕三趾鹑 Puyuh Biasa 17cm

DESCRIPTION ssp. *atrogularis*. Superficially resembles King Quail (see p.20), but has a less rounded appearance, pale irises and a much thicker bill. Male is heavily streaked on back and barred on neck, flanks and breast; female similar but has distinct black throat patch. In flight, contrasting pale wing coverts and dark primaries differ from the uniformly dark upperwing of King Quail. **DISTRIBUTION** Much of Indian sub-continent to as far north as Ryukyus, S China and Southeast Asia, east to Philippines, Sulawesi and Lesser Sundas. **HABITS AND HABITATS** Common resident of open grassland, open scrub

and old plantations, including scrub on newly reclaimed land. Difficult to see well due to habit of keeping to thick vegetation. May occasionally come out to feed in the open. Breeds May–July, laying up to 5 eggs in ground scrape. A polyandrous species: the more brightly marked females initiate courtship, leaving the males to incubate and tend to chicks. **SITES** Most suitable habitats across Singapore (e.g. Lorong Halus wetlands, Changi coast). **CONSERVATION** Adaptable, one of few open-country species to colonise newly reclaimed land in Singapore.

LEFT: *Male* RIGHT: *Female*

Black-winged Stilt ▪ *Himantopus himantopus* 黑翅长脚鹬
Kedidi Kaki Panjang 38cm

DESCRIPTION An unmistakable, elegant wader with thin black bill and disproportionately long pinkish-red legs. Non-breeding adults are black on mantle, scapulars and wings, and white on the head, neck and underparts. First-winter bird (shown) is dark brown on back and wings, with greyish wash on crown and hindneck. **DISTRIBUTION** Breeds in S Europe, Middle East, Central Asia, NW China, Africa, Madagascar, Indian sub-continent and parts of Southeast Asia. Northern populations winter in N Africa, eastwards to S China and Southeast Asia. **HABITS AND HABITATS** Rare winter visitor and passage migrant to coastal mudflats, freshwater marshes and ponds with well-vegetated fringes. Usually seen singly, but occasionally joins mixed flocks of waders. **SITES** Sungei Buloh Wetland Reserve. **CONSERVATION** No issues.

Red-wattled Lapwing ▪ *Vanellus indicus* 肉垂麦鸡
Cerewit Duit-duit 33cm

DESCRIPTION ssp. *atronuchalis*. An unmistakable, lanky plover with black hood, red facial skin and black-tipped red bill. Legs yellow. Upperparts sandy-brown, underparts white. In flight, note prominent white wing bar, black flight feathers, white band across rump and uppertail coverts, and black tail. **DISTRIBUTION** Parts of Middle East, east to Indian sub-continent, SW China, mainland

Southeast Asia and Thai–Malay Peninsula. **HABITS AND HABITATS** Previously a very rare non-breeding visitor, this species has undergone a major expansion in the last decade and is now an uncommon resident of freshwater marshes, wet grasslands, open grassy scrub. Breeding first reported from the Poyan Reservoir area in 2003. Breeds April–June. Nest is a scrape on stony, barren ground, usually containing 4 eggs. Call is a loud, rapid 'did-he-do-it', especially when alarmed. **SITES** Changi coast, Kranji marshes, Pulau Ubin. **CONSERVATION** Nationally endangered, but appears to have become more widespread in recent years.

Pacific Golden Plover ▪ *Pluvialis fulva* 金鸻 Kerinyut Pasifik 25cm

DESCRIPTION A medium-sized, somewhat small-headed plover. Non-breeding birds (shown) are brown with golden-yellow, black and white spangling on upperparts, buffish brow, and pale brown underparts. Some birds arrive in partial breeding plumage, showing a broad white band extending from brow to neck and flanks, separating upperparts from

black undersides. In flight, note plain brown upperparts, dull underwing and narrow pale wing bar. **DISTRIBUTION** Breeds in Arctic tundra across NE Russia and Alaska. Winters in East Africa, Indian sub-continent and across S China and Southeast Asia, east to SW Pacific. **HABITS AND HABITATS** Very common winter visitor and passage migrant, usually the most abundant wader counted annually. Coastal mudflats, sandy shores, wet grasslands and open scrubby fields, including playing fields. Birds begin to arrive in July and depart by May. Usually seen in flocks of a few hundred, occasionally mixing with other waders. **SITES** Sungei Buloh Wetland Reserve, Seletar mudflats, Pulau Ubin. **CONSERVATION** No issues.

Grey Plover ■ *Pluvialis squatarola* 灰鸻 Kerinyut Kelabu 28cm

DESCRIPTION ssp. *squatarola*. A medium-sized plover, similar to Pacific Golden Plover but larger, bigger-headed with a stout bill and whitish, not buffish, brow. Non-breeding birds (shown) appear greyish, with silvery-white and black spangling on upperparts. Underparts mostly white. In flight, note prominent white wing bar and uppertail coverts, boldly barred tail and distinctive black axillaries contrasting with whitish underwing.

DISTRIBUTION Breeds in tundra across N Eurasia and North America. Winters on the coasts of the Americas, Africa and across much of East and Southeast Asia, east to Australia. **HABITS AND HABITATS** Uncommon winter visitor and passage migrant, occurring on sandy beaches, occasionally mudflats. Roosts in dense flocks on isolated rocky outcrops, but forages either singly or in widely spaced flocks for invertebrates (e.g. small crabs), mixing with *Charadrius* plovers. **SITES** Changi coast, offshore islands (e.g. Pulau Semakau, Pulau Ubin). **CONSERVATION** Extensive loss of coastal sandy shores has reduced much wintering habitat.

Little Ringed Plover ■ *Charadrius dubius* 金眶鸻
Rapang Gelang Kecil 17cm

DESCRIPTION ssp. *curonicus*. A small brown plover with a white collar, complete greyish-brown breast band, yellowish eye-ring and yellowish to pinkish legs. Non-breeding birds (shown) are greyish brown on upperparts and head, with indistinct pale forehead and brow; underparts mostly white. Birds in breeding plumage show black breast band, black band across forecrown and prominent yellow eye-ring. **DISTRIBUTION** Breeds across much of

Eurasia, from North Africa and Europe to Indian sub-continent, East Asia, Philippines and New Guinea. Northern populations migrate to winter on coasts of Africa, Middle East, Indian sub-continent and much of East and Southeast Asia to N Australia. **HABITS AND HABITATS** Uncommon winter visitor and passage migrant, occurring on coastal mudflats, sandy beaches, canals and open muddy ground adjacent to ponds. Usually solitary or in pairs, and typically does not join mixed flocks with other waders. **SITES** Sungei Buloh Wetland Reserve, Lorong Halus wetlands. **CONSERVATION** No issues.

Kentish Plover ■ *Charadrius alexandrinus* 环颈鸻 Rapang Pantai 16cm

DESCRIPTION ssp. *alexandrinus, dealbatus*. A small plover with sandy-brown upperparts and narrow lateral breast patch in non-breeding plumage (top). Breeding males have rufous-brown crown to nape, white collar, black forecrown and lateral breast patch. Similar Malaysian Plover has thinner black lateral patch, which joins to form complete band bordering collar. In flight, white wing bars contrast with dark flight feathers. Ssp. *dealbatus*, or 'White-faced' Plover (bottom) from S China is paler, larger-headed, with broader white brow and forehead, but genetic evidence has not supported elevation to species level. **DISTRIBUTION** Breeds across Eurasia, from Europe to Indian sub-continent and East Asia. Northern populations migrate to winter in Africa, Middle East, Indian sub-continent, S China and Southeast Asia. **HABITS AND HABITATS** Uncommon winter visitor and passage migrant to sandy beaches, occasionally mudflats. Forages by scampering along beaches, stopping every now and then to pick up prey such as small crabs. Ssp. *dealbatus* apparently forages more actively, and with a more upright stance. Often joins flocks of other small waders. Arrives mostly in October, departing by April. **SITES** Seletar mudflats, Tuas coast. **CONSERVATION** Extensive loss of coastal sandy shores has greatly reduced wintering habitat.

Malaysian Plover ■ *Charadrius peronii* 马来鸻 Rapang Pasir 15cm

DESCRIPTION A small plover with mottled sandy-brown upperparts and a complete white collar. Male has black lateral band on breast sides which extends round the neck, unlike Kentish Plover (above). Also note white forehead with black patch at mid-crown and black spot behind ear coverts. Legs and feet are often tinged yellowish or pinkish. Female lacks the black markings of the male, appearing generally drabber. **DISTRIBUTION** Coastal Southeast Asia, Greater and Lesser Sundas, Philippines, Sulawesi. **HABITS AND HABITATS** Uncommon resident of undisturbed sandy beaches, including on offshore islands. Usually seen in pairs. Breeds March–April. Nest is a scrape on sandy ground with 2–3 eggs. **SITES** Tuas coast, Marina Barrage, Pulau Semakau. **CONSERVATION** Globally near threatened as populations are threatened by coastal development in the region. Nationally critically endangered.

LEFT: *Female* RIGHT: *Male*

Lesser Sand Plover ■ *Charadrius mongolus* 蒙古沙鸻
Rapang Mongolia 20cm

DESCRIPTION ssp. *schaeferi*, *atrifrons*. A small plover with uniform sandy greyish-brown upperparts, mostly white underparts, white forehead and brow in non-breeding plumage (shown). Dark grey to greenish-grey legs, with tibia obviously shorter than tarsus, appearing stockier than Greater Sand Plover (below). Bill short, black and blunt, and the bulge on the upper mandible occurs on the final third of the bill. In flight, toes project only slightly beyond tail tip. Birds in breeding plumage show distinctive black mask and

orange sides of neck and breast band. **DISTRIBUTION** Breeds from NE Siberia to Chukotka, and NE China, with disjunct populations in Central Asia and Tibetan Plateau. Winters along coasts of S and E Africa eastwards to much of Southeast Asia, New Guinea and Australia. **HABITS AND HABITATS** Common winter visitor and passage migrant occurring in large numbers on sandy beaches and mudflats, rarely inland. Often seen in large, packed flocks, and together with other calidrid sandpipers. Arrives in July and departs by May. Early-arriving birds are often seen in their breeding or partial breeding plumage. Call is a soft trilling 'prrrrrp'. **SITES** Sungei Buloh Wetland Reserve, Seletar mudflats. **CONSERVATION** No issues.

Greater Sand Plover ■ *Charadrius leschenaultii* 铁嘴沙鸻
Rapang Besar 23cm

DESCRIPTION ssp. *leschenaultii*. In non-breeding plumage (shown) resembles Lesser Sand Plover (above), but is noticeably larger and taller, with a squarer head, more robust-looking bill with a bulge on the upper mandible starting midway along the bill. Longer tibia gives it a more lanky appearance. Legs and feet are tinged greenish. In flight, toes project beyond

tail. **DISTRIBUTION** Breeds in Turkey, Middle East and parts of Central Asia, east to Mongolia, S Siberia and N China. Winters along E coast of Africa, Middle East, Indian sub-continent, Southeast Asia, Wallacea and Australia. **HABITS AND HABITATS** Uncommon winter visitor and passage migrant to coastal sandy beaches and mudflats. Often forms mixed flocks with other small waders. Tends to moult earlier than Lesser Sand Plover, and hence is already in non-breeding plumage by the time it arrives in July. **SITES** Sungei Buloh Wetland Reserve, Seletar mudflats, Pulau Ubin. **CONSERVATION** Extensive development in coastal areas has greatly reduced suitable habitat.

Greater Painted-snipe ■ *Rostratula benghalensis* 彩鷸 Meragi Biasa 24cm

DESCRIPTION An unmistakable, plump-looking snipe-like wader. Exhibits reversed sexual dimorphism. Female is bright and boldly marked, with white spectacles contrasting with maroon head and chest, white belly and white band around shoulder. Bill is long, pale pink and droops slightly at tip. Male is paler and shows more variegated plumage, buffish spectacles and greyish-brown head sides, neck and upper breast. **DISTRIBUTION** Widespread from Africa, Madagascar, parts of Middle East and Indian sub-continent, east to Greater and Lesser Sundas. **HABITS AND HABITATS** Uncommon resident of wet grassland and overgrown ditches. Very secretive and mainly crepuscular, thus likely overlooked. Gives an explosive 'kek' when flushed and flies a short distance with slow erratic wing-beats. Polyandrous, females mate with multiple males, after which the males incubate and tend chicks alone. Breeding reported February–October. **SITES** Jurong West, Lorong Halus wetlands. **CONSERVATION** Nationally critically endangered due to extensive habitat loss.

ABOVE: *Male.* BELOW: *Female*

Pheasant-tailed Jacana ■ *Hydrophasianus chirurgus* 水雉
Teratai Ekor Panjang 30cm

DESCRIPTION An unmistakable rail-like wader with very long toes. Non-breeding adult (shown) is brownish on much of upperparts with whitish brow extending into a yellowish patch down the neck side; underparts white with black eye-stripe extending down the side of neck and broadly across the breast. Feet greenish with prominently long toes. In flight, mostly white wings diagnostic. **DISTRIBUTION** Indian sub-continent, S China and much of Southeast Asia. Northern populations migrate to winter in S India and Southeast Asia east to Java. **HABITS AND HABITATS** Rare winter visitor occurring in marshes, flooded grasslands and freshwater ponds with dense fringing and floating vegetation, where it forages for insects and other invertebrates. Polyandrous, with females breeding with multiple males. **SITES** Sungei Buloh Wetland Reserve, Kranji marshes, Western Catchment area. **CONSERVATION** Extensive loss of freshwater marshes has greatly reduced wintering habitat.

Pin-tailed Snipe ■ *Gallinago stenura* 针尾沙锥 Berkik Ekor Runcing 26cm

DESCRIPTION Similar to Common Snipe and best separated by shorter bill, buffish brow always broader than dark eye-stripe at base of bill, narrower pale brown to whitish edges to scapulars and tail only projects slightly beyond closed wing tips. In flight, tail appears shorter and almost entire length of toes extends beyond tail tip. Also note less distinct whitish trailing edge to secondaries. Best separated from the similar-looking Swinhoe's

Snipe G. *megala* in hand by extremely narrow pin-like outer tail feathers. **DISTRIBUTION** Breeds across central and E Siberia, Mongolia and NE China. Winters in Indian sub-continent, S China and much of Southeast Asia. **HABITS AND HABITATS** Fairly common winter visitor to open freshwater marshes, wet grasslands, muddy banks of canals, and occasionally wet playing fields. Avoids dense vegetation, taller than a standing bird. Takes off quickly when flushed, uttering a short, raspy 'squok'. **SITES** Lorong Halus wetlands, Sungei Buloh Wetland Reserve. **CONSERVATION** Extensive loss of freshwater marshes and wet grasslands has greatly reduced wintering habitat.

Common Snipe ■ *Gallinago gallinago* 扇尾沙锥 Berkik Ekor Kipas 26cm

DESCRIPTION ssp. *gallinago*. Has a longer bill than similar-looking Pin-tailed Snipe (above). Dark eye-stripe at base of bill usually broader than buffish brow. Note also prominent buffish white lateral stripes on upperparts. Tip of tail projects beyond closed wings. In flight, note prominent white trailing edge to secondaries. **DISTRIBUTION** Breeds across Eurasia, from W Europe to NW India, NE China and E Russia. Winters in Africa, Middle East and Indian sub-continent, east to S China and much of Southeast

Asia. **HABITS AND HABITATS** Fairly common winter visitor to freshwater marshes, wet grasslands and playing fields, often in proximity to Pin-tailed Snipe. Sometimes seen foraging on muddy banks of streams and ditches. Takes off quickly when flushed, flying off in an erratic and zigzagging manner unlike the more direct flight of Pin-tailed Snipe. **SITES** Lorong Halus wetlands, Sungei Buloh Wetland Reserve. **CONSERVATION** Extensive loss of freshwater marshes and wet grasslands has reduced wintering habitat.

Asian Dowitcher ■ *Limnodromus semipalmatus* 半蹼鹬
Kedidi Paruh Tegak 34cm

DESCRIPTION Resembles Bar-tailed Godwit *Limosa lapponica* but smaller and shorter-necked. In non-breeding plumage, upperparts mostly greyish brown, with light barring on underparts. Note also distinctive long straight black bill, slightly swollen at the tip. In flight, secondaries and greater coverts paler than rest of wing, and white underwing coverts.

DISTRIBUTION Breeds in SE Siberia, Mongolia, and NE China. Winters on coasts of central Thailand, Thai–Malay Peninsula and Greater Sundas, east to Australia. **HABITS AND HABITATS** Rare passage migrant occurring on coastal mudflats. Feeds with a distinctive continuous vertical probing action. Most pass through Singapore in September–October, though some arrive as early as August. Much of world population stage on coastal mudflats off E Sumatra. **SITES** Sungei Buloh Wetland Reserve. **CONSERVATION** Globally near threatened due to loss of coastal mudflats in staging grounds.

Black-tailed Godwit ■ *Limosa limosa* 黑尾塍鹬 Kedidi Ekor Hitam 40cm

DESCRIPTION ssp. *melanuroides*. Large sandpiper with straight bicoloured bill, with pinkish basal half, unlike slightly upcurved bill of similar Bar-tailed Godwit *L. lapponica*. In non-breeding plumage, upperparts plain brownish-grey, becoming paler at the head-sides. Underparts mostly whitish. Legs black, longer than Bar-tailed Godwit's. In flight shows prominent white upperwing bars and white band across rump contrasting with black tail. **DISTRIBUTION** Breeds across Eurasia, from W Europe discontinuously to NE China and E Russia. Winters in parts of Europe, N and central Africa, Middle East and Indian sub-continent, east to New Guinea, Australia and SW Pacific. **HABITS AND HABITATS** Uncommon migrant to coastal mudflats. Commoner of the two godwits, but sightings in Singapore appear to have declined. Now usually seen in very small groups, and sometimes only singles. Occurs mostly August–March, and mainly as a passage migrant. **SITES** Sungei Buloh Wetland Reserve, Pulau Ubin. **CONSERVATION** Globally near threatened. Has suffered significant habitat loss in staging areas in China and Korea.

Whimbrel
■ *Numenius phaeopus* 中杓鷸 Kendi Pisau Raut 44cm

DESCRIPTION ssp. *phaeopus*. Large shorebird with long, decurved bill with pinkish base, and bluish-grey legs. Upperparts mostly dark greyish brown. Combination of prominent dark brown lateral crown-stripe and eye-stripe and broad whitish brow distinguishes from rarer Eurasian Curlew (below). In flight, dark above with contrasting white back and rump and plain whitish underwing coverts. **DISTRIBUTION** Breeds in Arctic tundra across N Eurasia and North America. Winters on the coasts of SW Europe, Africa, Middle East and Indian sub-continent, east to Australia and the Pacific. **HABITS AND HABITATS** Common migrant to coastal mudflats, sandy beaches, reefs and tidal ponds, with larger numbers overwintering annually. Feeds by probing its long decurved bill into the mud for crabs and other invertebrates. Congregates in large noisy flocks. Call is a loud whinnying trill in flight. Arrives in early July and departs by late May. A few oversummer annually. **SITES** Sungei Buloh Wetland Reserve, Pulau Ubin. **CONSERVATION** No issues.

Eurasian Curlew ■ *Numenius arquata* 白腰杓鷸 Kendi Besar 55cm

DESCRIPTION ssp. *orientalis*. One of the largest shorebirds. Resembles Whimbrel (above) but is much larger and has a longer bill. Female is larger and longer-billed than male. In flight, shows white back and rump contrasting with dark brown upperparts, and largely white underwing coverts, unlike the densely barred underwing coverts of the much rarer Far Eastern Curlew *N. madagascariensis*. **DISTRIBUTION** Breeds across Eurasia, from W Europe discontinuously to NE China and E Russia. Winters on the coasts of Africa, Middle

East, Indian sub-continent, S and E China, Southeast Asia and Philippines. **HABITS AND HABITATS** Rare migrant to coastal mudflats and sandy beaches, very rarely in wet grasslands. Previously regular, there are few recent records. Forages by deeply probing mud for invertebrates. Regularly joins Whimbrel and other medium-sized waders in mixed flocks, although individuals also forage alone. Occurs mostly September–March. **SITES** Sungei Buloh Wetland Reserve, Changi coast. **CONSERVATION** Globally near threatened. Loss of sandy shores has reduced wintering habitat.

Common Redshank ■ *Tringa totanus* 红脚鹬 Kedidi Kaki Merah 28cm

DESCRIPTION ssp. *craggi, eurhina, terrignotae, ussuriensis.* A medium-sized sandpiper with prominent red legs and feet. Lightly mottled grey-brown upperparts and whitish underparts with fine dark breast streaks. In flight shows distinctive white secondaries, a feature absent in the rare Spotted Redshank *T. erythropus*. Note that the four ssp. can only be confidently distinguished in breeding plumage. **DISTRIBUTION** Breeds across Eurasia, including much of Europe, Central Asia, Tibetan Plateau, NE China and E Russia. Winters in Africa and the Middle East, east to Southeast Asia and Australia. **HABITS AND HABITATS** Very common migrant to coastal mudflats, freshwater marshes and wet grassland. Often seen in big flocks and among the most abundant waders. Gregarious and frequently forms mixed flocks with other waders Birds arrive from early July and mostly depart by May. Small numbers oversummer annually. **SITES** Suitable habitat across Singapore (e.g. Sungei Buloh Wetland Reserve). **CONSERVATION** No issues.

Marsh Sandpiper ■ *Tringa stagnatilis* 泽鹬 Kedidi Paya 24cm

DESCRIPTION A medium-sized, graceful-looking sandpiper, washed greyish brown on upperparts; underparts white. Resembles Common Greenshank (see p.58) but smaller and daintier, with a thin 'needle-like' black bill, and lacks bold streaks on head, neck and mantle. Broad white brow. Legs and feet light greenish yellow. In flight, shows a prominent white patch from back to rump. **DISTRIBUTION** Breeds from E Europe and Central Asia to NE China and E Russia. Winters in Africa, SW Europe, Middle East, Indian sub-continent, much of Southeast Asia and Australia. **HABITS AND HABITATS** Common migrant to coastal mudflats, sandy beaches, freshwater marshes, wet grasslands and ponds with fringing vegetation. Often seen in mixed flocks with other waders. Forms large flocks, and up to 550 birds have been counted. Birds arrive from August and mostly depart by May. **SITES** Suitable habitat across Singapore (e.g. Sungei Buloh Wetland Reserve, Pulau Ubin). **CONSERVATION** No issues.

Common Greenshank ■ *Tringa nebularia* 青脚鹬
Kedidi Kaki Hijau 32cm

DESCRIPTION Similar to Marsh Sandpiper but much larger and stockier. Bill greenish grey, slightly upturned with dark tip. Legs long and greenish yellow. Upperparts mostly greyish; crown, ear-coverts, hindneck, mantle and sides of breast heavily streaked, unlike Marsh Sandpiper. In flight, note prominent white rump and back. **DISTRIBUTION** Breeds

across N Eurasia, from Scandinavia to E Russia. Winters in Africa, Middle East and Indian subcontinent, east to S China, Southeast Asia and Australia. **HABITS AND HABITATS** Common migrant to coastal mudflats, sandy beaches, rocky shores and occasionally wet grassland and ponds with fringing vegetation. One of the commonest shorebirds here. Often in mixed flocks with other waders, especially Common Redshank and Marsh Sandpiper. Birds arrive mostly in August–September and depart by late April. **SITES** Suitable habitat across Singapore (e.g. Sungei Buloh Wetland Reserve, Pulau Ubin). **CONSERVATION** No issues.

Grey-tailed Tattler ■ *Tringa brevipes* 灰尾漂鹬
Kedidi Ekor Kelabu 26 cm

DESCRIPTION A stout-looking shorebird, superficially similar to Common Sandpiper (see p.60), but much larger. In non-breeding plumage, upperparts mostly dark grey, underparts white with a greyish wash across breast and flanks. Bill greenish-yellow; broad white brow contrasts strongly with black eye-stripe. Legs yellowish, and short, not projecting beyond tail if seen in flight. Breeding birds are darker, and boldly barred on pale underparts.

DISTRIBUTION Breeds C Siberia, east to Chukotka and Kamchatka. Winters S and E China, Taiwan to much of Southeast Asia, and eastwards to Australia and Polynesia. **HABITS AND HABITATS** Uncommon migrant to coastal mudflats, sandy beaches and rocky shores, including on offshore islands (e.g. Semakau). Often seen singly, but sometimes in mixed flocks with other waders, especially plovers. Forages mostly for small crabs and other shellfish. Birds arrive mostly in August and depart by late April. **SITES** Sungei Buloh Wetland Reserve, Pulau Ubin, Pulau Semakau. **CONSERVATION** Globally near threatened.

Wood Sandpiper ■ *Tringa glareola* 林鷸 Kedidi Kayu 21cm

DESCRIPTION A medium-sized, slender-looking sandpiper with distinctive heavily spotted greyish-brown upperparts. Note also long broad whitish brow, straight greyish bill and yellow legs. In flight, uniformly brown upperparts contrast with white rump; also several narrow bars on tail. Underwings pale, unlike the much rarer Green Sandpiper *T. ochropus*, which has almost black underwings. **DISTRIBUTION** Breeds across N Eurasia, from Scandinavia to NE China and E Russia. Winters in Africa, Middle East and Indian sub-continent, east to S China, Southeast Asia and Australia. **HABITS AND HABITATS** Uncommon migrant to brackish and freshwater wetlands, especially freshwater ponds with fringing vegetation, marshes, wet grasslands and flooded pools on reclaimed land. Avoids the intertidal zone. Seen singly or in small flocks. Birds arrive from July and usually depart by May. Call is a rapid and sharp 'sif-sif-sif'. **SITES** Suitable habitat across Singapore (e.g. Lorong Halus Wetlands). **CONSERVATION** Much of the wet grassland habitat favoured by this species is transient and slated for development.

Terek Sandpiper ■ *Xenus cinereus* 翹嘴鷸 Kedidi Sereng 24cm

DESCRIPTION A stocky-looking sandpiper with long, upturned blackish bill with pale pinkish base and short orangy-yellow legs. Upperparts plain brownish grey, underparts white with faint streaking on neck and breast. In flight, upperparts are uniform brownish grey with distinctive broad white trailing edge to secondaries. **DISTRIBUTION** Breeds across N Eurasia, from Scandinavia and much of Russia to E Siberia. Winters along the coast of Africa, Middle East, Indian sub-continent, east to S China, Southeast Asia and Australia. **HABITS AND HABITATS** Uncommon migrant to coastal mudflats, sandy beaches, tidal ponds. Occurs in small groups of 10–15 birds. Runs actively while foraging. Call is a rapid fluty 'twee-hwee-hwee'. Birds arrive as early as July and mostly depart by May. **SITES** Sungei Buloh Wetland Reserve, Mandai and Seletar mudflats. **CONSERVATION** Extensive loss of coastal mudflats has greatly reduced suitable habitat.

Common Sandpiper ■ *Actitis hypoleucos* 矶鹬 Kedidi Pasir 20cm

DESCRIPTION A small, brownish sandpiper with a straight black bill and short greenish-yellow legs. Underparts white with prominent white patch between wing and breast. Also has distinctive white eye-ring and broad white brow. In flight, uniform brown upperparts contrast with long white wing bars. Flies with stiff wing-beats, alternating with short glides on down-turned wings. Has an unusual habit of 'bobbing' its tail. **DISTRIBUTION** Breeds across much of Eurasia, from W Europe to E Siberia and Japan, as far south as Middle East. Winters across Africa, Middle East and Indian sub-continent, east to S China, Southeast Asia, Australia and SW Pacific.

HABITS AND HABITATS Very common, highly adaptable migrant to sandy shores, coastal mudflats, freshwater marshes, wet grassland and concretised canals, where it is usually the only wader present. Usually seen singly or in small groups. Call is a sharp, plaintive 'swee-swee-swee' with a ringing quality. Birds starts to arrive at the end of July and mostly leave by March. **SITES** Suitable habitat throughout Singapore (e.g. Sungei Buloh Wetland Reserve). **CONSERVATION** No issues.

Ruddy Turnstone ■ *Arenaria interpres* 翻石鹬 Kedidi Batu 24cm

DESCRIPTION ssp. *interpres*. A plump-looking, short-billed shorebird with short orange-red legs and feet. Bold black patches on head and neck sides extending across upper breast diagnostic. Upperparts mostly dark grey-brown, contrasting with mostly white underparts. In flight, note diagnostic white wing bar and wing-covert patch, white back, white-based black tail. **DISTRIBUTION** Breeds in coastal tundra across N Eurasia and North America. Winters in temperate and tropical regions across Americas, Africa, Asia and Australasia.

HABITS AND HABITATS Uncommon winter visitor in small numbers to mudflats, sandy shores and breakwaters. Wintering population appears to have declined in recent years. Usually seen singly or in pairs, rarely in groups. Often joins similar-sized waders like Curlew Sandpiper and Sanderling. Has a rather peculiar habit of foraging by flipping over stones and debris for small invertebrates. Birds start arriving in August and usually depart by April. **SITES** Sungei Buloh Wetland Reserve, Mandai Mudflats. **CONSERVATION** Extensive loss of coastal mudflats has greatly reduced suitable habitat.

Great Knot ■ *Calidris tenuirostris* 大滨鹬 Kedidi Dian Besar 27cm

DESCRIPTION A large, stocky sandpiper with downward-tapering black bill. Legs short and dull greenish-yellow. In non-breeding plumage, upperparts dark grey, with neck, upper breast and flanks spotted greyish brown, becoming sparser lower down. Rest of underparts white. In flight, distinct white wing bar contrasts with black outer wing; white rump and underwing coverts. **DISTRIBUTION** Breeds in NE Siberia, east to Chukotka. Winters along coasts of Indian sub-continent, S China and much of coastal Southeast Asia, east to Australia. **HABITS AND HABITATS** Rare passage migrant, occurring in coastal mudflats, sandy beaches and tidal ponds. Few records of overwintering. Gregarious, usually seen in small groups of as many as 10 birds. Mostly arrives in September, departing by March. Specialist feeder on snails and bivalves. **SITES** Sungei Buloh Wetland Reserve. **CONSERVATION** Globally endangered due to loss of staging habitat in Yellow Sea coast.

Sanderling ■ *Calidris alba* 三趾滨鹬 Kedidi Kapak 20cm

DESCRIPTION ssp. *rubida*. A small, very pale sandpiper, palest of *Calidris* sandpipers locally, with a short straight bill and grey ear coverts. In non-breeding plumage, upperparts pale grey, underparts white. Often shows a pronounced dark patch at bend of wing. Leg and feet black; lacks hind toe, but this is difficult to see. Juvenile (shown) has darker streaks on crown, and black and white spangles on mantle and scapulars. In flight, shows prominent broad white wing bar across upperwing. **DISTRIBUTION** Breeds in coastal tundra across N Eurasia and North America. Winters on coasts of temperate and tropical regions across Americas, Africa, Asia and Australasia. **HABITS AND HABITATS** Uncommon migrant to sandy shores, very rarely coastal mudflats. Gregarious, foraging in closely knit flocks, usually amongst other small shorebirds. Forages by running on the beach in a rather mechanical fashion, usually by the surf to pick up disturbed invertebrates. **SITES** Pulau Ubin. **CONSERVATION** Extensive loss of sandy beaches has greatly reduced wintering habitat.

Red-necked Stint ■ *Calidris ruficollis* 红颈滨鹬 Kedidi Luris Leher 15cm

DESCRIPTION A very small, dumpy sandpiper with a short black bill. In non-breeding plumage, upperparts brownish-grey. Underparts mostly white with greyish lateral breast patch. Smaller and darker than Sanderling (see p.61). Brow whitish. Legs and feet black. In flight, note narrow white wing bar and dark centre to rump and tail. **DISTRIBUTION**

Breeds in N-central and E Siberia, east to Chukotka. Winters in coastal Bangladesh, S and E China and much of Southeast Asia, east to Australia and New Zealand. **HABITS AND HABITATS** Uncommon migrant to coastal mudflats, sandy beaches and tidal ponds, rarely wet grassland. Feeds with rapid pecking action, usually in small parties, associating with other small sandpipers and plovers. Arrives mostly in September, and departs by April. **SITES** Sungei Buloh Wetland Reserve, Pulau Ubin. **CONSERVATION** Globally near-threatened.

Long-toed Stint ■ *Calidris subminuta* 长趾滨鹬 Kedidi Jari Panjang 15cm

DESCRIPTION A very small dumpy sandpiper with a longish neck, yellow legs and thin black bill with pale-based lower mandible. In non-breeding plumage, upperparts brown with dark-centred feathers. Underparts white with neck sides and breast brown-washed with dark streaks. **DISTRIBUTION** Breeds discontinuously from central Siberia and

Mongolia to Chukotka. Winters in Sri Lanka, S China and much of Southeast Asia, east to New Guinea and Australia. **HABITS AND HABITATS** Uncommon migrant to tidal ponds, coastal mudflats and freshwater ponds with fringing vegetation. Numbers appear to have declined. Often feeds in small groups in dense vegetation. When alarmed, may stand erect with outstretched neck. Arrives mostly in September, departing by April. **SITES** Sungei Buloh Wetland Reserve, Lorong Halus Wetlands. **CONSERVATION** Has declined in the past two decades due to loss of wintering habitat.

Curlew Sandpiper ■ *Calidris ferruginea* 弯嘴滨鹬 Kedidi Pasir Kendi 21cm

DESCRIPTION A medium-sized sandpiper with long decurved black bill and long black legs. In non-breeding plumage, upperparts pale grey with prominent white brow. Underparts white with faint greyish wash on breast. In flight, prominent white wing bars and white band on lower rump. Similar-looking Dunlin C. *alpina*, a very rare vagrant, shows a dark centre to the white rump. Juvenile (shown) is darker on underparts with neat pale fringes to feathers. **DISTRIBUTION** Breeds in tundra of N Russia. Winters across Africa, Middle Eastand Indian sub-continent, east to Southeast Asia and Australia. **HABITS AND HABITATS** Uncommon migrant to coastal mudflats, tidal ponds and sandy beaches. Gregarious, usually in large groups, forming mixed flocks with other waders. Feeds by pecking and vigorous probing, often wading belly-deep into water. Birds arrive mostly in August and depart around April. **SITES** Sungei Buloh Wetland Reserve, Mandai Mudflats **CONSERVATION** Wintering population here has declined sharply in recent years; also mean autumn arrival dates have delayed by around 2 days. Globally near-threatened.

Broad-billed Sandpiper ■ *Calidris falcinellus* 阔嘴鹬
Kedidi Paruh Lebar 17cm

DESCRIPTION ssp. *sibirica*. A small sandpiper resembling the stints but larger, with longer and broader black bill, kinked downward at the tip. Upperparts greyish-brown. Underparts white with greyish wash on chest. Prominent white brow and narrow white lateral crown-stripe gives the appearance of a split brow, which is diagnostic. **DISTRIBUTION** Breeds discontinuously across N Eurasia, from Scandinavia to central and E Siberia. Winters along coasts of East Africa, Middle East and Indian sub-continent, east to S China, Southeast Asia and Australia. **HABITS AND HABITATS** Uncommon migrant to coastal mudflats, sandy beaches and tidal ponds. Typically found in small numbers mixed with other waders. Passage birds usually occur between September and December. Feeds by walking quickly and actively jabbing bill vertically into mud to pick polychaete worms. **SITES** Sungei Buloh Wetland Reserve. **CONSERVATION** Extensive loss of wintering coastal mudflats means that suitable habitat is much reduced.

Oriental Pratincole ■ *Glareola maldivarum* 普通燕鸻
Kedidi-Padang Biasa 24cm

DESCRIPTION A graceful, tern-like shorebird with short black bill and red base to lower mandible, long pointed wings and short forked tail. Plumage mostly greyish brown, with a buffish throat bordered by a narrow black necklace. In flight, plain greyish-brown upperparts contrast with white rump. Underwing dark brown with chestnut coverts. **DISTRIBUTION** Breeds in parts of Indian sub-continent, to NE China, Mongolia and

Russian Far East, and parts of Southeast Asia (e.g. Philippines). Northern populations winter in Greater and Lesser Sundas, Sulawesi, New Guinea and Australia. **HABITS AND HABITATS** Uncommon passage migrant to open grasslands, scrub and barren ground on reclaimed land, rarely on mudflats and marshes. Rarely overwinters. Usually in small flocks, although numbers in the low hundreds have also been recorded. Autumn passage mostly September–October. **SITES** Tuas West, Seletar north. **CONSERVATION** Extensive loss of coastal grassland has greatly reduced suitable staging habitat.

Black-headed Gull ■ *Chroicocephalus ridibundus* 红嘴鸥
Camar Topeng Hitam 40cm

DESCRIPTION A small, 'tern-like' gull with black-tipped red bill. Wings and mantle pale

grey, legs and feet dark red. Head is white with dark ear spot, with grey smudging on crown. First-winter bird (shown) has paler bill, duller legs and a broad greyish-brown band across upperwing coverts. **DISTRIBUTION** Breeds across Eurasia, from much of W Europe to NE China, E Russia and Kamchatka. Winters across Africa, eastwards to much of E and Southeast Asia. **HABITS AND HABITATS** Uncommon migrant to inshore waters, coastal mudflats and estuaries. Often seen perching on 'kelong' poles by the coast. More regularly encountered than Brown-headed Gull *C. brunnicephalus*. Recorded November–March. **SITES** Mandai and Seletar mudflats. **CONSERVATION** No issues.

Greater Crested Tern ■ *Thalasseus bergii* 大凤头燕鸥
Camar Berjambul Besar 47cm

DESCRIPTION ssp. *cristatus*. A large, black-capped, crested tern. Similar to Lesser Crested Tern (below) but larger, stockier, and has a thick yellow, not orange-yellow, bill. Mantle and wings mostly grey. Non-breeding birds (shown) show more white on forecrown and around eye, with fine black spotting, while black cap starts from behind eye. **DISTRIBUTION** Throughout much of Indian and Pacific oceans, breeding colonially on small offshore islands. In Southeast Asia, colonies are known atolls in the China Sea.

HABITS AND HABITATS Common migrant to coastal and offshore waters around Singapore, especially the Straits of Johor and Singapore Straits. Flies rapidly with deep, slow wing-beats. Hunts by diving and plunging into the water. Sometimes seen roosting on intertidal mudflats, 'kelong' poles, rocky outcrops and floating objects. Records from most months, but commonest August–April. **SITES** Mandai mudflats, Pulau Ubin. **CONSERVATION** No issues.

Lesser Crested Tern ■ *Thalasseus bengalensis* 小凤头燕鸥
Camar Berjambul Kecil 38cm

DESCRIPTION ssp. *torresii*. A medium-sized white tern with black hindcrown and diagnostic orange-yellow bill. Upperparts and upperwings pale grey, underparts white. Non-breeding birds (shown) white on forecrown and much of crown, appearing more white-headed than Greater Crested Tern (above). Breeding birds have a black cap that extends from bill to nape, unlike breeding Greater Crested Tern, which has white patch on forecrown. **DISTRIBUTION** Breeds on coasts of N and NE Africa, Middle East, islands in Indian Ocean (e.g. Laccadives), east to New Guinea and Australia. Disperses widely across SW Pacific and Indian Ocean. **HABITS AND HABITATS** Fairly common migrant to coastal and offshore waters around Singapore. Sometimes seen roosting on coastal mudflats, 'kelong' poles, rocky outcrops and floating buoys. Recorded mostly August–April. On the islet of Pedra Branca, off E coast of Singapore, roosting flocks of up to 200 birds have been observed. **SITES** Mandai mudflats, Pulau Ubin, Pedra Branca. **CONSERVATION** No issues.

Little Tern ▪ *Sternula albifrons* 白额燕鸥 Camar Kecil Biasa 24cm

DESCRIPTION ssp. *sinensis*. A small, dainty-looking tern. Mantle and wings pale grey. Non-breeding birds have long black bill, black legs and feet. Lores and forecrown white while hindcrown, eye-stripe and nape black. Breeding birds (shown) have black crown, nape and eye-stripe with white forehead patch, and yellow bill with black tip. In flight, note grey wings with dark outermost flight feathers. **DISTRIBUTION** Breeds from W Europe, Africa and Middle East to Indian sub-continent, much of East Asia, Southeast Asia, New Guinea and Australia. Northern populations migrate to winter in the tropics. **HABITS AND HABITATS** Common resident and migrant to sandy beaches, coastal

mudflats, reservoirs and lakes. Flies with rapid wing-beats. Hunts by hovering, then diving into water. Breeding recorded May–September on Changi coast and also landfills in Tuas and Tampines. Nest consists of a slight depression in which 2–3 eggs are laid. Call is a high-pitched 'kik', usually given in flight. **SITES** Tuas West, Pulau Ubin, Kranji Reservoir, Lorong Halus wetlands. **CONSERVATION** Nationally endangered, as most known breeding sites are on areas slated for development.

Aleutian Tern ▪ *Onychoprion aleuticus* 白腰燕鸥 Camar Aleutian 33cm

DESCRIPTION A medium-sized grey and white tern very similar to Common Tern *Sterna hirundo*. Non-breeding birds have extensive white crown with black nape, unlike Common Tern, which has mostly black cap with limited white on forehead. In flight, note narrow black bar along trailing edge of secondaries, black outer primaries and white rump contrasting with grey mantle and wings. Breeding birds (shown) show diagnostic white forehead bounded by black cap and eye-stripe. **DISTRIBUTION** Breeds on coasts of easternmost Russia (Chukotka, Kamchatka), Sakhalin and Alaska, as well as islands

in Bering Sea. Apparently winters in coastal waters across Thai–Malay Peninsula, Greater Sundas, Sulawesi and Maluku. **HABITS AND HABITATS** Fairly common migrant to coastal and offshore waters. Recent pelagic surveys around the Singapore Straits found this species to be commoner than previously thought. Autumn passage September–October, and spring passage March–April. Often seen resting on pieces of flotsam. **SITES** Singapore Straits. **CONSERVATION** No issues.

Bridled Tern ■ *Onychoprion anaethetus* 褐翅燕鸥 Camar Batu 38cm

DESCRIPTION ssp. *anaethetus*. A dark, medium-sized tern with deeply forked tail. Upperparts mostly dark greyish brown, contrasting with white underparts. Breeding birds have black cap and nape, with thin white forehead band extending from behind eye, bounded below by black eye-stripe. Non-breeding birds (shown) have more extensive white forehead. **DISTRIBUTION** Breeds on small islands across tropical Atlantic, Indian and E Pacific oceans. **HABITS AND HABITATS** Uncommon non-breeding visitor to offshore and coastal waters, and breeds on Pedra Branca. Appears more common in Singapore Straits than Johor Straits. Breeding reported in April, and birds were observed incubating single eggs laid on bare concrete structures, with no nesting material. **SITES** Singapore Straits, Pedra Branca. **CONSERVATION** Its only known breeding site is unprotected and may be subject to human disturbance.

Black-naped Tern ■ *Sterna sumatrana* 黑枕燕鸥
Camar Tengkuk Hitam 31cm

DESCRIPTION ssp. *sumatrana*. A medium-sized, very pale tern appearing all white when seen from afar. Black stripe extending from before eyes to lower nape diagnostic. Upperparts and wings very pale grey; rest of body white. Legs, feet and bill black. Tail deeply forked. **DISTRIBUTION** Breeds on islands across tropical parts of Indian and Pacific oceans, including across much of Southeast Asia. **HABITS AND HABITATS** Uncommon resident of coastal and offshore waters. Appears to be commoner in Johor Straits than Singapore Straits. Breeding documented on a rocky stack off Changi Point since 1949. Clutches of 2 are laid on rocky surfaces with no nesting material. Usually more numerous during breeding months, April–August, after which numbers drop, suggesting post-breeding dispersal. **SITES** Changi Point, Pulau Ubin. **CONSERVATION** Nationally endangered, as only known breeding site is not protected and is regularly subject to human disturbance.

Whiskered Tern
■ *Chlidonias hybrida* 须浮鸥 Camar Bermisai 26cm

DESCRIPTION ssp. *hybrida*. A small tern of lakes and rivers. Non-breeding birds similar to White-winged Tern (below), but larger and has stouter black bill, black mask and hindcrown. Forecrown and lores white. Ear coverts, hindcrown and nape blackish. Note also dark reddish legs and feet. Juvenile (shown) has brownish mantle, scapulars and tertials. **DISTRIBUTION** Breeds discontinuously across much of Africa, Eurasia and Australia, from W Europe, Middle East and parts of Central Asia to NE China and Russian Far East. Winters across Africa, Indian sub-continent and Southeast Asia, east to New Guinea and Australia. **HABITS AND HABITATS** Uncommon migrant to inland lakes, rivers and reservoirs. May have been overlooked due to the resemblance to the commoner White-winged Tern. Feeds by dipping or hawking over water surface. Recorded September–February. **SITES** Kranji Reservoir, Lorong Halus wetlands. **CONSERVATION** No issues.

White-winged Tern ■ *Chlidonias leucopterus* 白翅浮鸥
Camar Hitam Sayap Putih 23cm

DESCRIPTION A small, stocky tern of lakes and rivers. Non-breeding birds (shown) distinguished from Whiskered Tern (above) by smaller size, finer bill and distinctive head pattern: an isolated black roundish ear-covert patch, appearing somewhat like a headphone, and thin black patch stretching down centre of nape. In flight, also note

darker outer primaries and dark bands across shoulders and secondaries. **DISTRIBUTION** Breeds discontinuously across much of Eurasia, from E Europe, Middle East and Central Asia to NE China and Russian Far East. Winters from Africa east to Southeast Asia, New Guinea and Australia. **HABITS AND HABITATS** Fairly common migrant to inland lakes, rivers and reservoirs, occasionally seen in coastal waters. Like Whiskered Tern, feeds by dipping to the water surface. Occurs mostly September–February. **SITES** Kranji Reservoir, Lorong Halus wetlands. **CONSERVATION** Wintering numbers in Singapore have declined greatly in recent years.

Parasitic Jaeger ▪ *Stercorarius parasiticus* 短尾贼鸥
Camar Kejar Arktik 42–54cm

DESCRIPTION Resembles a large dark gull but has long pointed wings capable of fast and manoeuvrable flight. Plumage highly variable. Pale-morph non-breeding adults are dark brown on upperparts and white below, with dark mottled breast band. May retain tail streamers. Juveniles (shown) are mostly brown. In flight shows pale-barred uppertail coverts, underwing coverts and axillaries, with a pale patch on the primaries. Two other species, Pomarine *S. pomarinus* and Long-tailed Jaeger *S. longicaudus*, can also be found in Singapore's seas, and can be difficult to distinguish from this species. **DISTRIBUTION** Breeds across North American Arctic and N Eurasia, east to Bering Sea coasts. Winters in seas throughout tropics and southern hemisphere. **HABITS AND HABITATS** Previously thought to be a rare vagrant, but recent pelagic surveys found this bird to be a regular passage migrant passing through offshore waters in the Singapore Straits in October–November. A well-known kleptoparasite, often seen chasing terns until they drop their food. **SITES** Singapore Straits. **CONSERVATION** No issues.

Juvenile

Red Turtle Dove ▪ *Streptopelia tranquebarica* 火斑鸠 Tekukur Merah 23cm

DESCRIPTION ssp. *humilis*. The only pigeon with a black collar on the hindneck, sometimes confused with Spotted Dove (see p.70) if poorly seen. Wings and back rufous, lightly contrasting with light bluish-grey head. Rump and tail grey, with white edge to tail tip which is visible in flight and a diagnostic feature. Female has a less rich plumage and are pale brown on the wings and back. **DISTRIBUTION** Much of Indian sub-continent, S and E China, mainland Southeast Asia and the Philippines. **HABITS AND HABITATS** Uncommon introduced resident of secondary forest edge, open grassy scrub, especially on reclaimed land and parkland. Usually gathers in large flocks, resting on *Casuarina* trees, or feeding on the ground with other pigeons. Nomadic and wanders widely. **SITES** Changi area, Pulau Ubin. **CONSERVATION** May compete with Peaceful Dove where they co-occur.

Spotted Dove
▪ *Spilopelia chinensis* 珠颈斑鸠 Tekukur Biasa 30cm

DESCRIPTION ssp. *tigrina*. The only pigeon with a white-spotted black collar on the hindneck. Head and breast pinkish brown, contrasting with dark brown upperparts. In flight, note contrasting paler wing coverts against darker flight feathers, and white tips to outer tail feathers. **DISTRIBUTION** Indian sub-continent, S and E China across mainland Southeast Asia, Thai–Malay Peninsula, Greater Sundas and Palawan. Widely introduced worldwide. **HABITS AND HABITATS** Very common resident of secondary scrub, mangrove edges, old plantations, grasslands, parkland and urban areas. Usually seen feeding on the ground, or perched on open branches or antennas on buildings. A commonly seen flight display involves birds flying vertically up with rapid wing-beats and slowly gliding down with wings spread out. Call is a low, pleasing series of 'croo' notes. **SITES** Suitable habitat across Singapore. **CONSERVATION** Poaching for the songbird trade may pose some threat to this species.

Common Emerald Dove ▪ *Chalcophaps indica* 绿翅金鸠
Punai Tanah 25cm

DESCRIPTION ssp. *indica*. A colourful pigeon of the forest floor. Head, neck and breast of male (shown) a rich vinous-pink contrasting with white forehead and shoulder patch. Bill bright red. Wings and back a rich iridescent green. Female is similar to the male,

but has a grey forehead patch. **DISTRIBUTION** Indian sub-continent, S China, mainland Southeast Asia and Thai–Malay Peninsula, east to New Guinea and Australia. **HABITS AND HABITATS** Common resident of primary and secondary forests, mangroves, old plantations and occasionally secondary scrub. Usually seen feeding quietly on the forest floor, flushing when approached too closely. Call is a low, deep 'coo'. **SITES** Central Catchment Nature Reserve, Pulau Ubin, Singapore Zoo. **CONSERVATION** No issues.

Zebra Dove ■ *Geopelia striata* 斑姫地鳩 Merbuk Aman 20cm

DESCRIPTION A petite-looking pigeon with a distinct blue ring around the eye. Upperparts sandy brown, contrasting with pale grey head and breast. Flanks washed pink. Heavily barred from neck to rump, and on breast and flanks.. **DISTRIBUTION** Thai–Malay Peninsula, Sumatra, Java, Philippines, Sulawesi, Lesser Sundas. **HABITS AND HABITATS** Very common resident of secondary scrub, mangrove edges, grasslands, parkland and urban areas. Usually seen on the ground and in pairs, quietly foraging for grass seeds. Call is a soft, pleasant series of 'coo' notes. A sought-after cagebird in much of Southeast Asia and commonly trapped for the pet trade. **SITES** Suitable habitat across Singapore. **CONSERVATION** Poaching for the songbird trade may threaten wild populations.

Cinnamon-headed Green Pigeon ■ *Treron fulvicollis* 棕头绿鸠
Punai Bakau 26cm

DESCRIPTION ssp. *fulvicollis*. The only green pigeon where male (shown) has a rich rufous-chestnut head, extending to breast and back. Shoulder rich maroon, contrasting with yellow-fringed, black wing feathers. Like Thick-billed Green Pigeon (see p.73), both sexes have a reddish bill base, but is less extensive in this species. Female is light green on the head, with a pale blue cap and greenish back and wings. **DISTRIBUTION** Thai–Malay Peninsula, Borneo, Sumatra. **HABITS AND HABITATS** Rare non-breeding visitor and probable resident, occurring in primary and secondary forests, forest edge, mangroves and secondary scrub near the coast. Call is a pleasant, gurgling warble very similar to Thick-billed Green Pigeon. Birds in Singapore most likely to have dispersed from coastal forests in S Malaysia. **SITES** Pulau Ubin. **CONSERVATION** Globally near threatened.

LEFT: *Female* RIGHT: *Male*

Little Green Pigeon ■ *Treron olax* 小绿鸠 Punai Siul 20cm

DESCRIPTION Smallest green pigeon. Male has bluish-grey head and neck, and a distinct orange patch on breast, while shoulder, mantle and back are rich maroon. Irises pale, but difficult to see in field. Female lacks the orange breast patch, and is largely green on the back and wings. **DISTRIBUTION** Thai–Malay Peninsula, Borneo, Sumatra. **HABITS AND HABITATS** Rare resident and possibly a non-breeding visitor from Malaysia,

occurring only in primary and secondary forests. The most recent sighting was a pair seen over a number of days in the MacRitchie forest area in 2010. Should be looked for among large groups of Thick-billed Green Pigeon (see p.73) in fruiting trees. **SITES** Central Catchment Nature Reserve. **CONSERVATION** Nationally critically endangered.

LEFT: *Male.* RIGHT: *Female*

Pink-necked Green Pigeon ■ *Treron vernans* 红颈绿鸠 Punai Gading 27cm

DESCRIPTION Commonest green pigeon in Singapore. Bluish-grey head of male intergrades into pinkish neck, which contrasts with the orange patch on the breast. Wings pale green with black flight feathers. Undertail coverts chestnut. In flight, black subterminal tail band distinguishes it from other green pigeons. Female is largely green. **DISTRIBUTION** Much of mainland Southeast Asia, Thai–Malay Peninsula and Greater Sundas east to Philippines, Sulawesi and Maluku. **HABITS AND HABITATS** Very

common resident of primary and secondary forests, forest edge, mangroves, old plantations, scrub, parkland and even urban greenery such as the trees lining Orchard Road. Often seen gathering in large flocks to feed on fruiting figs. Nest is a flimsy structure of sticks usually concealed in foliage. Call is a series of gurgling warbles that ends in two raspy notes. **SITES** Suitable habitat across Singapore. **CONSERVATION** No issues.

LEFT: *Male;* RIGHT: *Female*

Thick-billed Green Pigeon ■ *Treron curvirostra* 厚嘴绿鸠
Punai Daun 27cm

DESCRIPTION ssp. *curvirostra*. A colourful forest pigeon. The only green pigeon with a large greenish patch of skin around the eye; bill base red. Male (shown) is bluish grey on the head, contrasting sharply with rich maroon mantle, shoulder and back. Female has greenish back and shoulders. **DISTRIBUTION** Himalayan foothills and E India to S China, mainland Southeast Asia and Thai–Malay Peninsula, Greater Sundas and Palawan. **HABITS AND HABITATS** Uncommon resident of primary and secondary forests, and forest edge. Usually seen gathering to feed on fruiting figs, and as many as 40 individuals have been seen on one tree. Breeding has been recently documented in the MacRitchie area in September. Call is a series of pleasant, gurgling whistles. **SITES** Central Catchment and Bukit Timah nature reserves, Dairy Farm Nature Park. **CONSERVATION** Nationally endangered.

ABOVE: *Male*. BELOW: *Female*.

Jambu Fruit Dove ■ *Ptilinopus jambu* 粉头果鸠 Punai-Buah Jambu 27cm

DESCRIPTION A colourful pigeon with a distinct pinkish-red face in both sexes. Male is largely green on the upperparts, contrasting sharply with white underparts, washed pink at the breast. Female is mostly green except for underparts, which are dirty white. **DISTRIBUTION** Thai–Malay Peninsula, Borneo, Sumatra, W Java. **HABITS AND HABITATS** Uncommon resident and non-breeding visitor in primary and secondary forests, and in secondary scrub and parkland where there are fruiting trees. Wanders widely in search of fruiting figs. As many as 7 birds have been seen at the fig tree at the summit of Bukit Timah during fruiting. **SITES** Bukit Timah Nature Reserve, Bukit Batok Nature Park. **CONSERVATION** Globally near threatened.

LEFT: *Female*. RIGHT: *Male*

Green Imperial Pigeon ▪ *Ducula aenea* 绿皇鸠 Pergam Hijau 45cm

DESCRIPTION ssp. *polia*. Large, distinctive grey and green pigeon with white eye-ring. Head, breast and belly pale grey, contrasting sharply with iridescent green back, mantle and wings. As in other imperial pigeons, head distinctly shaped with high forehead and

'down-sloped' nape. **DISTRIBUTION** S, E and NE India, S China, mainland Southeast Asia and Thai–Malay Peninsula, east to Philippines and Sulawesi. **HABITS AND HABITATS** Uncommon non-breeding visitor and resident of primary and secondary forests. Has bred in the Loyang area in March-April 2014; the nest is a messy pile of sticks on a branch fork, clutch 1-2. Feeds mostly on figs, palm fruits and nutmegs. Call is a low, guttural 'croo'. **SITES** Pulau Ubin, Pulau Tekong, Loyang Woods. **CONSERVATION** Commonly hunted throughout Southeast Asia for food.

Pied Imperial Pigeon ▪ *Ducula bicolor* 斑皇鸠 Pergam Rawa 40cm

DESCRIPTION Unmistakable white pigeon with black wing tips and tail. Both sexes entirely creamy white, with black flight feathers and lower half of the tail. Bill and feet bluish grey. **DISTRIBUTION** Small islands off coastal Cambodia and S Myanmar, Thai–Malay Peninsula and Greater Sundas, east to Sulawesi, New Guinea and many

intervening islands. **HABITS AND HABITATS** Uncommon non-breeding visitor and possibly resident. Mangroves, coastal forests and occasionally secondary scrub. More often seen on small offshore islands than on the Singapore mainland. Usually seen in small flocks, and widely island-hop in search of fruiting trees. Small groups seen in the Jurong and West Coast area are likely to be free-flying birds from private collections. **SITES** Pulau Hantu, St John's Island. CONSERVATION No issues.

Tanimbar Corella

◾ *Cacatua goffiniana* 戈氏凤头鹦鹉　Kakatua Tanimbar 32cm

DESCRIPTION An all-white cockatoo with pink lores. Smaller than Yellow-crested Cockatoo C. *sulphurea*, which is also rarer. Male has darker iris than female, but this is hard to see in the field. In flight, birds appear entirely white with yellow-tinged underwings. **DISTRIBUTION** Tanimbar and Kai islands in S Maluku. Introduced to Taiwan and Singapore. **HABITS AND HABITATS** Common resident, originating from introduced stock and escapees. Occurs in secondary scrub, old plantations, parkland. Known to have bred, and competes with other local nest-cavity-dependent birds for nest holes. Small groups of up to 20 birds roost in wayside trees, especially in the Bukit Timah Road area. An adaptable species that has been observed to feed on fruits of ornamental trees, including the Pong-pong. **SITES** Roosts are known from the Dunearn Road, Ulu Pandan area. **CONSERVATION** Globally near threatened due to poaching for the pet bird trade.

Blue-crowned Hanging Parrot ◾ *Loriculus galgulus* 蓝顶短尾鹦鹉

Serindit Melayu 14cm

DESCRIPTION The smallest parrot in Singapore. Both sexes are entirely green with bright red uppertail coverts and a blue crown patch that is difficult to see in the field. Male has a red patch on the breast, which the female lacks. **DISTRIBUTION** Thai–Malay Peninsula, Sumatra, Borneo. **HABITS AND HABITATS** Common resident of primary and secondary forests, forest edge, old plantations, parkland and many urban green spaces, including roadside trees in the heart of Orchard Road. Breeds February–July, nesting in tree-holes. Call is a series of shrill metallic ringing, usually uttered in flight. Has apparently benefited from widespread planting of fruit trees across Singapore. **SITES** Suitable habitat across Singapore. **CONSERVATION** Formerly rare, but has undergone a dramatic comeback and is now a common parkland bird.

ABOVE: *Male.* BELOW: *Female.*

Coconut Lorikeet
■ *Trichoglossus haematodus* 彩虹鸚鵡 Perkici Pelangi 28cm

DESCRIPTION ssp. *haematodus*. A colourful, medium-sized parrot. Head and throat entirely blue with violet flecks, collar yellow. Rest of upperparts green. Breast to upper belly red with blue-back barring. Tail and undertail coverts yellowish green with green barring. Recently split from Rainbow Lorikeet *T. moluccanus* of Australia. **DISTRIBUTION** S Maluku and New Guinea, east to Vanuatu and Solomon Islands, and south to New

Caledonia. Widely introduced. **HABITS AND HABITATS** Common resident, originating from escaped birds. Occurs in secondary forests, scrub and parkland. Usually seen in flight, in small flocks. Roosts on roadside trees, and groups of up to 25 have been recorded. Given recent taxonomic revisions that have split Rainbow Lorikeet into multiple species, other *Trichoglossus* lorikeets may also occur in a feral state. **SITES** Singapore Botanic Gardens. There is a well-known roost in roadside trees by the Buona Vista MRT station. **CONSERVATION** No issues.

Blue-rumped Parrot ■ *Psittinus cyanurus* 蓝腰鹦鹉 Nuri Puling 19cm

DESCRIPTION ssp. *cyanurus*. Chunky, colourful parrot of forest canopy. Male (shown) is largely green with a blue head, black back and red bill. Female is drabber, brown-headed, and lack the black back patch. Both sexes have pale irises and a blue rump but these features are difficult to see well. In flight, the bright red underwing coverts are

diagnostic. **DISTRIBUTION** Thai–Malay Peninsula, Sumatra, Borneo. **HABITS AND HABITATS** Uncommon resident of primary and secondary forest, occasionally wandering into old plantations. Difficult to see well due to its habit of feeding high up in the canopy, and usually seen flying over the canopy. Occasionally descends lower to feed on fruits. Calls include a melodious ringing trill and also high-pitched 'zeet', usually uttered in flight. **SITES** Bukit Timah and Central Catchment nature reserves. **CONSERVATION** Globally near threatened; nationally endangered. Popularly trapped for the pet trade outside Singapore.

Red-breasted Parakeet

◼ *Psittacula alexandri* 绯胸鹦鹉 Bayan Dada Merah 36cm

DESCRIPTION ssp. *alexandri*. The only parakeet with a pinkish-red breast. Male (shown) is mostly green on the upperparts, with bluish-grey head, thick moustachial stripe and red bill. Female is similar, but has grey head and black bill. Juveniles are drabber, with buffy-brown head and thin moustachial striple. **DISTRIBUTION** Himalayan foothills, NE India, S China, mainland Southeast Asia, Borneo, Java. Introduced in Singapore. **HABITS AND HABITATS** Common resident, originating from introduced stock. Occurs in secondary scrub, old plantations and parkland, occasionally straying into urban green spaces. Formerly confined to a few sites (e.g. Changi), this introduced parakeet has increased in abundance in recent years and is now the most numerous parakeet in secondary scrub. Has benefited greatly from wayside trees, where it uses holes as nest cavities or feeds on fruits (e.g. Sea Almond). **SITES** Suitable habitat across Singapore. There are well-known congregation sites in the roadside trees in Clementi Central and Changi Point. **CONSERVATION** Globally near-threatened. Declining in Southeast Asia due to trapping for the pet trade.

Long-tailed Parakeet ◼ *Psittacula longicauda*

长尾鹦鹉 Bayan Nuri 41cm (M), 30cm (F)

DESCRIPTION ssp. *longicauda*. The only native parakeet in Singapore. Male (shown) is mostly green with bright red bill, pinkish-red face and thick black moustache. Crown is darker green than in other parakeets. Juveniles are entirely green and have weakly marked facial patterns. **DISTRIBUTION** Andaman Islands, Thai–Malay Peninsula, Sumatra, Borneo. **HABITS AND HABITATS** Common resident of primary and secondary forests, forest edge, old plantations, scrub and occasionally parkland. Nests in tree cavities, and thus faces competition from woodpeckers and other parrots. Attracted to oil palm, and small groups are regularly seen feeding at the Botanic Gardens visitor centre. Call is a high-pitched screech, usually uttered in flight. **SITES** Pulau Ubin, Singapore Botanic Gardens, Bottle Tree Park, Springleaf Park. **CONSERVATION** May be threatened by competition from the introduced Red-breasted Parakeet. Globally near threatened.

Greater Coucal

■ *Centropus sinensis* 褐翅鸦鹃 Bubut Besar 52cm

DESCRIPTION ssp. *bubutus*. Unmistakable large coucal of secondary woodland. Entirely black except for chestnut wings and mantle. Plumage colour resembles the smaller Lesser Coucal (below), but lacks streaking on head and back. Juveniles similar to adults (shown), but have fine black barring on wings. **DISTRIBUTION** Indian sub-continent, S China and Southeast Asia, east to Greater Sundas and Philippines. **HABITS AND HABITATS** Uncommon resident of secondary forest, forest edge, old plantations, scrub and occasionally mangroves. Usually near water. Birds forage walking on ground, or in low shrubs, for large insects, snails and lizards. Difficult to see well due to skulking habits. Call is a long, descending series of 'boop' notes. **SITES** Pulau Ubin, Central Catchment Nature Reserve. **CONSERVATION** Population in Singapore appears to have declined in recent years.

Lesser Coucal ■ *Centropus bengalensis*
小鸦鹃 Bubut Kecil 38cm

DESCRIPTION ssp. *javanensis*. A small coucal of open scrub. Entirely black except for chestnut wings and back. Unlike Greater Coucal (above), variably streaked on the head and back. Juveniles have brown, instead of black, head and back, finely streaked buff. **DISTRIBUTION** Indian sub-continent, S China and Southeast Asia, east to Greater Sundas, parts of Maluku and Lesser Sundas. **HABITS AND HABITATS** Common resident of open scrub and grassland, including that near wet areas. Especially common in scrub dominated by Giant Mimosa and tall grasses in recently cleared areas, and on reclaimed land. Seldom overlaps with Greater Coucal due to its preference for more open habitat. The nest is a ball-shaped structure covered with a dome of plant matter, usually in low vegetation and with a clutch of 2. Call is a light series of whooping hoots, usually made by birds on partly exposed perches. **SITES** Open grassy and scrubby areas across Singapore. **CONSERVATION** No issues. More resilient than Greater Coucal.

Chestnut-bellied Malkoha
■ *Phaenicophaeus sumatranus*　棕腹地鹃
Cenuk Perut Coklat　40cm

DESCRIPTION The only extant malkoha in Singapore. Large and long-tailed. Head and underparts mostly grey, contrasting with glossy green wings. Bright red facial patch and pale green bill distinctive. The chestnut belly and undertail coverts are difficult to see in the field. **DISTRIBUTION** Thai–Malay Peninsula, Sumatra, Borneo. **HABITS AND HABITATS** Uncommon resident of primary and secondary forests, and occasionally secondary scrub and mangroves. Forages in the middle levels of the forest for large insect (e.g. katydids and grasshoppers) and lizard prey. Appears lethargic as birds move around in the foliage, sometimes perching still for long moments, occasionally joining mixed flocks with woodpeckers and drongos. Seldom heard calling, but known to utter a soft 'kook'. Nest is a concealed, messy cup of sticks, built in low bushes. **SITES** Central Catchment and Bukit Timah nature reserves. **CONSERVATION** Globally near threatened; nationally endangered.

Chestnut-winged Cuckoo
■ *Clamator coromandus*　红翅凤头鹃
Sewah Berjambul　46cm

DESCRIPTION A large, distinctive long-tailed cuckoo with a prominent crest. Head black with long crest, throat washed warm orange. Most of upperparts black, broken only by white nape. Wings chestnut. Underparts mostly white. The far rarer Jacobin Cuckoo lacks the chestnut wings, and is mostly white on underparts. **DISTRIBUTION** Indian sub-continent, S China and mainland Southeast Asia east to Philippines and Sulawesi. Northern populations are migratory, wintering in Southeast Asia and S India. **HABITS AND HABITATS** Uncommon migrant, occurring in secondary forests, scrub, old plantations and occasionally parkland and mangroves. Frequently encountered in dense groves of Albizzia trees where birds forage quietly for caterpillars and large insect prey by gleaning leaves and branches, somewhat like a malkoha; sometimes joins mixed flocks. Usually silent. Occurs mostly November-April, with the earliest arrivals in October. **SITES** Sungei Buloh Wetland Reserve, Pulau Ubin, Jurong Eco-Park. **CONSERVATION** No issues.

Asian Koel ■ *Eudynamys scolopaceus* 噪鹃 Tahu Asia 42cm

DESCRIPTION ssp. *malayanus*. A familiar, long-tailed cuckoo of parkland and urban areas. Male is entirely glossy black. Female has dark brown upperparts, heavily spotted buff. Both sexes have bright crimson eyes and a pale greenish bill. Distinguished in flight from the two crows by its longer tail and more rapid wing-beats. **DISTRIBUTION** Much of Indian sub-continent, S and E China and Southeast Asia, east to Greater Sundas and Philippines. Northern populations are migratory, wintering in Southeast Asia. **HABITS AND HABITATS** Common resident and migrant. Occurs in secondary forests, old plantations, mangroves, scrub, parkland, and urban green spaces. Formerly a rare winter visitor, but has colonised suitable habitat following increased abundance of House Crow, a regular host. Also known to parasitise Large-billed Crow. A frugivore, often seen feeding in roadside

trees, including ornamental Alexandra palms. Call, a loud, disyllabic 'ko-el', is a familiar sound across Singapore, and is frequently uttered before dawn. **SITES** Suitable habitat across Singapore. **CONSERVATION** One of few species that have shown a marked increase in abundance in the past two decades.

LEFT: *Male*; RIGHT: *Female*

Violet Cuckoo ■ *Chrysococcyx xanthorhynchus* 紫金鹃 Sewah-Kilat Ungu 17cm

DESCRIPTION ssp. *xanthorhynchus*. An unmistakable cuckoo of the forest canopy. Head and upperparts of adult male (shown) iridescent violet. Belly white, with thick violet barrings. Females are dark bronzy-green on upperparts. Juveniles may be confused with the Little Bronze Cuckoo (see p.81), but have rich rufous upperparts with patches of glossy

green on the back and wings, while underparts are finely barred. **DISTRIBUTION** NE India, S China and mainland Southeast Asia to Thai–Malay Peninsula, Greater Sundas and Philippines. **HABITS AND HABITATS** Uncommon resident of primary and secondary forests, forest edge, old plantations and occasionally scrub and parkland, especially when near woodland. Difficult to see well due to its habit of keeping high up in the canopy. Usually calls a repeated 'swee-wit' when in flight. Recorded hosts in Singapore include Brown-throated, Van Hasselt's and Olive-backed Sunbird. **SITES** Central Catchment Nature Reserve, Bukit Batok Nature Park, Singapore Botanic Gardens. **CONSERVATION** Nationally endangered.

Horsfield's Bronze Cuckoo ■ *Chrysococcyx basalis* 霍氏金鹃
Sewah-Kilat Australia 15cm

DESCRIPTION A small cuckoo frequently confused with Little Bronze Cuckoo (below). Back and wings iridescent green, with crown to nape dark brown. Distinguished from Little Bronze Cuckoo by pale brow and brown eye-stripe. Underparts are barred with thin brown bars that are incomplete, leaving pale ventral patch from breast to belly; outer tail feathers are rufous. Juveniles lack the iridescent green and are largely dark brown on the upperparts. **DISTRIBUTION** Australia. Migrates north to Lesser Sundas, New Guinea, Maluku, Sulawesi and as far as the Thai–

Malay Peninsula. **HABITS AND HABITATS** A rare austral migrant usually encountered late May–August. Occurs in open secondary scrub, especially on reclaimed land near the coast, and occasionally in parkland and mangroves. Most records of the species are from open scrubby areas with few trees. Birds are often seen foraging low, frequently coming to the ground to pick caterpillars and other insects. **SITES** Open grassy and scrubby areas (e..g. Lorong Halus Wetlands, Tuas coast). **CONSERVATION** No issues.

Little Bronze Cuckoo
■ *Chrysococcyx minutillus* 棕胸金鹃 Sewah-Kilat Biasa 16cm

DESCRIPTION ssp. *peninsularis*. Smallest resident cuckoo in Singapore. Upperparts bronzy green, underparts mostly white with dark barring. Bill black. Head is finely barred, with dark eye-stripe that is incomplete or poorly defined in some individuals. Tail lined white, unlike Horsfield's Bronze Cuckoo, which has rufous tail lining. Only (shown) adults have reddish eye-ring. Juveniles have dull brownish upperparts and pale underparts, are weakly

to completely unbarred, and have a yellow eye-ring. **DISTRIBUTION** Mainland Southeast Asia, Thai–Malay Peninsula, Greater Sundas east to Maluku and N Australia. **HABITS AND HABITATS** Common resident of mangroves, scrub, old plantations and parkland, including coastal stands of *Casuarina* and wayside trees. In Singapore, the only confirmed host is the Golden-bellied Gerygone. Most frequently heard call is a 3–5-note series of descending whistles. Young birds' call is a shrill high-pitched whistle. **SITES** Kranji marshes, Lorong Halus wetlands. **CONSERVATION** No issues.

Banded Bay Cuckoo ▪ *Cacomantis sonneratii* 栗斑杜鹃
Mati-Anak Takuweh 23cm

DESCRIPTION ssp. *sonneratii*. Medium-sized, finely barred cuckoo. Upperparts rufous, underparts white. Rufous facial mask is separated from crown by white brow, distinguishing it from similar-looking juvenile or hepatic morphs of Plaintive Cuckoo (below). Fine dark barring extends from head to tail. **DISTRIBUTION** Much of Indian sub-continent, S China and mainland Southeast Asia to Thai–Malay Peninsula, Greater Sundas and Palawan. **HABITS AND HABITATS** Uncommon resident of primary and secondary forests, forest edge, mangroves, scrub and old plantations. In Singapore, confirmed hosts include Common Iora and Ashy Tailorbird. Most vocal from January to May, when it breeds. Call is a repeated, rapid descending series of four notes. **SITES** Central Catchment Nature Reserve, Bukit Batok Nature Park. **CONSERVATION** No issues.

Plaintive Cuckoo ▪ *Cacomantis merulinus* 八声杜鹃 Mati-Anak Biasa 22cm

DESCRIPTION ssp. *threnodes*. A medium-sized cuckoo most easily confused with the similar Rusty-breasted Cuckoo (see p.83). Head to upper breast grey, rest of upperparts

from back onwards dark brown. Underparts from lower breast rusty orange. Juveniles finely barred and resemble Banded Bay Cuckoo (above), but lack the prominent white brow. **DISTRIBUTION** NE India, S China, and mainland Southeast Asia to Thai–Malay Peninsula, Greater Sundas, Philippines and Sulawesi. **HABITS AND HABITATS** Uncommon resident of secondary forests, mangroves, scrub, old plantations and occasionally parkland. No hosts observed in Singapore, but likely to include tailorbirds and Yellow-bellied Prinia based on extralimital data. Call is a series of 7–8 whistles, more hurried towards the end. Another call, which is a series of ascending, increasingly hurried whistles, is also shared by other *Cacomantis* cuckoos. **SITES** Lorong Halus wetlands, Pulau Ubin. **CONSERVATION** No issues.

Rusty-breasted Cuckoo

■ *Cacomantis sepulcralis* 胸胸丛杜鹃
Mati-Anak Dada Oren 24cm

DESCRIPTION ssp. *sepulcralis*. Similar to the Plaintive Cuckoo (see p.82), but marginally larger. Upperparts from head onwards grey, underparts orangy rufous. Juveniles are finely barred like Plaintive Cuckoo, but are generally darker, with bars that tend to be darker and broader. Both adults and juveniles have a prominent yellow eye-ring. **DISTRIBUTION** Thai–Malay Peninsula, Greater and Lesser Sundas, Philippines, Sulawesi. **HABITS AND HABITATS** Uncommon resident of primary and secondary forests, forest edge, mangroves, scrub and old plantations. Prefers more wooded habitats than Plaintive Cuckoo. In Singapore, the only confirmed host is the Malaysian Pied Fantail. In one well-documented instance, the cuckoo chick was observed to engage in a wing-shaking begging display in the presence of the fantail. Call is a long, descending series of a melancholy 'sweet', uttered up to 15 times. **SITES** Lorong Halus wetlands, Pulau Ubin, Kranji marshes. **CONSERVATION** Nationally endangered.

Asian Drongo-Cuckoo

■ *Surniculus lugubris* 乌鹃 Sewah-Sawai Biasa 25cm

DESCRIPTION ssp. *brachyurus*. An unmistakable, glossy black cuckoo. Superficially similar to a 'racket-less' Greater Racket-tailed or Crow-billed Drongo (see p.112), but lighter built, with a thin bill. Fine white bands on the undertail coverts and tail feathers can be difficult to see. Juveniles are finely spotted on head, upperparts and breast, and are also more strongly marked on undertail coverts. **DISTRIBUTION** NE India, mainland Southeast Asia, Thai–Malay Peninsula, Greater Sundas, Palawan. Some northern populations are migratory, wintering in the Thai–Malay Peninsula and Greater Sundas. **HABITS AND HABITATS** Uncommon resident and migrant. Residents occur mostly in primary and secondary forests, while migrants may show up in forests, old plantations, scrub and even parkland. Known hosts in Singapore include Pin-striped Tit-Babbler and Chestnut-winged Babbler. Migrants are usually silent, but residents sing an ascending series of up to 8 'pip' notes. **SITES** Central Catchment Nature Reserve. **CONSERVATION** Nationally endangered.

Large Hawk-Cuckoo

■ *Hierococcyx sparverioides* 鹰鹃
Sewah-Tekukur Besar 39cm

DESCRIPTION A large migratory cuckoo, superficially similar to the *Accipiter* hawks. Breast streaked rufous, contrasting with brown barring on belly and flanks. Upperparts largely dark brown, contrasting with grey head. Tail has four dark bars, with white tip. Larger bodied than similar Hodgson's Hawk-Cuckoo (below), giving it a small-headed appearance. Young birds are heavily streaked on underparts, while brown upperparts show fine barring. **DISTRIBUTION** Breeds in Himalayas, S, C and E China and mainland Southeast Asia. Northern populations are migratory, wintering across Southeast Asia. **HABITS AND HABITATS** Rare, but probably overlooked migrant of secondary forest and scrub. A bird observed in January 2012 was in secondary scrub, keeping to denser areas and descending to pick prey from the ground. Usually silent. Occurs mostly November–March. **SITES** Pasir Ris Park, Pulau Ubin. **CONSERVATION** No issues.

Hodgson's Hawk-Cuckoo ■ *Hierococcyx nisicolor* 棕腹杜鹃

Sewah-Tekukur Hodgson 29cm

DESCRIPTION A medium-sized cuckoo, often confused with very similar Malaysian Hawk-Cuckoo *H. fugax*. Adults upperparts mostly greyish. Variable rufous to orange on breast, extending to belly. Inner tertial is whitish. Usually 4 dark bands visible on tail, of which 2nd lowest band is narrowest. Upperparts of juveniles are chestnut-brown. Underpart streaks more elongated, unlike Malaysian Hawk-Cuckoo which is more spot-like. **DISTRIBUTION** Breeds Himalayan foothills, E India to S China and mainland Southeast Asia. Northern populations are migratory, wintering across Southeast Asia. **HABITS AND HABITATS** Uncommon migrant of mainly primary and secondary forests, forest edge, old plantations, scrub and occasionally parkland. Usually silent, and perches quietly for long periods. Occurs mostly November–March. **SITES** Bukit Timah and Central Catchment nature reserves. **CONSERVATION** No issues.

LEFT: *Juvenile Hodgson's Hawk-Cuckoo.*
RIGHT: *Juvenile Malaysian Hawk-Cuckoo.*

Indian Cuckoo

■ *Cuculus micropterus* 四声杜鹃 Sewah India 33cm

DESCRIPTION ssp. *micropterus*. A medium-sized cuckoo, somewhat similar to Oriental Cuckoo. Head grey. Back, mantle and wings greyish brown. White underparts barred with widely spaced black bands from breast to vent. Upper breast washed brown, with finer barring then rest of underparts. Grey tail ends with a prominent broad black subterminal band that is tipped white. Juveniles paler. **DISTRIBUTION** Indian sub-continent and across East Asia as far north as Russian Far East. Also across Southeast Asia, Greater Sundas and Philippines. Northern populations are migratory, wintering in Southeast Asia, parts of India and Sri Lanka. **HABITS AND HABITATS** Fairly common migrant; most regularly seen of the migratory cuckoos. Occurs in primary and secondary forests, forest edge, old plantations and scrub in parkland, especially during passage. Feeds mainly on caterpillars. Occurs mostly September–April. **SITES** Central Catchment Nature Reserve, Pasir Ris Park. **CONSERVATION** No issues.

Himalayan Cuckoo ■ *Cuculus saturatus* 中杜鹃 Sewah Pupu 33cm

DESCRIPTION A medium-sized cuckoo, similar to Indian Cuckoo. Head grey, with rest of upperparts and wings dark grey. White underparts barred with black bands (thinner than in Indian Cuckoo, which extend to vent. Tail black with narrow white tips. Hepatic-morph birds are barred rufous and dark brown, with brown barring on the underparts. Distinguished from similar-looking Oriental Cuckoo *Cuculus optatus* which should occur, by longer wing length (possible only in hand for males) and song (only in breeding range). **DISTRIBUTION** Breeds from Himalayas, N Myanmar, east to across much of S, C China and Taiwan. Winters across Southeast Asia, east to W New Guinea. **HABITS AND HABITATS** A rare migrant, occurring mostly in secondary forests, woodland and scrub. Much rarer than Indian Cuckoo. Usually silent. Occurs mostly October–January. **SITES** Pasir Ris Park, Central Catchment Nature Reserve. **CONSERVATION** No issues.

LEFT: *Hepatic morph*. RIGHT: *Adult normal morph*.

Eastern Barn Owl

■ *Tyto javanica* 东方仓鸮 Jampuk Putih 35cm

DESCRIPTION ssp. *javanica*. A medium-sized, pale owl. Upperparts pale brown with fine buff markings. Underparts white, with sparse fine spotting. Heart-shaped face pale white with large dark eyes. In flight, appears pallid white from below, except for dark wing tips. **DISTRIBUTION** Indian sub-continent, much of Southeast Asia, eastwards to New Guinea, Australia and SW Pacific Islands. **HABITS AND HABITATS** Uncommon resident of open scrub, grasslands and urban areas, and has colonised newly reclaimed land with stands of *Casuarina* trees. A predator of small ground mammals, especially rats and large insects. A well-watched pair was observed roosting and nesting in the shaded platforms beneath a major flyover in the city for many years. Call is an infrequently uttered hissing screech. **SITES** Changi coast, Tanjong Rhu. **CONSERVATION** Population in Singapore likely to be augmented by individuals dispersing from Malaysia, where it remains common in oil-palm plantations.

Sunda Scops Owl ■ *Otus lempiji* 领角鸮 Jampuk Kubur 23cm

DESCRIPTION ssp. *cnephaeus*. A small, 'eared' owl. Overall plumage brown, with distinct dark collar around head. Distinguished from smaller, migratory Oriental Scops Owl O. *sunia* by its dark brown eyes which can appear black in poor light. The taxonomy of this species is confused, and some authors treat it as a race of the widespread Collared Scops Owl O. *lettia*. **DISTRIBUTION** Thai–Malay Peninsula, Sumatra, Borneo, Java. **HABITS**

AND HABITATS Commonest and most widespread owl. Common resident in primary and secondary forests, forest edge, old plantations, scrub and occasionally parkland. In Singapore, observed to take largely insects and geckos. Breeds January-June, nesting mainly in natural tree cavities; clutch 1-3. Call is a soft 'ooo', usually repeated at fairly long intervals. **SITES** Suitable habitat across Singapore. **CONSERVATION** No issues.

LEFT: *Sunda Scops Owl*; RIGHT: *Oriental Scops Owl*

Buffy Fish Owl ▪ *Ketupa ketupu* 马来渔鸮 Tumbuk Ketampi 45cm

DESCRIPTION ssp. *ketupu*. A large, scruffy-looking owl. Underparts buffy-brown, with prominent black streaks on the breast; streaks are finer on the belly. Upperparts rich brown, with dark brown mantle and wing feathers that are buff-margined. Long 'ear' tufts, yellow eyes and white frontal patch diagnostic. Legs unfeathered. **DISTRIBUTION** E India, Mainland Southeast Asia, Thai–Malay Peninsula, Greater Sundas. **HABITS AND HABITATS** Uncommon resident of primary and secondary forest, old plantations and occasionally scrub. Birds are usually seen by reservoirs or rivers, hunting for fish, frogs, crustaceans and very rarely bats. In the daytime, birds perch quietly in shaded tree crowns. Usually nests in cavities in tree trunks. Call is a rattling series of 'kutook' or a single ascending shriek. **SITES** Central Catchment Nature Reserve, Singapore Botanic Gardens, Pasir Ris Park. **CONSERVATION** Nationally endangered.

Spotted Wood Owl
▪ *Strix seloputo* 点斑林鸮
Carik-Kafan Berbintik 46cm

DESCRIPTION ssp. *seloputo*. A large, 'earless' owl. Upperparts dark brown and finely spotted white. Underparts finely barred. Heart-shaped facial disc pale brown. Eyes dark brown, but appearing nearly black. Legs feathered. **DISTRIBUTION** Parts of mainland Southeast Asia, Thai–Malay Peninsula, C Sumatra, Java, Palawan. **HABITS AND HABITATS** Uncommon resident of secondary forests, forest edge, old plantations, secondary scrub and urban parkland. Feeds largely on rodents. Nests in cavities in tree trunks but there are also records of nests built on large epiphytic ferns. Call is a powerful, growling 'whoo', often uttered at dawn and dusk (between 1900 and 1930h). Birds only call sporadically after dark. **SITES** Pulau Ubin, National University of Singapore, Pasir Ris Park. **CONSERVATION** Nationally endangered. Historically unrecorded in Singapore; likely to have colonised when oil-palm plantations, a favoured habitat, became more widespread in Peninsular Malaysia.

Brown Wood Owl ■ *Strix leptogrammica* 褐林鸮
Burung Hantu Punggur 46cm

DESCRIPTION ssp. *maingayi*. The largest owl in Singapore. Upperparts dark brown, with dark bands on wing and mantle feathers. Underparts pale buff with fine barring. Heart-shaped facial disc pale brown, contrasting sharply with dark brown, unspotted head, unlike Spotted Wood Owl (see p.87). **DISTRIBUTION** Himalayan foothills, S and E India, S China to Taiwan, mainland Southeast Asia, Thai–Malay Peninsula, Greater Sundas. **HABITS AND HABITATS** Rare resident. Known only from secondary forests and old plantations in western Pulau Ubin. Call is a series of deep 'whoo', usually repeated twice, and may be confused with that of the Barred Eagle-Owl *Bubo sumatranus*, which also occurs on Ubin. Has bred, and 2 chicks were found in a cavity on an old Angsana tree. **SITES** Pulau Ubin and Bukit Batok Nature Park. **CONSERVATION** First discovered in Singapore in 2007 on Pulau Ubin. Nationally endangered.

LEFT: *Adult.*
RIGHT: *Juvenile*

Brown Hawk-Owl ■ *Ninox scutulata* 鹰鸮 Pungguk 30cm

DESCRIPTION ssp. *scutulata*. A medium-sized, 'earless' owl that lacks a defined facial disc. Upperparts and head dark brown. Underparts white with bold rufous heart-shaped streaks, unlike the teardrop-shaped streaks of the very similar migratory Northern Boobook *N. japonica*, which was discovered in Singapore in 2014. **DISTRIBUTION** Much of Indian sub-continent, mainland Southeast Asia, Thai–Malay Peninsula, Greater Sundas, east to Sulawesi. **HABITS AND HABITATS** Common resident of primary and secondary forests, old plantations and occasionally secondary scrub. Hunts for large insects and small mammals, including bats. Call is a disyllabic series of 'whoo-up', usually repeated for minutes on end; most vocal at dusk and dawn. **SITES** Central Catchment and Bukit Timah nature reserves. **CONSERVATION** Forest-dependent.

LEFT: *Brown Hawk-Owl*. RIGHT: *Northern Boobook*.

Grey Nightjar ■ *Caprimulgus jotaka* 普通夜鷹 Tukang Kelabu Jepun 28cm

DESCRIPTION ssp. *jotaka*. A dark, greyish nightjar. Crown darker than Large-tailed Nightjar (below), white throat patch smaller to the point of being indistinct. Buff patches on wing coverts and flight feathers give it a 'spotted' appearance. In flight, white patch on flight feathers and tail is smaller, compared to Large-tailed Nightjar. **DISTRIBUTION** Widespread across the Indian sub-continent and mainland Southeast Asia, to NE Asia in the Russian Far East, Japan and NE China, and east to Palau. Northern populations are migratory, wintering across much

of Southeast Asia. **HABITS AND HABITATS** Uncommon migrant to primary and secondary forests, old plantation, secondary scrub and occasionally well-wooded parkland. Usually roosts on trees and seldom seen on ground, unlike the other two *Caprimulgus* nightjars. Sallies quietly over the forests at dusk. Usually silent. **SITES** Central Catchment Nature Reserve, Bidadari Cemetery. **CONSERVATION** No issues.

Large-tailed Nightjar ■ *Caprimulgus macrurus* 长尾夜鹰
Tukang Biasa 30cm

DESCRIPTION ssp. *bimaculatus*. Most frequently encountered and largest nightjar. Buff-grey crown contrasts with rich brown face and white throat patch. Scapulars dark with pale edges and wing-covert feathers pale-tipped, giving it a spotted appearance. At rest, wings extend to midway along tail, unlike other nightjars. In flight, large white patches on flight feathers and white tips to outer tail feathers diagnostic. **DISTRIBUTION**

Indian sub-continent, S China, across mainland Southeast Asia, Thai–Malay Peninsula and Greater Sundas, east into New Guinea and N Australia. **HABITS AND HABITATS** Common resident of secondary forests, forest edge, old plantations, secondary scrub and well-wooded parkland. Usually seen resting on the ground, occasionally sallying low to catch flying insects. Breeds February–October; clutch 1-2. Call is a series of monotonous, regularly uttered 'chonk' notes. **SITES** Suitable habitat across Singapore. **CONSERVATION** No issues.

Savanna Nightjar

■ *Caprimulgus affinis* 林夜鷹 Tukang Padang 25cm

DESCRIPTION ssp. *affinis*. Smallest and palest nightjar. Plumage is greyish brown and finely mottled. At rest, wings extend to two-thirds along tail. In flight, note white wing patches on flight feathers and entirely white outer tail feathers. Female (shown) has a richer plumage than male and lacks the white outer tail feathers. **DISTRIBUTION** Indian sub-continent, S China and Taiwan, much of Southeast Asia east to Philippines and Sulawesi. **HABITS AND HABITATS** Common resident of scrub, barren land, grasslands and occasionally urban areas, resting on the roofs of buildings at night. Call, uttered from perch and in flight, is a ringing 'chweet'. Known to breed in April–May. **SITES** Suitable habitat across Singapore. **CONSERVATION** No issues. Unknown from Singapore prior to the 1980s, and is likely to have colonised from the Riau islands.

Malaysian Eared-Nightjar ■ *Lyncornis temminckii* 马来毛腿夜鷹
Taptibau Melayu 27cm

DESCRIPTION A rich-brown nightjar, generally darker than other nightjars. Buff-grey ear tufts and collar diagnostic, contrasting with rich chestnut facial mask. White collar

graduates to buff on hind neck. Wing-coverts dark, but rich brown with pale spotting. Underparts pale with dark barring. Lacks the pale throat patch and malars of other nightjars. **DISTRIBUTION** Thai–Malay Peninsula, Sumatra, Borneo and intervening islands (e.g. Bangka). **HABITS AND HABITATS** Rare resident mainly of primary and secondary forests, occasionally seen at the forest edge. Usually roosts on trees and thus seldom encountered. Sallies over forest at dawn and dusk, uttering a distinctive 'tip-tee-teuw'. **SITES** Central Catchment Nature Reserve. **CONSERVATION** Nationally endangered. Few records in recent years, mostly in the MacRitchie area.

Grey-rumped Treeswift
■ *Hemiprocne longipennis* 雨燕
Lelayang Berjambul Kelabu 21cm

DESCRIPTION ssp. *harterti*. A large swift-like bird of secondary woodland. Plumage mostly pale grey, with greenish gloss on crown, mantle and shoulders. Has a frontal crest, red ear patch and pale tertials, visible only when perched. In flight, appears like a large, slender swift with pale rump and a thin, tapered tail. **DISTRIBUTION** Thai–Malay Peninsula, Greater Sundas, Sulawesi. **HABITS AND HABITATS** Uncommon resident of secondary forest, forest edge, scrub, old plantations and occasionally parkland. Perches frequently on tall exposed branches of trees by the forest edge, often in small groups of up to 40 birds. Nest is a tiny cup much smaller than the adult bird, usually built on an exposed branch and contains a single egg. Call is a shrill series of 'kip' notes, made in flight and on perch. **SITES** Singapore Botanic Gardens, Bukit Batok Nature Park, Bishan Park. **CONSERVATION** Has declined in recent years.

Plume-toed Swiftlet ■ *Collocalia affinis* 白腹金丝燕
Lelayang Perut Putih 10cm

DESCRIPTION ssp. *cyanoptila*. Formerly known as Glossy Swiftlet, which has been revealed to be a complex of multiple distinct species. A small swiftlet with glossy, nearly black upperparts. Dark throat and breast contrast with white belly. Can be confused with the two resident *Aerodramus* swiftlets, but flight is more 'fluttery', often with rapid wing flapping, and glides less frequently. **DISTRIBUTION** Thai–Malay Peninsula, Greater Sundas and intervening islands. **HABITS AND HABITATS** Uncommon resident, occurring over primary and secondary forests and secondary scrub. Appears to be localised to Bukit Batok and Bukit Timah areas, where nesting colonies probably occur. Likely to be overlooked due to the difficulty in distinguishing from other small swiftlets. **SITES** Bukit Batok Nature Park, Bukit Timah Nature Reserve. **CONSERVATION** Nationally critically endangered.

Black-nest Swiftlet

■ *Aerodramus maximus* 大金丝燕
Lelayang Sarang Hitam 14cm

DESCRIPTION ssp. *maximus*. Very similar to Germain's Swiftlet (below), but darker with longer wings. Rump typically darker, but can be variable, and tail less notched. Lower leg (tarsus) is feathered, but this can only be seen when birds are perched at nests or roost sites. **DISTRIBUTION** Thai–Malay Peninsula, Greater Sundas, Philippines. **HABITS AND HABITATS** Uncommon resident occuring over primary and secondary forests, secondary scrub and occasionally parkland. Nest (shown) is very dark and contains many feathers, unlike that of Germain's Swiftlet.In Singapore, small nesting groups have been found in abandoned bunkers on some of the offshore islands. Navigates by echolocation. **SITES** Sentosa, Pedra Branca. **CONSERVATION** Unlike Germain's Swiftlet, not threatened by nest-collecting as nest has little commercial value.

Germain's Swiftlet ■ *Aerodramus germani* 爪哇金丝燕
Lelayang Sarang Putih 13cm

DESCRIPTION ssp. *germani*? Taxonomy confused, often lumped with Edible-nest Swiftlet *A. fulciphaga*. Plumage dark brown, with a pale rump patch and underparts. Tail more notched than Black-nest Swiftlet. Lower leg (tarsus) is unfeathered, unlike that of the Black-nest Swiftlet (above), but this can only be seen when birds are at nest.

DISTRIBUTION Coastal mainland Southeast Asia, Thai–Malay Peninsula, Greater Sundas. **HABITS AND HABITATS** Very common resident. Occurs over all kinds of terrestrial habitats, including coastal scrub and urban areas, and is also frequently seen out at sea. Nest is pale translucent, made entirely of the birds' saliva, and does not contain feathers; prized delicacy in the region. Navigates in dark areas, especially caves where they naturally nest, by echolocation. Probably the most abundant of the small swifts as a result of widespread swiftlet farming across Malaysia, where abandoned buildings are left for the species to nest in. Call is a raspy series of chattering clicks. **SITES** All suitable habitats across Singapore. **CONSERVATION** Illegal harvesting of nests may threaten small accessible colonies in built-up areas.

Asian Palm Swift ■ *Cypsiurus balasiensis* 棕雨燕 Lelayang Palma Asia 13cm

DESCRIPTION ssp. *infumatus*. A small, dark brown swift with slender body, and narrow wings and tail, giving it a rather dainty and long-winged appearance. Tail is well forked, but this is usually clearly seen only when tail is fanned. Flight rapid and manoeuvrable. **DISTRIBUTION** Indian sub-continent, S China and mainland Southeast Asia, east to Greater Sundas and Philippines. **HABITS AND HABITATS** Common resident occurring over forest edges, secondary scrub, parkland and urban areas, especially where *Borassus* fan palms are present. Nest is a flimsy half-cup made of saliva and plant matter, attached to the underside of the palm frond. Clutch size is 2. **SITES** Singapore Botanic Gardens, Kent Ridge Park. **CONSERVATION** No issues.

House Swift ■ *Apus nipalensis* 小白腰雨燕 Lelayang Rumah 15cm

DESCRIPTION ssp. *subfurcatus*. A dark, medium-sized swift with a distinct white rump. Appears almost black in flight, with pale throat and white rump. Similar to the migratory Pacific Swift (see p.94) but tail is only slightly notched and wings are broader. Flight tends to involve a lot of gliding with little wing flapping. **DISTRIBUTION** Much of East and Southeast Asia (including Thai–Malay Peninsula), extending east to Greater Sundas and Philippines. **HABITS AND HABITATS** Uncommon resident, seen over secondary scrub, old plantations, mangroves, parkland and urban areas. Associated with old buildings, where small colonies can be found, notably the former railway station. The call is a series of monotonous twittering. **SITES** Sungei Buloh Wetland Reserve, Lorong Halus wetlands, Changi coast. **CONSERVATION** Has clearly declined in Singapore in recent years and is now greatly outnumbered by *Aerodramus* swiftlets.

Pacific Swift
▪ *Apus pacificus* 白腰雨燕
Lelayang Ekor Cabang Pasifik 15 cm

DESCRIPTION ssp. *pacificus kurodae?* Slender-looking and distinctive swift with deeply forked tail and white rump patch. Overall blackish-brown, underparts mottled buff, with pale throat. Resident House Swift (see p.93) is smaller and darker while tail is slightly notched, not forked. **DISTRIBUTION** Breeds from C Siberia to Yakutia, Russian Far East, much of eastern China, Korea and Japan. Northern populations winter in S India and Southeast Asia eastwards to New Guinea and Australia. **HABITS AND HABITATS** Uncommon passage migrant and winter visitor, occurring mostly over forest, and secondary scrub, but also in open country habitats during migratory passage. Usually seen in small groups. Arrives from mid-September, mostly departing by April. **SITES** Bukit Timah and Central Catchment nature reserves, Tuas West. **CONSERVATION** No issues.

Oriental Dollarbird
▪ *Eurystomus orientalis* 三宝鸟 Tiong Batu 30cm

DESCRIPTION ssp. *orientalis* (shown), *cyanocollis*. A darkish roller, with a diagnostic red bill that can appear all black if seen under poor light conditions. Plumage dark glossy bluish-green, paler on belly. Head dark brown to nearly black at the cap. Pale bluish patches on flight feathers visible only in flight. **DISTRIBUTION** Widespread across much of E India, E Asia to as far north as the Russian Far East, and Southeast Asia east to Australia and New Guinea. NE Asian populations (ssp. *cyanocollis*) populations migrate to winter in Southeast Asia. **HABITS AND HABITATS** Common resident and migrant of secondary forests, forest edge, scrub, old plantations and parkland, occasionally venturing into mangroves. A hole nester, competing aggressively with cockatoos, parakeets and woodpeckers for cavities. Commoner in winter as residents are augmented by migrants. Call is a harsh series of cough-like cackles. **SITES** Most suitable habitat across Singapore. **CONSERVATION** Has benefited from the increase in open secondary woodland.

Stork-billed Kingfisher

■ *Pelargopsis capensis* 鶴嘴翡翠 Pekaka Emas 37cm

DESCRIPTION ssp. *malaccensis*. The largest kingfisher across much of Southeast Asia. Thickset red bill, blue upperparts, rich orangy underparts and pale brown head distinctive. Turquoise blue rump only visible when in flight. **DISTRIBUTION** Indian sub-continent, mainland Southeast Asia, Thai–Malay Peninsula, Greater Sundas east to Philippines and Sulawesi. **HABITS AND HABITATS** Uncommon resident occurring along mangrove creeks, ponds and reservoirs with forest fringes and suitably large water bodies in secondary scrub and old plantations. Known to take fish, small reptiles and crustaceans. Call is a mournful series of 6–8 descending whistles, or a harsh raucous cackle. **SITES** Sungei Buloh Wetland Reserve, Singapore Botanic Gardens, Singapore Zoo. **CONSERVATION** Extensive loss of mangroves has reduced suitable habitat for this species.

Ruddy Kingfisher ■ *Halcyon coromanda* 赤翡翠 Pekaka Ungu 25cm

DESCRIPTION ssp. *minor*, *coromanda* (shown), migratory *major* may occur. The only kingfisher that is entirely rufous-violet on the upperparts and rich orange on the underparts, with a bright red bill. Pale blue patch on back and rump only visible in flight. Birds of the resident race *minor*, which inhabits mangroves, are smaller than the migratory *coromanda* as well as being darker overall, with a larger patch on the rump. **DISTRIBUTION** Widespread from E India to as far north as Japan and Russian Far East, and across most of Southeast Asia east to Philippines and Sulawesi. NE Asian populations are migratory, wintering mostly in Southeast Asia. **HABITS AND HABITATS** Uncommon migrant and very rare resident. Wintering and passage birds occur in secondary forests, scrub, old plantations and occasionally parkland. Residents are only known from mangroves on Pulau Tekong. Shy, perching unobtrusively on well-concealed perches. Wintering birds tend to be silent. **SITES** Central Catchment Nature Reserve. **CONSERVATION** Extensive loss of mangroves has reduced much suitable habitat. The resident population is on the verge of extinction. Nationally endangered.

White-throated Kingfisher ■ *Halcyon smyrnensis* 白胸翡翠
Pekaka Dada Putih 28cm

DESCRIPTION ssp. *perpulchra*. A medium-sized kingfisher of open country. Plumage distinctive, a combination of brown head and largely brown underparts broken by a large

white throat patch that extends to the breast. Wing and back largely a brilliant turquoise, wing coverts brown. A white patch on the outer wing feathers is visible only in flight, and is shared by the similar Black-capped Kingfisher (below). **DISTRIBUTION** Widespread across much of S Eurasia, from Turkey to S China and Taiwan, and much of Southeast Asia to the Philippines. **HABITS AND HABITATS** Common resident of secondary scrub, old plantations, reedy fringes of reservoirs, open playing fields and parkland. Can occur far from water bodies, foraging in open fields where lizards, arthropods and even small birds are taken. Call is a whinnying series of descending 'kli' notes. **SITES** Most suitable habitat across Singapore. **CONSERVATION** Highly adaptable. One of two kingfishers frequently encountered in urban parkland, foraging even in concretised canals.

Black-capped Kingfisher ■ *Halcyon pileata* 蓝翡翠
Pekaka Kepala Hitam 30cm

DESCRIPTION The only kingfisher with black head and red bill, although Collared Kingfisher (see p.97) may appear similar when seen poorly. Neck, throat and breast white, but belly rich orange. Most of upperparts from back to tail deep blue. As in White-throated

Kingfisher (above), white patch on the outer wing feathers is only visible in flight. **DISTRIBUTION** Widespread across much of Indian sub-continent, East Asia to as far north as Korea and Japan, and east through Southeast Asia to Sulawesi. Northern populations are migratory, wintering in Southeast Asia and parts of India and Sri Lanka. **HABITS AND HABITATS** Uncommon migrant. Mangroves, marshes, ponds and reservoirs with reedy fringes. A shy bird that is easily disturbed and flushed. Arrives in October, mostly departing by May. **SITES** Kranji marshes, Sungei Buloh Wetland Reserve, Lorong Halus wetlands. **CONSERVATION** Extensive loss of marshland and mangroves has greatly reduced the wintering habitat for this species.

Collared Kingfisher
■ *Todiramphus chloris* 白领翡翠 Pekaka Bakau 24cm

DESCRIPTION ssp. *humii*. The most abundant kingfisher in Singapore. Upperparts and head mostly blue with variable turquoise wash on back and head, broken by thick white collar. Loral patch white, bill black with flesh-coloured mandible. Juveniles are duller, with buff fringes to wing coverts and flanks washed light brown. **DISTRIBUTION** Widespread across much of coastal Middle East, Indian sub-continent, Southeast Asia to Palau. **HABITS AND HABITATS** Very common resident of coastal mangroves, secondary scrub, old plantations, parkland and even urban areas. Primarily a coastal bird, it has spread inland with increase in open scrub habitat in recent years. Nests in tree holes and culverts on embankments; clutch about 3–4. Call is variable, but most commonly heard is a harsh series of 5–6 'kip' notes, somewhat like maniacal laughter. Other calls include a series of raspy chuckles. **SITES** Most suitable habitat across Singapore, including urban parks (e.g. Fort Canning Park). **CONSERVATION** Has benefited from increase in scrub habitat and parkland.

Blue-eared Kingfisher ■ *Alcedo meninting* 蓝耳翠鸟
Raja-Udang Binti-binti 17cm

DESCRIPTION ssp. *meninting*. A small, brilliant kingfisher of forest streams. Superficially similar to the Common Kingfisher (see p.98) but plumage deep blue (not turquoise-green), ear coverts blue (as name suggests), and underparts rich orange-red. **DISTRIBUTION** S, E India, SW China, mainland Southeast Asia, Thai–Malay Peninsula, Greater Sundas, Philippines and Sulawesi. **HABITS AND HABITATS** Uncommon resident of forested streams and swampy forest. Occasionally wanders to ponds in parkland and mangrove creeks. Call is a thin ringing 'tseep' that is higher pitched than Common Kingfisher, and usually uttered in flight. Nests in burrows excavated along the sandy banks of streams. Has apparently become more widespread in recent years, colonising well-wooded parks such as Bukit Batok Nature Park. **SITES** Central Catchment Nature Reserve, Bukit Batok Nature Park, Neo Tiew Lane. **CONSERVATION** Nationally endangered. Appears to have adapted to wooded streams outside the reserves.

Common Kingfisher ■ *Alcedo atthis* 普通翠鸟 Raja-Udang Cit-cit 17cm

DESCRIPTION ssp. *bengalensis*. A small kingfisher with turquoise-green upperparts contrasting with orange underparts and white throat. Blue-green back and paler rump visible when seen in flight. Male has an all-black bill, while female (shown) has orange on the lower mandible. Somewhat similar to Blue-eared Kingfisher (see p.97), which is deeper blue with blue ear coverts and much richer orange underparts. **DISTRIBUTION** Widespread across much of Eurasia, with many races; occurs east to Solomon Islands. A winter visitor to the Indian sub-continent and Southeast Asia, although there are also resident populations on a number of islands (e.g. Sulawesi). **HABITS AND HABITATS** Common migrant, occurring in all kinds of water bodies on migration, including open streams, canals, reservoir edges, ponds with reedy fringes and mangrove creeks, but seldom in forest streams. Call is a high-pitched 'tseep'. Like many kingfishers, has a habit of bobbing its head while perched. Birds usually arrive in August, departing March–April. **SITES** Most suitable habitat across Singapore. **CONSERVATION** No issues.

Oriental Dwarf Kingfisher ■ *Ceyx erithaca* 三趾翠鸟 Raja-Udang Api 14cm

DESCRIPTION ssp. *erithaca*. A petite-looking, colourful kingfisher with a bright red bill. Underparts rich yellow, contrasting with diagnostic blackish-blue mantle and dark iridescent blue wings. Note also blue patch on forehead and head sides. Rump pinkish red,

only visible when in flight. **DISTRIBUTION** NE India, SW China, mainland Southeast Asia, Greater Sundas, Palawan. **HABITS AND HABITATS** Uncommon passage migrant occurring in primary and secondary forests, usually along streams or in swampy areas. Birds have also wandered into urban areas on migration. Passage mostly late September to early November, and again mid-February to March. Call is a shrill, high-pitched whistle, higher than the two *Alcedo* kingfishers. **SITES** Central Catchment Nature Reserve. **CONSERVATION** Mortality of birds crashing into lighted buildings while on nocturnal migration may affect the population.

Blue-tailed Bee-eater ■ *Merops*
philippinus 栗喉蜂虎 Berberek Ekor Biru 30cm

DESCRIPTION ssp. *javanicus*. A greenish bee-eater
with a prominent orangy-brown throat. Black eye-stripe
contrasts with pale throat and cheek. Upperparts mostly
green. Underparts lighter green, grading into light blue
on the lower belly and vent. Lower back, flight feathers
and tail rich blue. Juveniles are less strongly marked.
DISTRIBUTION Indian sub-continent, S China,
mainland Southeast Asia and Greater Sundas east to
Philippines and New Guinea. Northern populations
migrate to winter across Southeast Asia. **HABITS AND
HABITATS** Common migrant of secondary forests,
forest edge, scrub, old plantations, parkland and even
urban gardens. Commoner than Blue-throated Bee-
eater (below). Birds usually arrive in August and stay
to March. Northbound migration starts from March
and usually does not extend past mid-April, with large
congregations often seen during this period along the
Malay Peninsula. Small groups are often seen perched at
the top of tall trees and TV antennae, from where birds
launch sorties to catch flying insects. **SITES** Suitable
habitat across Singapore. **CONSERVATION** No issues.

Blue-throated Bee-eater
■ *Merops viridis* 蓝喉蜂虎 Berberek Leher Biru 28cm

DESCRIPTION ssp. *viridis*. Combination of blue, green and
brown makes this bee-eater unmistakable. Bright blue throat
contrasts with rich chestnut head and back. Underparts
and wing feathers mostly green. Lower back, rump and
tail brilliant blue. Juveniles have a bluish green head, and
lack tail streamers. **DISTRIBUTION** S China, mainland
Southeast Asia to Thai–Malay Peninsula, Greater Sundas and
Philippines. **HABITS AND HABITATS** Common breeding
migrant, occurring in secondary forest, scrub, old plantations
and occasionally parkland. Birds nest communally, excavating
nest burrows in sandy banks on quarry faces and man-made
sand piles. Birds seen in Singapore breed March–June, most
migrate to winter in Indonesia from September onwards, so
there is limited overlap with Blue-tailed Bee-eater (above).
SITES Suitable habitat across Singapore (e.g. Bukit Batok
Nature Park). **CONSERVATION** No issues.

Oriental Pied Hornbill ▪ *Anthracoceros albirostris* 冠斑犀鸟
Enggang Belulang 70cm

DESCRIPTION ssp. *convexus*. The commoner of two hornbills. Overall plumage black with white lower breast, belly and outer tail feathers. Light blue facial skin around

eye and cheeks. Black patch on casque tends to be less extensive but more clearly defined in male (shown) than female. **DISTRIBUTION** Himalayan foothills, E India to S China and mainland Southeast Asia, Thai–Malay Peninsula and Greater Sundas. **HABITS AND HABITATS** Uncommon resident of secondary forests, old plantations and occasionally mangroves and parkland. Usually in small groups, and can be seen feeding at fruiting trees. Call is a tuneless series of staccato cackles. Besides natural tree cavities, has also utilised nest boxes. Feeds on fruits, small lizards, snakes and large arthropods. **SITES** Pulau Ubin, Sungei Buloh Wetland Reserve. **CONSERVATION** Nationally endangered. Extinct here for nearly a century, then recolonised Pulau Ubin in the early 1990s and has since spread widely on mainland Singapore thanks to an extensive reintroduction programme.

Lineated Barbet ▪ *Megalaima lineata* 绿拟啄木鸟 Takur Kukup 27cm

DESCRIPTION ssp. *hodgsoni*. A large barbet with heavy brown streaking on the head

and most of its underparts, but largely green on its back, wings and tail. Bright yellow facial skin and pinkish-yellow bill are distinctive features. Sexes similar. **DISTRIBUTION** Himalayan foothills, E India to S China and mainland Southeast Asia. Also Thai–Malay Peninsula to northern half of Peninsular Malaysia. Also in Java and Bali. Introduced in Singapore. **HABITS AND HABITATS** Common resident, originating from escapes. Secondary forests, scrub, old plantations and occasionally parkland. Has spread widely across Singapore since it was first discovered in Bukit Batok. Like most barbets, excavates holes in trees for nesting, but may also use holes left by woodpeckers. Typical calls include a 2-note 'koo-kook' and a long, resonant trill. **SITES** Bukit Batok Nature Park, Bukit Timah Nature Reserve, Singapore Botanic Gardens. **CONSERVATION** Has adapted well to scrub, especially in W Singapore.

Red-crowned Barbet ■ *Megalaima*
rafflesii 花彩拟啄木鸟 Takur Ubun Merah 27cm

DESCRIPTION The only forest-dwelling barbet in
Singapore. Predominantly green with colourful facial
patterns. Crown red, with blue throat and yellowish
neck-sides. **DISTRIBUTION** Thai–Malay Peninsula,
Sumatra, Borneo. **HABITS AND HABITATS**
Uncommon resident of primary and mature secondary
forests only. Appears to be locally common in low-lying
swampy forest, especially in the Nee Soon-Seletar area.
Regularly encountered at fruiting fig trees in the Bukit
Timah Nature Reserve. While mainly frugivorous,
has been known to take large insects like beetles.
Nests in excavated tree cavities. Call is a monotonous
series of 'took' notes. **SITES** Central Catchment and
Bukit Timah nature reserves. **CONSERVATION** May
face competition from Lineated Barbet (opposite) if
that species invades the Central Catchment Nature
Reserve. Globally near threatened.

Coppersmith Barbet ■ *Megalaima haemacephala* 赤胸拟啄木鸟
Takur Tukang Besi 16cm

DESCRIPTION ssp. *indica*. A small barbet with
a distinctive facial pattern. Two yellow patches
surrounding the eye give it a 'spectacled' appearance.
Forehead crimson. Throat yellow, separated from
breast by red band. Underparts streaked green against
overall yellow. Sexes similar. **DISTRIBUTION**
Indian sub-continent, S China, mainland Southeast
Asia, Sumatra, Java, Philippines. **HABITS AND
HABITATS** Common resident of secondary scrub,
parkland and occasionally mangroves. The only
species of barbet to be expected in most urban
gardens, where they are often seen at fruiting figs,
but can be very unobtrusive as birds perch high.
Often in small parties, but groups with more than
30 individuals have been reported. Call is a long,
monotonous series of soft 'took' notes, like a copper
sheet being lightly struck. **SITES** Singapore Botanic
Gardens, Pasir Ris Park. **CONSERVATION** Has
benefited from the increase in parkland and scrub
across Singapore.

Sunda Pygmy Woodpecker
■ *Dendrocopos moluccensis* 褐头啄木鸟
Belatuk-Belacan Kecil 13cm

DESCRIPTION ssp. *moluccensis*. The smallest and most frequently encountered woodpecker in Singapore. Brown cap, nape, back and wing with extensive spotting. Dark brownish patch over eye extends down neck and contrasts with white brow and cheek. Faint brown streaks on underparts. Male has fine red streak on rear crown sides, which is absent in female (shown). **DISTRIBUTION** Thai–Malay Peninsula and Greater Sundas, east to the Lesser Sundas (Alor). **HABITS AND HABITATS** Common resident of mangroves, coastal scrub and urban parkland, including narrow strips of ornamental trees beside car parks and along roadside verges. Usually seen foraging in pairs or family groups on the Yellow Flame. Has been observed to join mixed flocks with other garden birds such as Common Iora. Call is a soft, chattering trill. **SITES** Most suitable habitat across Singapore. **CONSERVATION** One of few mangrove birds that have spread widely across Singapore.

White-bellied Woodpecker
■ *Dryocopus javensis* 白腹黑啄木鸟 Belatuk Gajah 41cm

DESCRIPTION ssp. *javensis*. The largest resident woodpecker in Singapore. Highly distinctive given its large size and pied appearance. Both sexes largely black with a diagnostic white belly, with red crest and crown. Male has a red moustachial stripe, absent in female (shown). **DISTRIBUTION** Indian sub-continent east to mainland Southeast Asia, Thai–Malay Peninsula, Greater Sundas and Philippines. An isolated population occurs in Korea. **HABITS AND HABITATS** Probably a non-breeding visitor. Occurs in primary and mature secondary forests, but occasionally wanders into old plantations near the forest edge. Usually in pairs or small groups of up to 5 birds. Recent unconfirmed sightings may have involved birds that have strayed from Johor. Call is a repeated series of 'keow' notes when perched, or a rapid series of 'kek-kek-kek' uttered in flight. **SITES** Central Catchment Nature Reserve. **CONSERVATION** Nationally critically endangered.

Banded Woodpecker ■ *Chrysophlegma miniaceum* 镶红绿啄木鸟 Belatuk Merah 25cm

DESCRIPTION ssp. *malaccense*. A medium-sized, rufous-brown woodpecker with a distinct yellow nape. Both sexes have red crown and rich maroon wings, contrasting with olive-green back, but male (shown) also red on neck sides. Female white speckled on face. Belly to vent buff-white, finely barred olive-green. May be confused with similar-looking Crimson-winged Woodpecker *Picus puniceus*, which has been reported in recent years, but that species is predominantly olive-green and possesses a blue eye-ring. **DISTRIBUTION** Thai–Malay Peninsula, Sumatra, Borneo, Java. **HABITS AND HABITATS** Common resident of primary and secondary forests, forest edge, scrub and old plantations. Call is a single 'kwee', repeated at irregular intervals. Commonest woodpecker in the forests. **SITES** Bukit Batok Nature Park, Central Catchment Nature Reserve, Kent Ridge Park. **CONSERVATION** Extinction of other forest woodpeckers may have benefited this species, allowing it to spread widely.

Laced Woodpecker ■ *Picus vittatus* 花腹绿啄木鸟 Belatuk-Hijau Bakau 30cm

DESCRIPTION ssp. *vittatus*. A medium-sized greenish woodpecker. The largely green plumage, grey face, yellow rump and fine speckling on the belly distinguish it from other woodpeckers. Crown and nape red in male, black in female. **DISTRIBUTION** E India, mainland Southeast Asia, Thai–Malay Peninsula, Sumatra, Java.

HABITS AND HABITATS Common resident of secondary forests, scrub, old plantations, mangroves and occasionally urban parks. Absent from primary forests. Usually forages lower than other woodpeckers, occasionally descending to the ground. Call is a series of staccato 'kek' notes repeated about 8–10 times. **SITES** Occurs in most suitable habitats across Singapore (e.g. Bukit Batok Nature Park). **CONSERVATION** An adaptable woodpecker that has colonised secondary woodland.

LEFT: *Female.* RIGHT: *Male.*

Common Flameback ▪ *Dinopium javanense* 金背三趾啄木鸟
Belatuk-Pinang Kecil 30cm

DESCRIPTION ssp. *javanense*. Easily recognised by its combination of facial pattern, bright golden-yellow mantle, back and wings, red crest and fine black scaling on the underparts. Both sexes possess a black eye-stripe and thinner moustachial stripe. Male has a red crest, female a black crest finely spotted with white. **DISTRIBUTION** SW India; Himalayan foothills and NE India east to mainland Southeast Asia, Thai-Malay Peninsula and Greater Sundas. **HABITS AND HABITATS** Common resident of secondary forests, scrub, old plantations, mangroves and occasionally urban parks near woodland. Call is a rapid trilling series of ringing 'keek' notes. **SITES** Widespread in suitable habitat across Singapore. **CONSERVATION** An adaptable woodpecker that has colonised secondary woodland and parklands.

LEFT: *Male*. RIGHT: *Female*.

Rufous Woodpecker
▪ *Micropternus brachyurus* 栗啄木鸟
Belatuk Biji Nangka 25cm

DESCRIPTION ssp. *badius*. A small, reddish-brown woodpecker with an indistinct crest (unlike many other woodpeckers) and fine black bars from the upper back to the wings, breast and tail. Male (shown) has a red patch below the eye that can only be seen if observed closely. **DISTRIBUTION** S China, Himalayan foothills to E India, mainland Southeast Asia, Thai–Malay Peninsula and Greater Sundas. **HABITS AND HABITATS** Uncommon resident of primary and secondary forests, scrub and old plantations. Has unusual symbiotic relationship with tree ants, building its nest within the ants' nest, yet feeding on ants of other nests. Call is a rapid, laughter-like series of 7–9 'hee' notes. **SITES** Most suitable habitat across Singapore. **CONSERVATION** A forest woodpecker that has adapted to secondary forest habitats.

Hooded Pitta
■ *Pitta sordida* 绿胸八色鸫
Burung Pacat Hijau 18cm

DESCRIPTION ssp. *cucullata*. A mostly greenish pitta, with black head and chestnut-brown crown. Vent to lower belly bright red. Shoulders and rump blue. Flight feathers black with large white wing patch, visible only in flight. **DISTRIBUTION** NE India, SW China, mainland Southeast Asia, Thai–Malay Peninsula, Greater Sundas, Philippines, Sulawesi, New Guinea. Northern populations migrate to winter in Southeast Asia. **HABITS AND HABITATS** Uncommon migrant to primary and secondary forests, scrub and occasionally parkland. Shy, difficult to see well. Forages for invertebrates, especially worms in the leaf litter. Birds mostly arrive in November and depart by April. Silent when wintering. **SITES** Central Catchment and Bukit Timah nature reserves, Singapore Botanic Gardens. **CONSERVATION** Mortalities suffered when migrating birds crash into lighted buildings may significantly affect the migrant population.

Blue-winged Pitta ■ *Pitta moluccensis* 蓝翅八色鸫
Burung Pacat Sayap Biru 19cm

DESCRIPTION A colourful pitta with black facial mask, buff crown sides and black crown-stripe. Mantle, back and wing coverts green, shoulders blue and underparts orange-buff, with red centre of belly and vent. **DISTRIBUTION** S China, mainland Southeast Asia and Thai-Malay Peninsula. Northern populations winter S Thai-Malay Peninsula and Greater Sundas. **HABITS AND HABITATS** Uncommon migrant and probable resident. Occurs in primary and secondary forests, old plantation, scrub and occasionally parkland. Arrives in October and departs by April. Unclear if birds breeding in Singapore migrate elsewhere Mostly silent when wintering and may only call briefly at dawn or dusk. Breeding activity reported from July-August, with clutch of 4. Call is a loud fluty 'tu-teew, tu-teew' usually uttered from a high perch. Forages for earthworms and snails in the leaf litter. **SITES** Central Catchment and Bukit Timah nature reserves, Pulau Ubin, Singapore Botanic Gardens. **CONSERVATION** Prone to colliding with glass and other structures on migration.

Mangrove Pitta ■ *Pitta megarhyncha* 红树八色鸫 Burung Pacat Bakau 20cm

DESCRIPTION A colourful pitta with a long, thickset bill. Very similar to Blue-winged Pitta (see p.105) but bill is longer and more robust; black crown-stripe is narrower and less distinct; crown sides darker and richer brown, unlike buff of Blue-winged Pitta, and broader. **DISTRIBUTION** Coastal E India, Bangladesh and Myanmar, Thai–Malay

Peninsula, Sumatra. **HABITS AND HABITATS** A rare resident occurring only in mangroves and confined mainly to the islands of Pulau Tekong and Pulau Ubin. Also sporadic records of birds on mainland Singapore most recently at Pasir Ris Park and the Botanic Gardens. A mangrove specialist, adapted to take crabs (which explains its robust bill). Call is similar to that of Blue-winged Pitta; most vocal during breeding season, March–August. Nest is a dome of sticks, built near ground with 2–3 eggs. **SITES** Pulau Ubin, Pulau Tekong. **CONSERVATION** Globally near threatened; nationally critically endangered. Now extinct from mainland Singapore due to loss of mangroves.

Golden-bellied Gerygone ■ *Gerygone sulphurea* 黄胸噪刺莺
Kelicap Perepat Asia 10cm

DESCRIPTION ssp. *sulphurea*. A small, nondescript warbler-like bird with plain greyish-brown upperparts and pale yellowish underparts. Note also pale lores and short, black bill.

DISTRIBUTION Mainland Southeast Asia, Thai-Malay Peninsula, Greater and Lesser Sundas, Sulawesi and Philippines. **HABITS AND HABITATS** Common resident of primary and secondary forests, forest edges, mangroves, scrub and parkland. Difficult to see well as it usually keeps to canopy. However, its high-pitched musical, wheezy song is often heard. Often parasitised by Little Bronze Cuckoo. Nest is purse-shaped with a side entrance, suspended from overhanging branch, with clutch of 2-3. **SITES** Suitable habitat throughout Singapore. **CONSERVATION** One of few forest/mangrove birds that have expanded its niche into urban greenery and parkland.

Common Iora ■ *Aegithina tiphia* 黑翅雀鹎 Kunyit-Kecil Biasa 13cm

DESCRIPTION ssp. *horizoptera*. The only iora in Singapore. Breeding male has mostly black upperparts from the cap onwards, with two white wing bars. Non-breeding male has olive-green upperparts. Female is less strongly marked with paler green upperparts.
DISTRIBUTION Indian sub-continent, S China, mainland Southeast Asia, Thai–Malay Peninsula, Greater Sundas, Palawan.
HABITS AND HABITATS Common resident of secondary forests, forest edge, mangroves, scrub, and urban parkland. A familiar bird, often seen foraging in roadside trees for caterpillars and insects.

During courtship, the males engage in a remarkable display in which the wings are drooped, tail fanned and body feathers erected. Vocal, with repertoire including a varied series of melodious whistles. A common call is a drawn-out trill that ends with an abrupt whistle.
SITES Suitable habitat across Singapore. **CONSERVATION** No issues.

ABOVE: *Female* RIGHT: *Male*

Pied Triller ■ *Lalage nigra* 黑鸣鹃鵙 Rembah Kening Putih 17cm

DESCRIPTION ssp. *striga*. A distinctive black and white bird with contrasting white brow and black eye-stripe. Male is black on crown, nape, mantle and parts of wing; mostly white on underparts. Back and uppertail coverts grey. Female is greyish brown on upperparts, not black, and finely scaled on underparts. Young birds are less strongly marked and are finely streaked on the underparts. **DISTRIBUTION** Thai–Malay Peninsula, Greater Sundas, Philippines. **HABITS AND HABITATS** Common resident of mangroves, parkland, urban areas and especially coastal scrub. Often seen foraging on roadside trees (particularly Yellow Flame) for insects and caterpillars, occasionally joining mixed flocks with other small birds. Nest is a small cup built fairly high above the ground. Call is a rapid series of about 20 'ngeh' notes. **SITES** Suitable habitat across Singapore. **CONSERVATION** No issues.

ABOVE: *Male* LEFT: *Female*

Ashy Minivet ▪ *Pericrocotus divaricatus* 灰山椒鸟 Matahari Kelabu 19cm

DESCRIPTION A grey-and-white minivet. Male is dark grey on upperparts with prominent white forehead contrasting with black eye-stripe and nape patch. Female (shown) is paler grey, with black lores and much smaller white patch on forehead. In flight, note long tail, white underparts and white patches on underwing. **DISTRIBUTION** Breeds

in Russian Far East, E China, Korea and Japan. Winters mostly in S India, mainland Southeast Asia, Thai–Malay Peninsula, Greater Sundas and Philippines. **HABITS AND HABITATS** Common migrant of primary and secondary forests, old plantations, mangroves, coastal scrub and parkland, occasionally urban areas. Feeds high up in the canopy. Birds usually arrive in early to mid-October, becoming particularly common by late October to early November when large flocks are seen. Small numbers overwinter. Often calls when about to take flight or flying, usually a series of fast, high-pitched trills of 5 'dee' notes, the last slightly lower. **SITES** Suitable habitat across Singapore. **CONSERVATION** No issues.

Scarlet Minivet ▪ *Pericrocotus speciosus* 赤红山椒鸟 Matahari Besar 19cm

DESCRIPTION ssp. *xanthogaster*. An unmistakable red and black minivet. Head, neck and back black, contrasting with bright red underparts and tail in male (shown). Wings with one large and two small red patches across secondaries and tertials. Female is grey on the crown, nape and back, with orangy forehead, and entirely orangy-yellow on

the underparts. **DISTRIBUTION** Himalayan foothills, NE India, S China, mainland Southeast Asia, Thai–Malay Peninsula, Greater Sundas, Philippines. **HABITS AND HABITATS** Very rare resident of primary and secondary forests. Forages in the forest canopy, regularly joining mixed flocks with malkohas, drongos and other canopy birds. Usually seen in small flocks. Call is a repeated series of 5–6 sweet 'weep' notes. **SITES** Bukit Timah and Central Catchment nature reserves. **CONSERVATION** Nationally critically endangered. There are very few recent records.

Mangrove Whistler

■ *Pachycephala cinerea* 红树啸鹟 Murai Bakau 16cm

DESCRIPTION ssp. *cinerea*. A drab, chunky greyish-brown bird of coastal vegetation. Upperparts dull brown with grey crown. Underparts white, with grey wash on the breast. Bill thick and uniformly black. Sexes alike. **DISTRIBUTION** E India and Bangladesh, coastal Southeast Asia, Thai–Malay Peninsula, Greater Sundas and Palawan. **HABITS AND HABITATS** Locally common resident of mangroves, coastal scrub, *Casuarina* woodland, secondary forests and occasionally parkland. Not an active feeder, and hops casually from branch to branch to glean insects, frequently perching still. Only seen on offshore islands in Singapore. Call is variable, but commonly sings a fluid 'chi-chi-chi-chi-chew', the last note being most explosive. **SITES** Pulau Ubin, Pulau Tekong. **CONSERVATION** Virtually extinct on mainland Singapore and Pulau Hantu.

Tiger Shrike ■ *Lanius tigrinus* 虎纹伯劳 Tirjup Harimau 19cm

DESCRIPTION Adult male wears a thick black mask, and is grey from head to mantle, with dark scaling on mostly rufous upperparts. Female duller, but shows more prominent black bars on flanks than male, and has white lores and brow. First-winter bird has dark scaling on warm-brown upperparts and white underparts, and lacks the dark facial mask. **DISTRIBUTION** Breeds in NE China, Russian Far East, Korea and Japan. Winters in S China, mainland Southeast Asia, Thai–Malay Peninsula and Greater Sundas. **HABITS AND HABITATS** Common migrant of primary and secondary forests, mangroves, scrub and parkland. Immature birds are more commonly seen than adults. Call is a harsh scolding chatter when alarmed. A predator of large insects, lizards and small birds. Arrives from August and departs by May. Especially common in October during peak passage period. **SITES** Suitable habitat throughout Singapore. **CONSERVATION** Dependent on forests in the wintering range.

LEFFT: *Male;* RIGHT: *First winter bird*

Brown Shrike ■ *Lanius cristatus* 红尾伯劳 Tirjup Coklat 19cm

DESCRIPTION Combination of black mask, white brow and forehead, and plain brown, not barred, upperparts distinguishes this from Tiger Shrike (see p.109). Crown either grey (ssp. *lucionensis*) or brown (ssp. *cristatus*). Underparts off-white to buff. Female *cristatus* (shown) has dark brown mask, brown upperparts and off-white underparts with dark scaling. **DISTRIBUTION** Breeds across C Siberia, east to NE China, Korea, Japan and Kamchatka, and south to E Tibetan Plateau. Winters in Indian sub-continent, S China and most of Southeast Asia, east to Sulawesi and Lesser Sundas. **HABITS AND HABITATS** Common migrant of secondary forests, old plantations, mangroves, open scrub, grasslands and parkland. Often seen perched on exposed stakes or fences, scanning for large insect prey. Immature birds more commonly seen than adults. Call is a harsh scolding 'chak-chak-chak' when alarmed. Birds arrive mostly in September and depart by May. **SITES** Suitable habitat throughout Singapore. **CONSERVATION** No issues.

Long-tailed Shrike ■ *Lanius schach* 棕背伯劳 Tirjup Ekor Panjang 26cm

DESCRIPTION ssp. *bentet*. The shrike with the longest tail. Large black facial mask extends from forecrown to head sides, with hindcrown and mantle grey, edged rufous. Wings black with small white patch. Throat white and rest of underparts washed pale rufous. Young birds plain, mostly dark brown with blackish face and throat. **DISTRIBUTION** Parts of Central Asia, Indian sub-continent, S China, mainland Southeast Asia, east to Greater and Lesser Sundas, Philippines and New Guinea. **HABITS AND HABITATS** Uncommon resident of open scrub, grasslands and playing fields. Hunts from open perches including fence lines, branches and posts for insects, lizards and small birds. Song consists of a series of rather nondescript squeaks and whistles, calls a harsh 'chak-chak' when alarmed. Breeding reported patchily throughout the year in January, April and July–October. **SITES** Lorong Halus wetlands, Changi coast. **CONSERVATION** Has declined in recent years, Trapped for the pet trade in parts of Indonesia.

Black-naped Oriole ■ *Oriolus chinensis* 黑枕黄鹂 Kunyit Besar 26cm

DESCRIPTION ssp. *maculatus*, *diffusus?* The only oriole in Singapore, thus unmistakable. Male (shown) plumage is rich golden-yellow, with diagnostic black band from lore to nape and a pinkish bill. Wing dirty yellow with black fringes and tip. Female has upperparts washed olive-yellow. Young birds are duller yellow, finely streaked black from throat to lower belly. **DISTRIBUTION** Indian sub-continent and much of China north to SE Russia and Japan. Also across much of Southeast Asia, east to Sulawesi and the Lesser Sundas.

HABITS AND HABITATS Very common resident and migrant to secondary forests, mangroves, old plantation, scrub, parkland and urban areas. One of the commonest parkland birds. An omnivore that takes mostly fruits, but opportunistically raids nests. Calls variable, but usually a series of fluty whistles, and occasionally a harsh 'kyaaarr'. **SITES** Suitable habitat across Singapore. **CONSERVATION** No issues.

Ashy Drongo ■ *Dicrurus leucophaeus* 灰卷尾 Cecawi Kelabu 27cm

DESCRIPTION ssp. *leucogenis* (shown), *salangensis* The only grey drongo with a forked tail. Plumage ashy grey, with white patch around red eye. Two rather similar-looking races occur in Singapore. Ssp. *leucogenis* shows white facial patch around eye, extending to ear coverts. Ssp. *salangensis* is similar, but facial patch is much smaller, not reaching ear coverts, while plumage is darker grey. Ssp. *nigrescens* is slate-grey, appearing almost black, and may occur. **DISTRIBUTION** Much of Indian sub-continent and Himalayan foothills, north to S and E China. Also mainland Southeast Asia, Thai–Malay Peninsula and Greater Sundas. Northern populations are migratory, wintering in Southeast Asia. **HABITS AND HABITATS** Rare migrant to secondary forests, old plantations, scrub and occasionally parkland. Feeds by flycatching for insects from a perch, regularly returning to original position. Usually silent in winter, but occasionally calls a harsh 'kip'. **SITES** Parks in the Southern Ridges (Mount Faber), Western Catchment area. **CONSERVATION** No issues.

Crow-billed Drongo ■ *Dicrurus annectans* 鸦嘴卷尾
Cecawi Paruh Tebal 30cm

DESCRIPTION A glossy black drongo with a forked tail. Plumage black with glossy sheen, long bill. Forked tail is usually upcurled at the tip, separating it from other black drongos. Also note lack of black tuft on forehead, a consistent feature of the Greater Racket-tailed Drongo (below). Young birds (shown) show white spots on the breast to undertail.

DISTRIBUTION Breeds in Himalayan foothills, E India, S China and mainland Southeast Asia. Winters across mainland Southeast Asia, Thai–Malay Peninsula, Sumatra and Java. **HABITS AND HABITATS** Uncommon migrant to primary and secondary forests, forest edge, old plantation and scrub, occasionally entering parkland. Shy, often seen under dense cover. Occasionally joins mixed flocks in search of insects, but usually forages alone. Calls include a ringing whistle, followed by harsh raspy notes similar to Greater Racket-tailed Drongo. **SITES** Bukit Timah and Central Catchment nature reserves. **CONSERVATION** No issues.

Greater Racket-tailed Drongo ■ *Dicrurus paradiseus* 大盘尾
Cecawi Anting-anting Besar 34cm (+ 30cm tail)

DESCRIPTION ssp. *platurus*. A large drongo with prominent tail feathers. Plumage glossy black, with conspicuous tuft on forehead. Tail lightly forked, unlike Crow-billed Drongo (above), with shafts of outer feathers extending, and ending with a curled 'racket'. Recently moulted birds may not possess these rackets. **DISTRIBUTION** Much of Indian sub-continent, S China, mainland Southeast Asia, Thai–Malay Peninsula and Greater Sundas. **HABITS AND HABITATS** Common resident of primary and secondary forests, forest edge, scrub and old plantations. One of the commonest forest birds, frequently joining mixed flocks with malkohas and woodpeckers to forage for insects. Also known to follow Long-tailed Macaques to feed on insects flushed. Vocal, repertoire varied, uttering many different metallic whistles and harsh raspy notes, and frequently mimicking other birds. **SITES** Bukit Batok Nature Park, Bukit Timah Nature Reserve, Central Catchment Nature Reserve. **CONSERVATION** No issues.

Malaysian Pied Fantail ■ *Rhipidura javanica* 斑扇尾鶲 Murai Gila 18cm

DESCRIPTION ssp. *longicauda*. The only fantail in Singapore. Upperparts entirely black. Underparts white with broad black band across breast. Prominent rictal bristles. Long tail with white tips, repeatedly fanned and closed as bird moves. Formerly known as Pied Fantail, but now split from Philippine ssp. which is treated as Philippine Pied Fantail *R. nigritorquis*. **DISTRIBUTION** Mainland Southeast Asia, Thai–Malay Peninsula, Sumatra, Borneo, Java. **HABITS AND HABITATS**
Common resident of mangroves, old plantations, forest edge, secondary scrub and occasionally parkland, usually near water (e.g. ponds, abandoned quarries). One of the dominant insectivorous birds in mangroves, sometimes foraging with Ashy Tailorbird. A known host of the Rusty-breasted Cuckoo. The song is a series of high-pitched rising and falling squeaks, 'chi-chi-chi-wit-chi-weet', the first two notes very soft. **SITES** Lorong Halus wetlands, Bukit Batok Nature Park, Sungei Buloh Wetland Reserve. **CONSERVATION** No issues.

Black-naped Monarch

■ *Hypothymis azurea* 黑枕王鶲 Kelicap Ranting 16cm

DESCRIPTION ssp. *prophata*. A chunky blue bird with a large head. Male (shown) is bright blue, with a prominent black tuft at the back of the head and base of upper mandible, and a thin black 'necklace' at the base of throat. Female is duller, lacking the black patches, and greyish brown on much of the breast and upperparts. **DISTRIBUTION** Indian sub-continent, S China, mainland Southeast Asia, Thai–Malay Peninsula, Greater and Lesser Sundas, Philippines. **HABITS AND HABITATS** Locally common resident of secondary forests forests, forest edge and old plantations. An insectivore that forages alone by flycatching, occasionally joining mixed flocks. Very rare on the mainland, known from very few records from the Central Catchment Nature Reserve, but remains common on Pulau Tekong, where it is one of the dominant forest birds. Builds a small cup-shaped nest of plant fibres, usually on a fork of thin branches; clutch size 2–3. Call is a ringing series of 'whit' notes. **SITES** Pulau Tekong. **CONSERVATION** Nationally critically endangered.

Blyth's Paradise Flycatcher ▪ *Terpsiphone affinis* 中南寿带
Murai-Ekor-Gading Asia 21cm (+ 27cm tail)

DESCRIPTION ssp. *indochinensis, affinis?* Commonest of three similar-looking black and chestnut monarchs. Male sports long tail streamers and is rich chestnut on wings and back, with head and crest slate grey, becoming paler towards breast. Female lacks tail streamers and has a less prominent crest. Rare white-morph birds are entirely white except for black head. Similar-looking Amur Paradise Flycatcher (formerly ssp. *incei*) has black hood that contrasts strongly with grey breast. **DISTRIBUTION** Breeds NE India, S China and much of Southeast Asia, east to Lesser Sundas. Northern populations winter in Thai-Malay Peninsula and Greater Sundas. **HABITS AND HABITATS** Common migrant of forests, forest edge, mangroves, old plantations, scrub and well-wooded parkland,

especially during passage. Commonest in mid-October, becoming progressive rarer thereafter. Wintering birds mostly confined to forest. Frequently joins Pin-striped Tit-Babblers, warblers and drongos in mixed flocks. Commonly heard call is a harsh, raspy 'chi-chuu. **SITES** Suitable habitat across Singapore. **CONSERVATION** Extinct as a resident in Singapore.

LEFT: *Blyth's Paradise Flycatcher.*
RIGHT: *Amur Paradise Flycatcher.*

Japanese Paradise Flycatcher ▪ *Terpsiphone atrocaudata* 紫寿带鸟
Murai-Ekor-Gading Jepun 19cm (+ 23cm tail)

DESCRIPTION ssp. *atrocaudata*. Similar to Blyth's Paradise Flycatcher. Males unmistakable, purplish black from mantle to rump, with black tail. Head and breast black, contrasting sharply with white belly. Female very similar to Asian Paradise Flycatcher, but appears duller and darker on mantle, wings and tail. **DISTRIBUTION** Breeds in Japan, Korea and islands off Taiwan. Winters in Thai–Malay Peninsula,

Sumatra, Borneo and Java. **HABITS AND HABITATS** Rare passage migrant to primary and secondary forest, old plantation, scrub and occasionally parkland. Most birds encountered in Singapore are females. Occurs mostly October–March. **SITES** Central Catchment Nature Reserve. **CONSERVATION** Globally near threatened, forest dependent in winter range.

LEFT: *Male.* RIGHT: *Female.*

House Crow ■ *Corvus splendens* 家鸦 Gagak Rumah 42cm

DESCRIPTION ssp. *splendens*. Commoner of the two crows. Plumage entirely blackish with a broad dull collar around neck, mantle and breast. Appears black in poor light, but can be distinguished from Large-billed Crow by its different head profile, with shorter bill and less steep forehead. **DISTRIBUTION** Coastal Iran, Indian sub-continent and Myanmar. Widely introduced elsewhere, including many parts of Southeast Asia. **HABITS**

AND HABITATS Very common resident, originating from introduced stock, of old plantations, scrub, mangroves, parkland and urban areas. Scavenges on refuse and carcasses, but opportunistically hunts small animals and birds. Call is a dry 'aaa, aaa', higher-pitched than Large-billed Crow. Systematic shooting has reduced the population greatly in recent years, but it remains common at some sites (e.g. Orchard Road). A frequent host of the Asian Koel. **SITES** Suitable habitat across Singapore. **CONSERVATION** Considered a pest, and one of 6 species not protected by law in Singapore.

Large-billed Crow ■ *Corvus macrorhynchos* 大嘴乌鸦
Gagak Paruh Besar 50cm

DESCRIPTION ssp. *macrorhynchos*. A large crow with a massive thickset bill. Plumage entirely black with purple sheen. Head profile different from House Crow, showing steep forehead and long bill with arched upper mandible. In flight, tail appears slightly wedge-shaped, while wings appear fingered. **DISTRIBUTION** Himalayan foothills, E

India and much of China north to E Russia and Japan. Also across much of Southeast Asia, east to the Lesser Sundas. **HABITS AND HABITATS** Common resident of secondary forests, mangroves, forest edge, scrub, old plantations and parkland, occasionally straying into urban areas. Usually seen in pairs or small groups, never forming large flocks. Nest is a large messy structure of sticks. Call is a deep 'gaa, gaa…', with tail raised, sometimes throaty guttural notes. **SITES** Suitable habitats across Singapore. **CONSERVATION** No issues.

Straw-headed Bulbul ■ *Pycnonotus zeylanicus* 黄冠鹎 Barau-barau 29cm

DESCRIPTION Largest bulbul in the region. Upperparts greyish brown with fine streaking from nape to back. Wings, tail and rump olive green. Breast finely streaked white, extending onto belly. Crown and cheeks rich orange. Thick black moustachial stripe contrasts with white throat. Sexes similar. **DISTRIBUTION** Thai–Malay Peninsula, Sumatra, Borneo, Java. **HABITS AND HABITATS** Locally common resident of secondary

forests, forest edge, scrub and plantations along water bodies including rivers, lakes, reservoirs and abandoned quarries. Nest is a cup of sticks, usually high up a tree from March to May. Frugivorous, and pairs or small groups are frequently seen at fruiting trees by forest edge. Song is a rich and varied series of far-carrying resonant warbles. Other calls include a soft double whistle, 'wheet-wheet', and a bubbly trill. **SITES** Bukit Batok Nature Park, Central Catchment Nature Reserve, Pulau Ubin. **CONSERVATION** Globally endangered. Nationally endangered. Extirpated from most of its global range due to the pet bird trade.

Black-headed Bulbul

■ *Pycnonotus atriceps* 黑头鹎 Merbah Siam 18cm

DESCRIPTION ssp. *atriceps*. A small yellowish bulbul with a glossy black head. Plumage bright yellow, becoming yellowish-green on hindneck, back, breast and wing coverts. Iris pale blue. Also note black flight feathers and thick subterminal tail band, both absent in the similar-looking introduced Black-crested Bulbul *P. flaviventris*. **DISTRIBUTION** NE India, mainland Southeast Asia, Thai–Malay Peninsula, Greater Sundas, Palawan. **HABITS AND HABITATS** Rare resident of secondary forests and forest edge, occasionally wandering into nearby scrub and parkland. Omnivorous, and known to take many insects, especially when nesting. Usually seen feeding at fruiting figs in small groups and not associating with other bulbuls. Nest is a small cup of sticks and dried leaves, built in low shrubs. Call is a series of toneless 'chew' notes. **SITES** Central Catchment Nature Reserve, Bukit Brown. **CONSERVATION** Nationally critically endangered Reasons for its rarity here unclear as it is known to occur in heavily degraded forests in region.

Red-whiskered Bulbul ▪ *Pycnonotus jocosus* 红耳鹎
Merbah Telinga Merah 20cm

DESCRIPTION ssp. *pattani/emeria*? A familiar brown, black and white bulbul with a prominent crest. Upperparts dark brown, contrasting with mostly white underparts and bright red undertail coverts. Unmistakable black crest, red 'whiskers' and large white cheek patch demarcated from throat by thin black malar stripe. Young birds are less strongly marked and lack the red whiskers. **DISTRIBUTION** Indian sub-continent, S China, mainland Southeast Asia, Thai–Malay Peninsula. Widely introduced elsewhere (e.g. Hawaii). **HABITS AND HABITATS** Uncommon resident, originating from escapes, occurring in scrub and parkland, occasionally secondary forests. Population established since the 1910s, but likely that it is continually augmented by recent escapes. Usually seen in pairs, but small flocks of as many as 20 have been recorded. Nesting has been reported from April to May. **SITES** Lorong Halus wetlands, Kranji marshes. **CONSERVATION** No issues.

Yellow-vented Bulbul ▪ *Pycnonotus goiavier* 白眉黄臀鹎
Merbah Kapur 20cm

DESCRIPTION ssp. *analis*. An unmistakable medium-sized bulbul with black crown and lores. Head white, contrasting with black crown and lore patches. Rest of upperparts greyish-brown. Underparts dirty white with faint brown streaking on breast, belly and flanks, and vent bright yellow. Young birds are less strongly marked. **DISTRIBUTION** Parts of mainland Southeast Asia, Thai–Malay Peninsula, Greater Sundas, Philippines. **HABITS AND HABITATS** Very common resident of secondary forests, forest edge, scrub, old plantations, mangroves, parkland and urban areas. Commonest bulbul in Singapore, and often the only bulbul in urban areas. Breeds February–August. Nest is an untidy cup of sticks and dried leaves, usually in low dense shrubs. Some birds even nest on potted plants in balconies. Commonly heard calls include a series of bubbly 'chic' and 'chweek' notes. **SITES** Suitable habitat across Singapore. **CONSERVATION** No issues.

Olive-winged Bulbul

■ *Pycnonotus plumosus* 橄榄褐鹎 Merbah Belukar 20cm

DESCRIPTION ssp. *plumosus*. A brownish bulbul with olive-green wings. Head, neck, mantle and tail dark brown, with underparts buffy brown, becoming dull yellowish towards the vent. Back, wings and tail dull olive-green, with yellowish-olive flight feathers. Also note white streaking on cheeks and red eyes. Similar-looking Asian Red-eyed Bulbul (see p.119) lacks olive-green in plumage and is browner. Young birds appear more uniformly brown. **DISTRIBUTION** Thai–Malay Peninsula, Sumatra, Borneo, Java. **HABITS AND HABITATS** Common resident of secondary forests, forest edge, old plantations, scrub, occasionally straying into parkland; seldom in primary forests. Commonest bulbul in secondary forests and scrub. Usually keeps to understorey, but occasionally joins other bulbuls to feed in low fruiting trees. Breeds February–April. Nest is a cup-shaped nest made of sticks in low shrubs. Call is a series of sweet 'whip' notes. **SITES** Suitable habitat across Singapore. Particularly common in woodland at Singapore Zoo and Sentosa. **CONSERVATION** No issues.

Cream-vented Bulbul ■ *Pycnonotus simplex* 白眼褐鹎
Merbah Mata Putih 18cm

DESCRIPTION ssp. *simplex*. A drab brown bulbul with white irises. Upperparts brownish and underparts mostly creamy buff, with pale brownish wash on chest. Young birds are paler. Buff-vented Bulbul (see p.119) also has pale irises but is very rare in Singapore and has a distinct black brow, also appearing longer-billed. **DISTRIBUTION** Thai–Malay Peninsula, Sumatra, Borneo, Java. **HABITS AND HABITATS** Uncommon resident of primary and secondary forests, and forest edge. Appears to have declined in recent years, and now less frequently encountered than Asian Red-eyed Bulbul in the central forests. Forages mostly in canopy, occasionally descending lower to feed on low trees. Often seen feeding at fruiting figs and flowering *Macaranga* trees. Breeds April–October. Builds a cup-shaped nest, usually containing clutch of 2. Call is a dry, bubbly 'trrrr' and a quick series of 'whit' notes. **SITES** Bukit Timah and Central Catchment nature reserves. **CONSERVATION** Forest dependent in Singapore.

Asian Red-eyed Bulbul ■ *Pycnonotus brunneus* 红眼褐鹎
Merbah Mata Merah 19cm

DESCRIPTION ssp. *brunneus*. A nondescript brown bulbul with orangy-red eyes.
Upperparts dark brown, underparts brownish buff. Generally darker than Cream-vented
Bulbul (see p.118) and has orangy-red, not white, irises. Young birds have brownish
eyes and paler plumage than adults.
DISTRIBUTION Thai–Malay Peninsula,
Sumatra, Borneo. **HABITS AND
HABITATS** Uncommon resident of
primary and secondary forests and forest
edge. Like Cream-vented Bulbul, often
seen at fruiting figs or flowering *Macaranga*
trees, sometimes in loose groups of
as many as 10 birds. Appears to have
become commoner in recent years; more
numerous than Cream-vented Bulbul.
Breeds March–July. Call is a series of
high-pitched, bubbly notes, with the final
note the highest. **SITES** Bukit Timah
and Central Catchment nature reserves.
CONSERVATION Nationally endangered.

Buff-vented Bulbul ■ *Iole crypta* 黄臀灰胸鹎 Merbah Riang 20cm

DESCRIPTION An unmistakable bulbul with a bristly crown. Upperparts brown,
underparts pale grey. Combination of head features diagnostic, with pale iris, black brow
patch, pale lores and long bill. Raised
feathers on crown give it a 'spiky-
headed' appearance. **DISTRIBUTION**
Thai–Malay Peninsula, Sumatra.
HABITS AND HABITATS Very rare
non-breeding visitor and probable
resident, known from a handful
of recent records in primary and
secondary forests. Most sightings of
the species are of lone individuals
at the fruiting fig tree at the summit
of Bukit Timah. Call is a quick
nasal, upward inflected 'whe-ic'.
SITES Bukit Timah Nature Reserve.
CONSERVATION Globally near
threatened. Nationally critically
endangered.

Streaked Bulbul

■ *Ixos malaccensis* 纹羽鹎 Bebarau Lorek 23cm

DESCRIPTION A rather long-billed bulbul with extensive underpart streaking. Upperparts olive-brown, contrasting with paler underparts, notably white vent. Throat and breast pale grey, with thick white streaking. Bill longer than in most other bulbuls. Lacks a distinct crest, but has loose crown feathers giving it a 'spiky-headed' appearance. **DISTRIBUTION** Thai–Malay Peninsula, Sumatra, Borneo. **HABITS AND HABITATS** Rare non-breeding visitor to primary and secondary forests. Apparently nomadic, and birds seen here may have originated from Peninsular Malaysia, where it is common in hill forests. Scattered records suggest wandering behaviour. Usually seen in pairs or parties at fruiting fig trees. Call is a rapid, dry 'chee-ree'. **SITES** Bukit Timah Nature Reserve, Pulau Ubin. **CONSERVATION** Globally near threatened, forest dependent.

Cinereous Bulbul ■ *Hemixos cinereus* 灰黑短脚鹎
Bebarau Kelabu Melayu 21cm

DESCRIPTION ssp. *cinereus*. A crested bulbul with a puffy white throat. Upperparts greyish brown, underparts pale grey. Combination of short grey crest, black cheek and lore patches gives it a 'black-faced' appearance. Formerly treated as a race of Ashy Bulbul *H. flavala*. **DISTRIBUTION** Thai–Malay Peninsula, Sumatra, Borneo. **HABITS AND HABITATS** Uncommon non-breeding visitor to primary and secondary forests, occasionally mangroves and scrub. Often seen in small groups, but large flocks of over 100 birds have been reported in 2014. Apparently a nomadic species, with most records September–January. Birds seen in Singapore are probably wanderers from Peninsular Malaysia, where it is common in hill forest. Calls include a repeated 'treeh' note with a nasal, ringing quality. **SITES** Bukit Timah and Central Catchment nature reserves, Pulau Ubin. **CONSERVATION** Forest dependent.

Barn Swallow ■ *Hirundo rustica* 家燕 Layang-layang Hijrah
15cm (+ 5cm tail streamers)

DESCRIPTION ssp. *gutturalis, saturata*? A familiar swallow, the only one with largely white underparts. Upperparts glossy blue with brick-red forehead and throat patch, separated from white breast and belly by blue-black breast band. Adults have tail streamers, longer in males. **DISTRIBUTION** Widespread across much of the Americas, Eurasia, Africa and Australia. Populations across Eurasia migrate to winter in Africa, Indian sub-continent, Southeast Asia, Australia and W Pacific. **HABITS AND HABITATS** Very common migrant, occurring over all habitats. Roosts in large groups of a few hundreds to the low thousands in reedbeds and buildings. An active aerial insectivore, often seen feeding over water bodies, where it regularly descends to drink. Usually arrives from August onwards, with small numbers overwintering. Groups of several thousands have been seen roosting in housing estates (e.g. Yishun). The call is a squeaky twittering. **SITES** Suitable habitats across Singapore. **CONSERVATION** No issues.

Pacific Swallow ■ *Hirundo tahitica* 洋燕 Layang-layang Pasifik 14cm

DESCRIPTION ssp. *javanica*. The only resident swallow. Upperparts glossy blue. Underparts buff-grey. Forehead and throat brick-red. Superficially similar to Barn Swallow (above), but lacks blue-black breast band, has darker underparts and lacks the tail streamers. **DISTRIBUTION** Parts of mainland Southeast Asia and Thai–Malay Peninsula, east to Maluku, New Guinea and W Pacific islands. **HABITS AND HABITATS** Very common resident, occurring over nearly all habitats except for tall primary forests. An active aerial insectivore often seen in mixed groups with the Barn Swallow, but foraging lower than that species on average. The neat cup nest, made of mud, is usually built under roofs and eaves of buildings. Clutch size 3–4. **SITES** Suitable habitat across Singapore. **CONSERVATION** No issues.

LEFT: *Underparts*. RIGHT: *Upperparts*.

Red-rumped Swallow ■ *Cecropis daurica* 金腰燕
Layang-layang Api 17cm (+ 3cm tail streamers)

DESCRIPTION ssp. *japonica*. A large swallow with a prominent pale rump. Upperparts glossy blue-black, contrasting with red rump patch, particularly visible during flight. Brow, head sides and nape brick-red. Underparts pale buff with fine streaking from throat to belly. Can also be distinguished from other swallows by distinctive flight pattern, consisting of periods of gliding interspersed with occasional wing flapping, recalling a bee-eater. **DISTRIBUTION** Widespread across Eurasia, breeding from S Europe and Middle East to Central Asia, China and E Russia. Winters in Africa, Indian sub-continent and Southeast Asia, south to Australia. **HABITS AND HABITATS** Fairly common migrant, occurring over secondary forests, forest edge, scrub and plantations along water bodies including rivers, lakes, reservoirs and abandoned quarries. Generally less numerous than Barn and Pacific Swallows, but can be common in open scrubby areas near water. An active aerial insectivore, but less manoeuvrable in flight than the other two common swallows. **SITES** Suitable habitat across Singapore (e.g. Lorong Halus). **CONSERVATION** No issues.

Arctic Warbler ■ *Phylloscopus borealis* 极北柳莺 Cekup-Daun Artik 12cm

DESCRIPTION ssp. *borealis*. Most abundant *Phylloscopus* warbler in Singapore. Upperparts olive-green to greenish brown. Underparts white with brownish wash on flank and belly. Vent white, not yellow as in next species. Long black eye-stripe, and pale brow reaching nape. Two whitish wing bars, but upper one usually faint. Birds in worn plumage may not show any visible wing bars. **DISTRIBUTION** Breeds from Fennoscandia to Russian

Far East, N Mongolia, NE China and Korea. Winters across S China, and most of Southeast Asia. **HABITS AND HABITATS** Very common migrant to primary and secondary forests, forest edge, mangroves, old plantations, scrub, parkland and urban areas, including on small islands. Usually the only warbler expected in urban areas, and the dominant warbler in all habitats. Sometimes joins mixed feeding flocks in the middle storey and canopy. Call is a short, repeated, ringing 'chit'; from March, many birds in song, which consists of a series of trills. Occurs mostly September–April. **SITES** Suitable habitat across Singapore. **CONSERVATION** No issues.

Eastern Crowned Warbler ■ *Phylloscopus coronatus* 冕柳莺
Cekup-Daun Tongkeng Kuning 11.5cm

DESCRIPTION An olive-green warbler rather similar to Arctic Warbler (see p.122). Upperparts olive-green, with yellowish-green fringes to flight feathers giving it a much richer plumage colour than Arctic Warbler. Thin white brow extends from bill to nape, contrasting with dark lateral crown-stripe. Median crown paler green, contrasting with lateral crown-stripe, and is diagnostic. **DISTRIBUTION** Breeds in SE Russia, NE China, Korea and Japan. A disjunct population occurs in central China. Winters in parts of mainland Southeast Asia, Thai–Malay Peninsula, Sumatra and Java. **HABITS AND HABITATS** Uncommon migrant to primary and secondary forests, forest edge, old plantations, scrub and occasionally parkland. Starts to arrive from early September, peaking in October. Overwintering birds usually occur in forest, but on passage show up in most habitats, including small islands in Singapore Straits. Forages singly but also joins mixed feeding flocks. **SITES** Bukit Timah and Central Catchment Nature Reserve. **CONSERVATION** Largely dependent on forests in wintering range.

Yellow-browed Warbler ■ *Phylloscopus inornatus* 黄眉柳莺
Cekup-Daun Paruh Pendek 10cm

DESCRIPTION Small, well-marked warbler with two wing bars. Upperparts olive-green while underparts whitish. Brow long and yellowish-buff, grading to white towards nape and contrasts with weak black eye-stripe. Crown stripe poorly-defined. Two wing bars, that on the greater coverts broader and with dark border. Tertials pale-edged. **DISTRIBUTION** Breeds Urals east to E Siberia, NE China. Winters from NE India, S, SE China to mainland Southeast Asia and Thai–Malay Peninsula. **HABITS AND HABITATS** Rare winter visitor to primary and secondary forests, forest edge and occasionally in parkland. Very active; while foraging, often flicks wings and tail. Regularly joins mixed-species flocks. Arrives late September, departs by March. Call is a high-pitched 'chwewii', up-slurred at the end. **SITES** Bukit Timah and Central Catchment nature reserves. **CONSERVATION** No issues.

Sakhalin Leaf Warbler ■ *Phylloscopus borealoides* 库页岛柳莺
Cekup-Daun Sakhalin 11.5 cm

DESCRIPTION Medium-sized leaf warbler with pale legs. Plumage darker and more strongly washed green than Arctic Warbler (see p.122), due to olive-green fringes of flight feathers. Brow whitish and thin with buff wash above eye, and extends to hind-crown; contrasts strongly with dark eye-stripe. Crown dark olive but visibly paler towards crown ridge. Underparts cool white, unlike Arctic Warbler which is often light grey. Legs

pale pink. **DISTRIBUTION** Breeds Sakhalin, Kuril Islands, Hokkaido and N Honshu. Winters Thai-Malay Peninsula and possibly Sumatra. **HABITS AND HABITATS** Uncommon migrant, first discovered in Singapore in 2013. Occurs in primary and secondary forests. Forage near forest floor, gleaning insects from the leaf-litter; also low shrubs and vines. While foraging, birds climb vertical branches and stems, picking off small insects from leaves. Arrives November, departs by March. Call is a high-pitched 'tsink'. **SITES** Bukit Timah and Central Catchment nature reserves. **CONSERVATION** Appears dependant on forests in wintering grounds.

Oriental Reed Warbler ■ *Acrocephalus orientalis* 东方大苇莺
Cekup-Paya Besar 19cm

DESCRIPTION Commoner of two reed warblers in Singapore. Upperparts mostly drab olive-brown. Underparts white, with brownish wash on flanks and vent. Birds with worn plumage tend to appear greyish brown. Note white brow extending beyond eye, and longish somewhat heavy bill with a pink lower mandible. **DISTRIBUTION** Breeds from SE Russia and Mongolia to E China, Japan and Korea. Winters in E India, S China, mainland Southeast Asia, Thai–Malay Peninsula and Greater Sundas east to N Maluku. **HABITS AND HABITATS** Common migrant to wet grasslands, marshes and ponds with fringing reeds, occasionally in scrub with nearby water bodies. Skulks in thick scrub and long grass, but easier to see than other reed warblers, sometimes on exposed perches. Call is a repeated series of raspy and croaking notes, usually with bird concealed in dense herbage. Occurs mostly September–April. **SITES** Suitable habitat across Singapore. **CONSERVATION** No issues.

Black-browed Reed Warbler ■ *Acrocephalus bistrigiceps* 黑眉苇莺
Cekup-Paya Kening Hitam 13.5cm

DESCRIPTION A brownish, skulking warbler with prominent black lateral crown-stripe.
Plumage greyish brown, with white throat and
pale buffy underparts. Note long white brow and
thick black lateral crown-stripe. **DISTRIBUTION**
Breeds in SE Russia Korea, Japan, NE and E
China. Winters in E India, S China, mainland
Southeast Asia, Thai–Malay Peninsula, Sumatra
and Java. **HABITS AND HABITATS** Uncommon
migrant to wet grasslands, marshes and ponds
with fringing reeds, occasionally in scrub. Appears
to be less widespread and more secretive than
Oriental Reed Warbler. Winters annually, with
birds arriving mostly in early/mid-October. Call
is a repeated series of disyllabic raspy notes,
usually less varied than Oriental Reed Warbler.
SITES Kranji marshes, Sengkang Wetlands.
CONSERVATION No issues.

Pallas's Grasshopper Warbler ■ *Locustella certhiola* 小蝗莺
Cekup-Tikus Berjalur 14cm

DESCRIPTION ssp. *certhiola*. A streaked, skulking warbler of damp grassland. Upperparts
rufous-brown, with streaking on crown, mantle, back and rump. Rump and tail distinctly
richer-hued than rest of upperparts, with tail white-tipped. Young birds tend to be
washed yellowish on underparts, with fine streaking on breast. Similar Lanceolated
Warbler (see p.126) is smaller, paler and heavily streaked both on upper- and underparts.
DISTRIBUTION Breeds from C Siberia to Russian Far East, Korea, W and NE China
and Japan. Winters in NE India, mainland Southeast Asia, Thai–Malay Peninsula and
Greater Sundas. **HABITS AND HABITATS**
Fairly common migrant to open scrub, wet
grasslands, marshes and ponds with fringing
reeds, including in parkland. Arrives from
mid-September, mostly departing by April.
Skulks in dense vegetation, where it feeds on
insects, usually keeping very low and hence
more difficult to see than reed warblers. Sings
a melodious warble consisting of a rising and
falling series of trills and chirps. Also calls a
dry, four-note trill 'ti-tit-tit-tit'. **SITES** Lorong
Halus wetlands, Kranji marshes, Gardens-by-
the-Bay. **CONSERVATION** No issues.

Lanceolated Warbler ■ *Locustella lanceolata* 矛斑蝗鶯
Cekup-Tikus Pinggul Perang 12 cm

DESCRIPTION ssp. *lanceolata*. Heavily-streaked, skulking warbler of grassland. Upperparts olive-brown, with bold streaking mantle; crown and neck sides finely streaked. Brow long and faint. Underparts white, washed buff on flanks, and streaked from throat to undertail coverts, with bolder streaking on flanks. Similar Pallas's Grasshopper Warbler (see p.125) is larger and less heavily streaked on underparts. **DISTRIBUTION** Breeds from W Russia eastwards to Yakutia, Kamchatka, NE China, Korea and Japan. Winters NE India, mainland Southeast Asia to the Greater Sundas and Philippines. **HABITS AND HABITATS** Rare migrant to open scrub, dry and wet grasslands; occasionally in marshes. Winters annually, with birds arriving in late September; departs by April. Skulks low in dense vegetation where it feed on insects, very difficult to flush. Call is a rapid series of 'chi-chi-chi-chi-chi-chi'. **SITES** Kranji marshes, Punggol Barat. **CONSERVATION** No issues.

Photographed in S Kamchatka, E Russia.

Zitting Cisticola ■ *Cisticola juncidis* 棕扇尾鶯　Burung Cekup Padi 11cm

DESCRIPTION ssp. *malaya*. A lanky warbler-like bird of grasslands. Upperparts buffy-brown. Underparts mostly clean white, with flanks washed brown. Crown chestnut with pale streaking, contrasting with whitish face and brow. Back boldly streaked black. Superficially similar to Pallas's Grasshopper Warbler (see p.125) but paler, and habits very different. **DISTRIBUTION** Breeds from S Europe, N Africa and Middle East to E Asia, Southeast Asia and N Australia. Also in Sub-Saharan Africa. **HABITS AND HABITATS** Common resident of scrub and grasslands, especially on reclaimed land, one of the first species besides Paddyfield Pipit to colonise scrub on newly reclaimed land. In display flight birds hover in the open before dropping into thick cover. Often perches on exposed positions on low bushes and tall grass, rendering it rather conspicuous. Breeds June–August. Nest is ball-shaped nest in low bushes or grasses. Call is a ringing series of soft 'tzit' or 'tink' notes. **SITES** Tuas west, Changi coast. **CONSERVATION** No issues.

Yellow-bellied Prinia ▪ *Prinia flaviventris* 黄腹山鷦莺
Perenjak Kuning 14cm

DESCRIPTION ssp. *rafflesi*. A long-tailed warbler-like bird of long grass. Head slate-grey with thin white brow and black bill, rest of upperparts greenish brown. Throat to upper breast white, rest of underparts yellow. Young birds are brownish on upperparts with yellow underparts and yellowish lores. **DISTRIBUTION** Himalayan foothills and much of N and E India, S China, mainland Southeast Asia, Thai–Malay Peninsula, Greater Sundas. **HABITS AND HABITATS** Common resident of scrub and grasslands, especially on reclaimed land. Tends to avoid wet grasslands. Often seen perched and singing from tall grass, diving into cover at the approach of danger. Nest is a small dome of dried plant fibres in tall grass or low bushes. Call is a melodious, descending series of sweet notes, repeated for minutes on end. Another frequently heard call is a soft, mewing 'ngeeee'. **SITES** Lorong Halus Wetlands, Sungei Buloh Wetland Reserve. **CONSERVATION** No issues.

Common Tailorbird ▪ *Orthotomus sutorius* 长尾缝叶莺
Perenjak Pisang 12cm

DESCRIPTION ssp. *maculicollis*. A lanky tailorbird with a long tail. Head greyish with pale streaking on cheek and neck, with rufous crown; rest of upperparts olive-green. Underparts dirty white with noticeable dark streaking on neck and upper breast. Similar-looking Dark-necked Tailorbird (see p.128) has more extensive rufous on head, and larger black patch extending from neck to upper breast. **DISTRIBUTION** Indian sub-continent, S China, mainland Southeast Asia, Thai–Malay Peninsula, Java. **HABITS AND HABITATS** Very common resident of forest edge, old plantations, scrub, parkland and urban areas, where it usually is the only tailorbird. Breeds January–October with multiple broods. Nest is a cup of dried plant material built within a cradle formed by stitching leaves together with fine threads of plant fibre. Clutch size 2–6. Forages for insects in dense shrubbery, occasionally taking flower nectar. Call is a long series of 'cheeup', repeated for minutes on end. **SITES** Suitable habitat across Singapore. **CONSERVATION** No issues.

Dark-necked Tailorbird ◾ *Orthotomus atrogularis* 黑喉缝叶莺
Perenjak Leher Hitam 11cm

DESCRIPTION ssp. *atrogularis*. A small tailorbird with a diagnostic black throat patch. Extensive orange-rufous on crown extends to lores and nape, more so than Common Tailorbird (see p.127), and lacks pale brow of that species. Male (shown) has a black patch from neck to upper breast. Much of upperparts olive-yellow. Female lacks the black patch, which is replaced by faint streaking. **DISTRIBUTION** NE India, mainland Southeast Asia,

Thai–Malay Peninsula, Sumatra, Borneo. **HABITS AND HABITATS** Common resident of primary and secondary forests, forest edge, old plantations and scrub, and usually the commonest tailorbird in well-wooded areas. One of the commonest forest birds on offshore islands. A frequent participant in mixed flocks, joining groups of Pin-striped Tit-Babbler and warblers foraging in the mid-storey. Nest similar to Common Tailorbird, built in low shrubs. An often heard call is a ringing trill 'trrrrrrrrrit', somewhat like a ringing phone. **SITES** Suitable habitat across Singapore. **CONSERVATION** No issues.

Rufous-tailed Tailorbird ◾ *Orthotomus sericeus* 红头缝叶莺
Perenjak Ekor Merah 13cm

DESCRIPTION ssp. *hesperius*. Combination of rufous head and tail with white underparts unmistakable. Head rich rufous, demarcated from white throat below eye. Tail rufous, and rest of upperparts ashy grey, contrasting with white underparts. Young birds are

similar to adults, but weakly marked. **DISTRIBUTION** Thai–Malay Peninsula, Sumatra, Borneo, Palawan. **HABITS AND HABITATS** Uncommon resident of primary and secondary forests, forest edge, scrub and old plantations. Regularly encountered in swampy forests, where it usually forages in shrubs by streams. Least common and most secretive of four tailorbirds, often skulking in dense vegetation. Sings a series of repeated 'chwee-ooo', sometimes in duet with the mate's low trill. Singing birds expose a large patch of dark bare skin on the neck. **SITES** Bukit Batok Nature Park, Central Catchment Nature Reserve. **CONSERVATION** No issues.

Ashy Tailorbird ■ *Orthotomus ruficeps* 灰缝叶莺 Perenjak Kelabu 12cm

DESCRIPTION ssp. *cineraceus*. An unmistakable grey tailorbird with a rufous head. Male plumage ashy grey, paler on underparts, but has a darker grey patch on throat. Face is orange-rufous, contrasting with rest of plumage. Female white-throated, and shows white centre to underparts. **DISTRIBUTION** S Myanmar, Thai–Malay Peninsula, Greater Sundas, islands off Palawan. **HABITS AND HABITATS** Common resident of mangroves, but also coastal scrub and parkland, especially near water.

The only tailorbird in mangrove forests. As with other tailorbirds, nest is a structure built under leaves sewn together. Forages singly or in pairs in the understorey of mangrove forests. Sings a ringing 'chwee-wip', in duet with the mate's short trill. **SITES** Sungei Buloh Wetland Reserve, Pasir Ris Park, Singapore Botanic Gardens. **CONSERVATION** Continuing loss of mangroves has reduced habitat for this species.

ABOVE: *Male* LEFT: *Female*

Chestnut-winged Babbler ■ *Stachyris erythroptera* 红翅穗鹛
Rimba Merbah Sampah 13cm

DESCRIPTION ssp. *erythroptera*. A greyish babbler with distinctive chestnut upperparts. Upperparts from nape onwards rich chestnut. Head to upper belly grey. Rest of underparts increasingly pale buff. Blue facial skin around eye and pale blue patch on throat diagnostic.

DISTRIBUTION Thai–Malay Peninsula, Sumatra, Borneo. **HABITS AND HABITATS** Uncommon resident of primary and secondary forests and forest edge. Forages in pairs or small groups of about 4–5 birds in the understorey, often keeping to dense patches of forest-edge ferns such as Resam (*Dicranopteris* sp), never descending to ground. Pairs are often engaged in a head-bobbing display where one bird, possibly the male, calls to its partner, continually exposing the blue neck patch. Call is a fairly rapid series of low-pitched 'hu' notes. **SITES** Central Catchment Nature Reserve. **CONSERVATION** Nationally endangered. May be extirpated from Bukit Timah Nature Reserve where there are no records for over a decade.

Pin-striped Tit-Babbler ■ *Macronus gularis* 纹胸巨鹛
Rimba Berjalur 13cm

DESCRIPTION ssp. *gularis*. Familiar babbler with streaking on yellowish underparts. Upperparts olive-brown with rufous crown. Underparts mostly pale yellow. Dark brown streaking extends from throat to breast, but less boldly marked in young birds. Some birds

may show bluish-grey skin around the eye. Split from Bold-striped Tit-Babbler M. *bornensis* of Borneo and Java. **DISTRIBUTION** Himalayan foothills and NE India, S China, mainland Southeast Asia, Thai–Malay Peninsula, Sumatra. **HABITS AND HABITATS** Very common resident of primary and secondary forests, forest edge, scrub and old plantations, occasionally entering wooded gardens and mangroves. Often seen in small family groups of about 4–5 birds, and regularly joins mixed flocks. Breeds December–August, building a concealed dome-shaped nest in forest undergrowth. Call is a repeated, monotonous series of 'chonk' notes, as well as harsh churrs. **SITES** Suitable habitat across Singapore. **CONSERVATION** No issues. The most adaptable babbler, occurring in many small isolated patches of secondary scrub.

Abbott's Babbler ■ *Malacocincla abbotti* 艾博特氏雅鹛 Rimba Riang 16cm

DESCRIPTION ssp. *olivacea*. A nondescript brown babbler. Upperparts brown. Underparts off-white, with rufous-buff wash on neck sides, flanks and vent. Grey brow may be difficult

to see well. Similar to White-chested Babbler (see p.131), but lacks clean white underparts and is shorter-tailed. **DISTRIBUTION** Himalayan foothills, NE India, mainland Southeast Asia, Thai–Malay Peninsula, Sumatra, Borneo. **HABITS AND HABITATS** Uncommon resident of secondary forests, forest edge, old plantations, scrub and occasionally mangroves. Forages singly or in pairs, mostly in the forest understorey, keeping to dense vegetation. With Pin-striped Tit-Babbler, this is a regular babbler of small secondary woodland and forest patches on offshore islands. Nest is a small cup built in low vegetation, with clutch of up to 3. Sings a cheerful 'wii-wu-wi-you' with regular variations. **SITES** Central Catchment Nature Reserve, Pulau Ubin, Sentosa. **CONSERVATION** No issues.

Short-tailed Babbler ■ *Malacocincla malaccensis* 短尾雅鶥
Rimba Ekor Pendek 15cm

DESCRIPTION ssp. *malaccensis*. Unmistakable babbler with very short tail and long pinkish legs. Upperparts brown with grey face, demarcated from white throat by thin black moustachial stripe. Underparts washed rufous. Similar-looking Abbott's Babbler (see p.130) is longer-tailed, and has brown rather than grey face. **DISTRIBUTION** Thai–Malay Peninsula, Sumatra, Borneo. **HABITS AND HABITATS** Common resident of primary and secondary forests, including swampy forest. Forages low, mostly in the understorey, and regularly descends to the forest floor. Usually seen singly or in pairs. Nest is a small cup built low, with clutch of 2. Call is a high-pitched series of 'teew', or a 6–7-note descending series of whistles, of a mournful quality. **SITES** Bukit Timah and Central Catchment nature reserves. **CONSERVATION** Globally near threatened. Recent studies have found low genetic variability in remnant populations in the Central Catchment.

White-chested Babbler ■ *Trichastoma rostratum* 白胸雅鶥
Rimba Dada Putih 16cm

DESCRIPTION ssp. *rostratum*. Unmistakable brown babbler with white underparts and somewhat long, thin bill. Upperparts mostly brown, with lower back and tail richer chestnut-brown. White underparts diagnostic, with faint grey wash on breast sides. face buff-brown. Similar-looking Abbott's Babbler (see p.130) has shorter tail, and is bright rusty-buff on flanks and vent. **DISTRIBUTION** Thai–Malay Peninsula, Sumatra, Borneo. **HABITS AND HABITATS** Rare resident of primary and secondary forests, scrub and occasionally mangroves. Often found in the vicinity of water, especially streams, or in swampy forest where it skulks in dense cover. Forages for insects in the understorey singly or in pairs, also regularly descends to the ground. Call is a high-pitched, three-note 'chwee-tu-dwee', the last note inflected upwards. Has declined significantly in the past decade. **SITES** Central Catchment Nature Reserve, Pulau Tekong. **CONSERVATION** Globally near threatened. Nationally critically endangered.

White-crested Laughingthrush ■ *Garrulax leucolophus*
白冠噪鹛 Rimba Jambul Putih 28cm

DESCRIPTION ssp. *diardi*. Unmistakable white and brown bird. White head and crest with contrasting black facial mask and lores. Nape grey, merging into rufous of back. Rest of upperparts rich rufous-brown. Throat to breast white, with rest of underparts to undertail coverts washed rufous. **DISTRIBUTION** Himalayan foothills to NE India, S China and much of mainland Southeast Asia. **HABITS AND HABITATS** Common resident, originating from escaped birds. Occurs in secondary forests, forest edge, scrub and old plantations. Forages for insects and fallen fruits in low shrubs or on ground in parties of 4–6 birds. May have originated from one or more populations in the Bukit Batok area in the 1990s, but now widespread across secondary scrub in W Singapore, where densities can exceed 1 individual/hectare. Vocalisations varied, but a commonly heard call is an outburst of chatters and raucous 'whee' and 'woot' notes, usually from a small group or a duetting pair. **SITES** Bukit Batok Nature Park, Kent Ridge Park. **CONSERVATION** A potential competitor with native babblers.

Oriental White-eye ■ *Zosterops palpebrosus* 灰腹绣眼鸟
Mata-Putih Bakau 11cm

DESCRIPTION ssp. *auriventer*. Only white-eye in Singapore. Unmistakable. Most of upperparts olive-green with white eye-ring. Throat, upper breast and forehead yellow. Lower breast and belly pale grey, with yellow undertail coverts and ventral stripe that extends up belly (difficult to see in the field). Japanese White-eye *Z. japonicus* has been reported occasionally as an escapee in Singapore, but lacks yellow ventral stripe and has a well-defined lore patch. **DISTRIBUTION** Much of Indian sub-continent, mainland Southeast Asia, Thai–Malay Peninsula, Greater Sundas. **HABITS AND HABITATS** A common resident, but given its popularity in the pet trade, likely that many birds are recent escapees. Occurs in secondary forests, forest edge, old plantations, scrub, mangroves and parkland, including urban areas. Usually seen in small flocks of up to 20 birds, gathered to feed at flowering trees. Nest is small and cup-shaped, in low bushes; clutch of up to 4. A commonly heard call is a shrill, plaintive 'chew'. **SITES** Suitable habitat across Singapore (Pulau Ubin). **CONSERVATION** No issues.

Asian Fairy-bluebird ■ *Irena puella* 和平鸟 Murai Gajah 25cm

DESCRIPTION ssp. *malayensis*. An unmistakable black and blue bird of the forest canopy. Male is mostly black with brilliant blue crown, back, rump and undertail coverts. Eye red. Female is duller, with turquoise-blue plumage and blue-black wings. **DISTRIBUTION** SW and E India, SW China, mainland Southeast Asia, Thai–Malay Peninsula, Greater Sundas, Palawan. **HABITS AND HABITATS** Fairly common resident occurring in primary and secondary forests and adjacent scrub, especially where there are fruiting trees. Forages in the canopy or mid-storey. Usually seen singly or in pairs, but small groups may be encountered at large fruiting trees, especially figs. Call is a loud, liquid 'wiit'. **SITES** Central Catchment and Bukit Timah nature reserves. **CONSERVATION** Forest-dependent species.

ABOVE: *Male* LEFT: *Female*

Asian Glossy Starling ■ *Aplonis panayensis* 亚洲辉椋鸟
Perling Mata Merah 20cm

DESCRIPTION ssp. *strigata*. A familiar dark, red-eyed starling. Plumage entirely glossy bluish-green, appearing black in poor light. Eye crimson-red. Young birds are greyish-brown on upperparts with dark, bold streaking on pale underparts, and a dark red eye. **DISTRIBUTION** E India, parts of mainland Southeast Asia, Thai–Malay Peninsula, Greater Sundas, Philippines, Sulawesi. **HABITS AND HABITATS** Very common resident of secondary forests, forest edge, scrub, old plantations, parkland and urban areas, where it is one of the commonest birds. Gathers in large noisy flocks to feed at fruiting figs, where it usually dominates. Often seen with flocks of Pink-necked Green Pigeons at fruiting trees in urban areas. Joins Javan Mynas and other starlings in large roosting flocks in roadside trees. Nest is a messy cup of sticks built in a tree-hole or under eaves of buildings. Calls varied, includes metallic ringing whistles and harsh squeaks. **SITES** Suitable habitat across Singapore. **CONSERVATION** No issues.

Common Hill Myna ■ *Gracula religiosa* 鹩哥 Tiong Emas 29cm

DESCRIPTION ssp. *religiosa*. A large, dark forest starling. Plumage glossy black with fleshy orange-yellow wattles on nape and below eye, and white patch on wings. Bill bright orange

with yellow tips. Flies with strong but shallow flapping, somewhat like a pigeon. **DISTRIBUTION** SW and E India, SW China, mainland Southeast Asia, Thai–Malay Peninsula, Greater and Lesser Sundas, Palawan. **HABITS AND HABITATS** Common resident of primary and secondary forests, forest edge and occasionally scrub. Seen in pairs or in large flocks of as many of 30 birds. Often seen perched on exposed branches, or feeding in small groups at fruiting trees. Nests in tree cavities, laying up to 3 eggs. Frequently calls a single, repeated piercing whistle, but also utters varied screeches and nasal-sounding growls. **SITES** Singapore Botanic Gardens, Central Catchment and Bukit Timah nature reserves. **CONSERVATION** Although common in Singapore, has clearly declined in other parts of its range due to widespread trapping for the pet bird trade.

Javan Myna ■ *Acridotheres javanicus* 爪哇八哥 Gembala-Kerbau Jawa 24.5cm

DESCRIPTION A familiar starling of urban areas and parkland. Plumage black, with white wing patch and white undertail coverts. Bill and iris yellow. White wing patch and tuft on forehead smaller than that of Crested Myna *A. cristatellus*, which is now very rare. Young bird similar to adult, but greyer. **DISTRIBUTION** Java and Bali. Widely introduced elsewhere (e.g. Taiwan, Sulawesi, Borneo), and spreading up the Thai–Malay Peninsula.

HABITS AND HABITATS Very common resident of secondary forests, forest edge, scrub, old plantations, parkland and urban areas, where it is easily the most abundant bird. Gathers in noisy flocks of hundreds to roost in large-crowned roadside trees, often mixed with other starlings. Very adaptable, nesting in natural tree cavities and the eaves of buildings and bridges. Omnivorous. Calls a variety of harsh shrieks, whistles and chatters. **SITES** Suitable habitat across Singapore. **CONSERVATION** Globally Vulnerable. One of 6 species not protected by law in Singapore. Competition with other urban birds has led to declines in their populations, but Javan Mynas have declined in their native range due to extensive trapping for the pet trade.

Common Myna ■ *Acridotheres tristis* 家八哥 Gembala-Kerbau Rumah 25cm

DESCRIPTION ssp. *tristis*. An unmistakable brown myna with yellow facial patch. Head black with prominent bare yellow skin around eye. Rest of body plumage brown, tail black. Note white patch on primary and underwing coverts. Young bird similar to adult, but less strongly marked, with a greyish head. Moulting bird may have unfeathered head. **DISTRIBUTION** Parts of Middle East and Central Asia, east to Indian sub-continent, Southeast Asia and Thai–Malay Peninsula. Widely introduced worldwide. **HABITS AND HABITATS** Common resident of scrub, grasslands, parkland and urban areas. One of the commonest birds in Singapore, though now visibly outnumbered by Javan Myna. Pairs or small groups can still be seen in urban areas. Nest is a shallow cup built into a tree-hole or artificial cavity. Calls a variety of harsh chatters and whistles. When alarmed, calls a subdued 'kweerh'. **SITES** Suitable habitat across Singapore. **CONSERVATION** One of 6 species not protected by law in Singapore. Has declined in recent years, possibly due to competition with Javan Myna.

Daurian Starling ■ *Agropsar sturninus* 北椋鸟 Perling Belakang Ungu 18cm

DESCRIPTION A pale starling with a dark back. Male grey on head, paler on rest of underparts, contrasting with dark back, wings and tail. Back purple. Wings dark green, broken by white scapular patch and smaller pale patches on flight feathers. Female similar, but with brownish wash on upperparts. Some birds may have pale yellow-orange head as a result of probing into flowers. **DISTRIBUTION** Breeds from SE Russia to NE China and Korea. Winters in mainland Southeast Asia, Thai–Malay Peninsula and Greater Sundas. **HABITS AND HABITATS** Common migrant to secondary forests, forest edge, mangroves, old plantations, scrub and parkland, occasionally in urban areas. Forages for nectar, fruits and insects in flocks, sometimes joined by Asian Glossy and White-shouldered Starlings. Forms large flocks of up to a thousand birds. Peak passage early/mid-October, departs mostly by March. Call is a harsh, quick 'krrrrrpp'. **SITES** Suitable habitat across Singapore. **CONSERVATION** One of 6 species not protected by law in Singapore.

LEFFT: *Female*. RIGHT: *Male*.

White-shouldered Starling
■ *Sturnia sinensis* 灰背椋鸟 Perling Bahu Putih 20cm

DESCRIPTION A pale starling with diagnostic white shoulder patches. Male (shown) pale grey on head and upper breast with rest of underparts white. Large white shoulder patch, contrasting sharply with black flight feathers, separates from similar Daurian Starling. Female mostly grey with smaller white patch on wings. Young bird similar to female, but lacks white wing patch. Note also pale iris when seen close. **DISTRIBUTION** Breeds in S China. Winters in parts of S China, Taiwan, mainland Southeast Asia and Thai–Malay Peninsula. **HABITS AND HABITATS** Uncommon migrant of secondary forests, coastal scrub, grasslands and occasionally parkland. Appears to favour coastal vegetation. Usually seen in groups of 5–10 birds, occasionally joining larger flocks of Daurian Starlings. Occurs mostly late September–March; overwinters in small numbers. **SITES** Lorong Halus wetlands, Changi coast. **CONSERVATION** No issues.

Orange-headed Thrush ■ *Geokichla citrina* 橙头地鸫
Murai-Belanda Dada Oren 21cm

DESCRIPTION ssp. *innotata, gibsonhilli*. Bright orange ground-thrush. Head and underparts to lower belly orange-rufous. Rest of upperparts, including wings, bluish grey. Two subspecies are known, *gibsonhilli*, which shows a distinct pale patch on the shoulder, and *innotata* (shown) which lacks this. Migratory *melli* shows dark brown patches below eye

and ear coverts, and may occur. **DISTRIBUTION** Himalayan foothills, SW and E India, S China, mainland Southeast Asia and Greater Sundas. Some populations are migratory, wintering in S parts of Southeast Asia and India. **HABITS AND HABITATS** Uncommon migrant of primary and secondary forests, scrub and occasionally parkland. Migrants arrive in December, and small numbers spend the winter here. A shy ground thrush often seen foraging quietly on the forest floor and along forested trails for arthropods and worms. Flushes and flies up to high perch if approached. Usually silent. **SITES** Central Catchment and Bukit Timah nature reserves, Singapore Botanic Gardens. **CONSERVATION** Dependent on forests in wintering grounds.

Siberian Thrush ▪ *Geokichla sibirica* 白眉地鸫 Murai-Belanda Hitam 22cm

DESCRIPTION ssp. *sibirica*, *davisoni*. A dark thrush with a prominent white brow. Male is entirely dark slaty blue, appearing almost black, with thick white brow. First-winter male is paler, with dark brown wings and pale buff brow, ear coverts and throat. Female (shown) is dark brown, finely scaled on the underparts, but not on the mantle and back.

DISTRIBUTION Breeds across C Siberia to Russian Far East, NE China, Korea and Japan. Winters in mainland Southeast Asia, Thai–Malay Peninsula, Sumatra and Java. **HABITS AND HABITATS** Rare passage migrant, occurring in primary and secondary forests, and occasionally in scrub. Occurs mostly November–early January. Regularly seen feeding at fruiting figs. Mostly arboreal but sometimes descends to forage on ground, occasionally joining Eyebrowed Thrush. Usually silent. **SITES** Bukit Timah Nature Reserve. **CONSERVATION** Dependent on forests in wintering grounds.

Eyebrowed Thrush ▪ *Turdus obscurus* 白眉鸫
Murai-Belanda Kening Putih 22cm

DESCRIPTION A medium-sized brownish thrush. Male has grey hood with distinctive white brow and white patch below eye, and is largely brown on the upperparts, with orange-brown underparts. Female (shown) is less strongly marked, lacks the grey hood and shows distinct white moustachial stripe and throat. **DISTRIBUTION** Breeds across much of C Siberia to Russian Far East and Kamchatka. Winters in NE India, S China, mainland Southeast Asia, Thai-Malay Peninsula and Greater Sundas. **HABITS AND HABITATS** Uncommon migrant to primary and secondary forests, and occasionally in scrub, especially during passage. Birds arrive in mid-November on passage to Sumatra, and small numbers overwinter; depart by end-March. Feeds on fruit and insects, occasionally descending to forage on the ground. Call is a sharp, thin 'seep', usually made by birds in flight. **SITES** Bukit Timah and Central Catchment nature reserves. **CONSERVATION** Dependent on forests in wintering grounds.

Siberian Blue Robin ▪ *Larvivora cyane* 蓝歌鸲 Murai-Kecil Biru 13.5cm

DESCRIPTION ssp. *cyane*. A dark blue robin of the forest floor. Male entirely dark blue on upperparts, white on underparts, with diagnostic thick black patch running from lores to breast sides. Female largely brownish-grey on upperparts, with blue tail, pale underparts, and faint scaling limited to throat and upper breast. Young bird like female, but lacks blue tail. **DISTRIBUTION** Breeds from C Siberia east to Russian Far East and Kamchatka, south to Korea. Winters in NE India, S and E China, mainland Southeast Asia, Thai–Malay Peninsula and Greater Sundas. **HABITS AND HABITATS** Common migrant to primary and secondary forests, forest edge, old plantations, and occasionally scrub. Peak passage is mid-October, when it becomes very common. Also overwinters, when surveys show it to be among the commonest migrant passerines in forests, but rare in other habitats. Feeds quietly on forest floor. Call is a soft 'tsit', or a series of dry 'tik' notes. **SITES** Bukit Timah and Central Catchment nature reserves. **CONSERVATION** Dependent on forests in wintering grounds.

ABOVE: *Male* RIGHT: *Female*

Oriental Magpie-Robin ▪ *Copsychus saularis* 鹊鸲 Murai Kampung 20cm

DESCRIPTION ssp. *musicus*. A familiar black and white chat. Head and upperparts black, contrasting with white underparts from lower breast backwards. Also note white wing patch and outer tail. Female (shown) similar to male, but with black parts replaced by slate-grey. **DISTRIBUTION** Indian sub-continent, S and E China, mainland Southeast Asia, Thai–Malay Peninsula and Greater Sundas. Philippine ssp. are now considered a distinct species. **HABITS AND HABITATS** Uncommon resident, occurring in forest edges, mangroves, forest edge, scrub, parkland and occasionally urban areas. Forages mostly on the ground, where it picks up insects and other small invertebrates. Has a habit of cocking its tail. Breeds March–November, building a cup-shaped nest of plant material. Clutch size 2–4. Song is a melodious series of sweet rising and falling whistles. Also calls a harsh 'keeeee' when alarmed. **SITES** Sungei Buloh Wetland Reserve, Singapore Botanic Gardens, Pulau Ubin. **CONSERVATION** Nationally endangered. A popular songbird that is sometimes trapped for the pet trade. Numbers have apparently increased in recent years.

White-rumped Shama ▪ *Copsychus malabaricus*
白腰鵲鴝　Murai Hutan　25cm (+ 6–7cm tail)

DESCRIPTION ssp. *tricolor*. A long-tailed, black and orange chat. Head, back, wings and tail dark glossy black, broken by large white patch on rump and uppertail coverts. Belly to undertail rufous-orange. Female similar to male (shown), but with black parts replaced by dark grey, and with rufous lining to wing feathers. Young bird mostly brown on upperparts with buff speckling. **DISTRIBUTION** Himalayan foothills, S and NE India, mainland Southeast Asia, Thai–Malay Peninsula, Greater Sundas. **HABITS AND HABITATS** Rare resident of primary and secondary forests, forest edge, scrub and old plantations. Shy, skulking in the understorey, where it can be difficult to see well. Remains locally common in secondary forests on Tekong and Ubin. Breeds March–August. Builds a cup-shaped nest on low branches or in tree cavities. Song is a variable series of rich, melodious warbling. Also known to mimic other birds. **SITES** Central Catchment Nature Reserve, Pulau Ubin. **CONSERVATION** Nationally critically endangered. A popular songbird that is frequently trapped for the pet trade. Populations in Central Catchment may have been established from released cagebirds.

Stejneger's Stonechat ▪ *Saxicola stejnegeri*　黑喉石鵰
Murai-Sawah Asia　13cm

DESCRIPTION A small brown chat of open country. Male black-headed with white neck sides. Back and wings dark with prominent white wing patch. Underparts buff, with rich rufous patch on breast. Non-breeding male has dark brown to black face, sometimes appearing patchy, and is pale brown on much of upperparts, with dark streaking on back. Female buff brown on upperparts with dark streaking on back, and pale orange from breast to belly. **DISTRIBUTION** Breeds C Siberia east to Yakutia, also NE China, Korea and Japan. Winters S China, mainland Southeast Asia and Thai-Malay Peninsula. **HABITS AND HABITATS** Uncommon migrant to open scrub, marshes and grasslands, including on reclaimed land. Perches on exposed branches in dense scrub and on tall grass. Small numbers winter in Singapore annually, mostly November–March. Most wintering birds are females. Call is a harsh 'chack'. **SITES** Tuas coast, Kranji marshes. **CONSERVATION** No issues.

ABOVE: *Male* LEFT: *Female*

White-throated Rock Thrush ■ *Monticola gularis* 白喉矶鸫
Murai Biru Leher Putih 18cm

DESCRIPTION A small, colourful chat. Male is blue-capped and rufous-orange on underparts and uppertail coverts, with white throat and patch on wing. Female is brown, with scaling on mantle, back and much of underparts. Distinguished from female Siberian Thrush (see p.137) by back scaling, lack of pale brow and more upright. **DISTRIBUTION** Breeds in Russian Far East, NE China and Korea. Winters in southern China, parts of mainland Southeast Asia and Thai–Malay Peninsula. **HABITS AND HABITATS** Rare migrant to primary and secondary forests. Easily overlooked due to its unobtrusive behaviour; perching still in the understorey for long periods and has a habit of wagging its tail, occasionally descending to ground to feed. Usually silent in winter. Occurs November–March. **SITES** Bukit Timah Nature Reserve. **CONSERVATION** Dependent on forests in wintering grounds.

ABOVE: *Male* RIGHT: *Female*

Brown-chested Jungle Flycatcher ■ *Cyornis brunneatus* 白喉林鹟
Sambar-Hutan Cina 15cm

DESCRIPTION A large, robust flycatcher with a slightly hooked bill. Upperparts greyish brown. Underparts dirty white, with brown patch on the breast contrasting with pale throat. Also note pale loral patch. Bill hooked at tip, and lower mandible fleshy orange, being partly black at the tip in young birds. Recent genetic analysis has found it to be a *Cyornis* flycatcher. **DISTRIBUTION** Breeds in S and C China. Winters in Thai–Malay Peninsula, Sumatra and Java. **HABITS AND HABITATS** Fairly common passage migrant to primary and secondary forests, old plantations, scrub and occasionally mangroves and well-wooded parkland. Peak passage in mid-October, when they become fairly common; there are very few records of wintering birds. Forages alone on low perches, dropping to the ground to pick up insect prey. Commonly heard call is a series of dry 'tik' notes, usually uttered during territorial encounters. **SITES** Central Catchment Nature Reserve. **CONSERVATION** Globally Vulnerable. Endemic breeder in China.

Dark-sided Flycatcher ∎ *Muscicapa sibirica* 乌鹟
Sambar-Perang Siberia 13cm

DESCRIPTION ssp. *sibirica*. A dark, boldly streaked flycatcher. Upperparts sooty grey, much darker than Asian Brown Flycatcher (below). Underparts dirty white with bold diffused dark streaking, especially on breast and flanks. White malars and half-collar bolder and more prominent than Asian Brown Flycatcher. **DISTRIBUTION** Breeds from C Siberia east to NE China, Korea and Japan. A disjunct population breeds in the Himalayas, S China and N Southeast Asia. Winters in S China, mainland Southeast Asia, Thai–Malay Peninsula and Greater Sundas. **HABITS AND HABITATS** Uncommon migrant to primary and secondary forests, forest edge, scrub, old plantations and occasionally parkland. Usually seen in forests, and less frequently encountered than Asian Brown Flycatcher. Occurs mostly late September–April. Perches fairly high in the canopy, where it flycatches for insects from a fixed, open perch. Call is a thin 'tsiii'. **SITES** Bukit Timah and Central Catchment nature reserves. **CONSERVATION** Dependent on forests in wintering grounds.

Asian Brown Flycatcher ∎ *Muscicapa dauurica* 北灰鹟
Sambar-Perang Biasa 13cm

DESCRIPTION ssp. *dauurica*. A nondescript brown flycatcher. Plumage mostly greyish brown on the upperparts and dirty white on the underparts, with a variable wash of grey-brown on the breast and flanks. Also pale lore patch and white eye-ring. Unlike Dark-sided Flycatcher, lacks the boldly marked malars and half-collar patches, and is shorter-winged. **DISTRIBUTION** Breeds across C Siberia east to NE China, Korea and Japan. Winters across S India to Southeast Asia, Thai–Malay Peninsula, Greater Sundas and Philippines. Non-migratory populations occur in Indian sub-continent, and mainland Southeast Asia. **HABITS AND HABITATS** Very common migrant to primary and secondary forests, mangroves, forest edge, scrub, old plantations, parkland and even urban green spaces. Occurs mostly early September–April. One of the commonest boreal migrants in Singapore, and usually the only flycatcher in urban areas. Call is a rattle consisting of a series of up to 5 descending 'chit' notes, and a faint 'tsii' that is easily missed. **SITES** Suitable habitat across Singapore. **CONSERVATION** No issues.

Brown-streaked Flycatcher

■ *Muscicapa williamsoni*　褐纹鹟　Sambar-Perang Lorek Perang　14cm

DESCRIPTION Similar to Asian Brown Flycatcher and formerly thought conspecific. Upperparts and wings brown, but more richly coloured than Asian Brown Flycatcher

(see p.141), although this can be difficult to see well. Lower mandible pale yellow. Diffused brown streaks from upper breast run down to flanks. Belly dirty white. **DISTRIBUTION** Breeds in S Myanmar and Thai-Malay Peninsula. Also N Borneo. Winters in S Thai–Malay Peninsula and possibly Sumatra? **HABITS AND HABITATS** Uncommon migrant to primary and secondary forests, forest edge, scrub, old plantations and occasionally parkland. Apparently a winter visitor in Singapore, although there are a handful of mid-year records, possibly of overstaying birds. Behaviour very similar to Asian Brown Flycatcher, keeping to high perches and flycatching for insects. Thought to be rare, but more likely under-recorded due to similarity to Asian Brown Flycatcher. **SITES** Central Catchment Nature Reserve. **CONSERVATION** No issues.

Ferruginous Flycatcher

■ *Muscicapa ferruginea*　棕尾褐鹟　Sambar-Perang Sampah　12.5cm

DESCRIPTION An unmistakable rich orange-brown flycatcher. Adult (shown) bluish-grey on head. Mantle, back and wings rich chestnut. Underparts orangey brown, graduating

to white on the belly. Note also white eye-ring, lores, malars and throat. Young birds are boldly streaked chestnut brown on the upper underparts. **DISTRIBUTION** Breeds in Himalayas, NE India, S China and Taiwan. Winters in mainland Southeast Asia, Thai–Malay Peninsula, Greater Sundas and Philippines. **HABITS AND HABITATS** Uncommon migrant to primary and secondary forests, forest edge and scrub. An unobtrusive flycatcher, usually perched low in understorey while foraging. When feeding, repeatedly returns to same perch. Occurs mostly October–March. Call is a high-pitched 'tsiii'. **SITES** Bukit Timah and Central Catchment nature reserves. **CONSERVATION** Dependent on forests in wintering grounds.

Yellow-rumped Flycatcher ■ *Ficedula zanthopygia* 白眉姬鹟
Sambar-Kunyit Kening Putih 13.5cm

DESCRIPTION A richly coloured flycatcher with a yellow rump patch. Male is boldly marked black on upperparts and bright yellow on underparts, lower back and rump, with a white brow and wing patch. Female is olive brown, with a much smaller yellow rump patch; similar to female Green-backed Flycatcher (below) but underparts paler yellow, and white on wing varying from one large patch to two broad bars. **DISTRIBUTION** Breeds across Russian Far East, E and NE China and Korea. Winters in mainland Southeast Asia, Thai–Malay Peninsula, Sumatra and Java. **HABITS AND HABITATS** Common migrant to primary and secondary forests, mangroves, forest edge, scrub, old plantations and occasionally parkland, often near water. Largely a passage migrant (peaking mid-October), with few overwintering. Most birds seen here are female. Forages from low shrubs to high up in trees. Call is a hard 'trrrrrr' and a weak high-pitched whistle. **SITES** Bukit Batok Nature Park, Central Catchment Nature Reserve. **CONSERVATION** No issues.

LEFT: *Female* ABOVE: *Male*

Green-backed Flycatcher ■ *Ficedula elisae* 绿背姬鹟
Sambar-Kunyit Hijau 13.5cm

DESCRIPTION A yellowish flycatcher with diagnostic olive-green back. Male yellow-browed, largely olive-greenish on the upperparts, with a white wing patch; underparts and rump rich yellow. Female (shown) similar to female Yellow-rumped Flycatcher, but yellower on underparts, usually showing two thin pale wing bars; also lacks yellow rump and has a more prominent eye-ring. **DISTRIBUTION** Breeds in N-central China, in Beijing, Shaanxi and Hebei provinces. Winters in Thai–Malay Peninsula and possibly Sumatra. **HABITS AND HABITATS** Rare migrant to primary and secondary forests, forest edge and scrub. An unobtrusive flycatcher that forages low, usually within a few metres of the ground. Most records are in November during passage; wintering birds are far rarer. Usually silent, but has been heard to call a weak 'cheep'. **SITES** Central Catchment Nature Reserve. **CONSERVATION** Likely to be threatened by the loss of forest habitat in winter range. Endemic breeder in China.

Mugimaki Flycatcher ■ *Ficedula mugimaki* 鸲鹟
Sambar-Perang Mugimaki 13cm

DESCRIPTION A small, dark flycatcher. Male is completely black on upperparts with white streak above eye; throat to breast bright orange, and rest of underparts white. Female is greyish brown on upperparts, lacks the white streak above eye, and usually showa one white wing bar. **DISTRIBUTION** Breeds from C Siberia to Russian Far East, south to NE China and Korea. Winters in S China, mainland Southeast Asia, Thai–Malay Peninsula and Greater Sundas. **HABITS AND HABITATS** Uncommon passage migrant to primary and secondary forests, forest edge, scrub and occasionally parkland. Arrives later than other flycatchers, usually in mid/late November, with no wintering records. Seen again in March–April during spring passage. Forages in canopy. **SITES** Bukit Batok Nature Park, Central Catchment Nature Reserve. **CONSERVATION** Dependent on forests in wintering grounds.

ABOVE: *Male.* BELOW: *Female*

Zappey's Flycatcher ■ *Cyanoptila cumatilis* 琉璃蓝鹟 Sambar Zappey 17cm

DESCRIPTION A large, striking blue flycatcher. Male is turquoise blue on upperparts, with sides of face to upper breast deep greenish blue, not black as in Blue-and-white Flycatcher. Both first winter male and female cannot be easily separated from that of Blue-and-white

Flycatcher. First winter males of both species mostly brown, with blue wings and tail. Females greyish-brown with rufous-brown tail. **DISTRIBUTION** Breeds in Central and NE China (Beijing, Hubei and Shaanxi Provinces). Winters in mainland Southeast Asia, Thai–Malay Peninsula, Sumatra. **HABITS AND HABITATS** Uncommon migrant to primary and secondary forests, forest edge and parks. Mostly occurs late October–December while on passage; few midwinter or spring records. Forages from the understorey to the canopy. Usually silent, but may call a soft 'tick'. **SITES** Bukit Timah and Central Catchment nature reserves. **CONSERVATION** Globally near-threatened. Dependent on forests in wintering grounds.

LEFT: *Adult Male* RIGHT: *Male Blue-and-white Flycatcher*

Mangrove Blue Flycatcher ▪ *Cyornis rufigastra* 红树仙鹟
Sambar-Biru Bakau 14.5cm

DESCRIPTION ssp. *rufigastra*. The only resident blue flycatcher. Male is deep blue on upperparts, with throat to belly rich orange-rufous. Female is similar but has distinctive white lore patch, white spot below eye and white chin. Young birds have pale buff spots on head, mantle and back. **DISTRIBUTION** Thai–Malay Peninsula, Greater Sundas, Philippines. **HABITS AND HABITATS** A rare resident. Occurs in mangroves, occasionally wandering into fringing secondary forests. Nest is a cup built in low tree cavities, usually 1.5–2m above ground.

An active feeder that flies from perch to perch to foliage-glean, usually keeping low in the understorey. Call is a melodious series of 5–6 notes. **SITES** Pulau Ubin, Pulau Tekong. **CONSERVATION** Nationally critically endangered. Extinct from Singapore mainland.

ABOVE: *Female*. RIGHT: *Male*

Greater Green Leafbird ▪ *Chloropsis sonnerati* 大绿叶鹎
Burung-daun Besar 21cm

DESCRIPTION ssp. *zosterops*. The largest leafbird. Male entirely green with black face and bib, and a bluish malar band only visible in good light. Separated from similar Lesser Green Leafbird (see p.146) by size, stouter bill and absence of yellow rim to bib. Female is mostly green, but shows diagnostic yellow eye-ring, yellow chin and throat. **DISTRIBUTION** Thai–Malay Peninsula, Sumatra, Borneo, Java. **HABITS AND HABITATS** Rare resident of primary and secondary forests. Forages in the canopy, regularly seen at large fruiting trees. Usually seen singly or in pairs. Call is a series of liquid, musical whistles and warbles. **SITES CONSERVATION** Globally Vulnerable; Nationally critically endangered. A familiar pet bird; faces trapping pressure across region.

LEFT: *Female*. ABOVE: *Male*

Lesser Green Leafbird

■ *Chloropsis cyanopogon* 小绿叶鹎 Burung-daun Kecil 18cm

DESCRIPTION ssp. *cyanopogon*. All-green leafbird with black mask. Resembles Greater Green Leafbird (see p.145) but smaller and has less robust bill. Male is yellow on forehead, with a thin yellow fringe to black face and bib, a feature absent in Greater Green Leafbird. Female is entirely green, and lacks yellow eye-ring and throat of Greater Green Leafbird.

LEFT: *Male*. ABOVE: *Female*

DISTRIBUTION Thai–Malay Peninsula, Sumatra, Borneo. **HABITS AND HABITATS** Rare resident of primary and secondary forests. Forages mostly in middle storey and canopy of forest for fruits, and rarely nectar. Also known to take small insects. Joins mixed foraging flocks. Usually seen singly or in pairs. Call is a series of loud, rich and varied warbling. **SITES** Central Catchment and Bukit Timah nature reserves. **CONSERVATION** Globally near threatened. Nationally critically endangered.

Blue-winged Leafbird

■ *Chloropsis cochinchinensis* 蓝翅叶鹎 Burung-daun Biru 17cm

DESCRIPTION ssp. *moluccensis*. Best separated from previous two species by combination of yellowish-green head, blue wings and tail. Male (shown) has bright yellow crown and nape, contrasting with black face and bib, with orange-bronze wash on hindcrown and neck sides. Female is green, with blue malar stripe, and faint orange wash on neck. **DISTRIBUTION** NE India, SE Bangladesh, SW China, mainland Southeast Asia, Thai–Malay Peninsula and Greater Sundas. **HABITS AND HABITATS** Uncommon resident of primary and secondary forest. Commonest of the 3 leafbirds in Singapore. Difficult to spot as it keeps to the middle storey and forest canopy, from where its trisyllabic 'ch-chirup' call can be heard. Best seen when birds descend low on fruiting trees while feeding. Nest a suspended deep cup, built high up; usually with clutch of 2. **SITES** Central Catchment and Bukit Timah nature reserves, Sentosa. **CONSERVATION** More tolerant of disturbance than other leafbirds.

Yellow-vented Flowerpecker

■ *Dicaeum chrysorrheum* 黄肛啄花鸟 Sepah Puteri Tongkeng Kuning 10cm

DESCRIPTION ssp. *chrysorrheum*. Unmistakable streaked flowerpecker of the forest canopy. Upperparts yellowish olive. Underparts white with bold blackish streaks, and yellow undertail coverts. Eye reddish-brown, note also white lores and black malar stripe. Sexes similar. **DISTRIBUTION** NE India, SW China, mainland Southeast Asia, Thai–Malay Peninsula, Greater Sundas. **HABITS AND HABITATS** Rare resident of secondary and primary forests, occasionally straying into well-wooded parkland. Birds are usually seen feeding at clumps of mistletoe in the canopy. Likely under-recorded because of its habit of keeping high in the canopy. Usually seen singly or in pairs. **SITES** Bukit Batok Nature Park, Central Catchment and Bukit Timah nature reserves. **CONSERVATION** Nationally critically endangered. A forest-dependent species.

Thick-billed Flowerpecker

■ *Dicaeum agile* 厚嘴啄花鸟 Sepah Puteri Paruh Tebal 10cm

DESCRIPTION ssp. *remotum*. Only brownish flowerpecker in Singapore. Head, upperparts and wing coverts greyish brown with olive wash on flight feathers. Underparts pale with diffused brown streaking on breast and flanks; tail tipped white. Eyes red; dark malar stripe distinctive. Bill stout, with lower mandible slightly shorter. **DISTRIBUTION** Indian Subcontinent, SW China, mainland Southeast Asia, Thai–Malay Peninsula, eastwards to Greater and Lesser Sunda Islands. **HABITS AND HABITATS** Rare resident or non-breeding visitor of secondary and primary forests. Usually seen feeding at clumps of mistletoe plants in the canopy with other flowerpeckers, also feeds on figs; sometime perched high in bare trees. Usually seen singly or in pairs. Has a distinctive habit of wagging tail sideways. Call is a ringing 'tseep'. **SITES** Bukit Batok Nature Park, Central Catchment Nature Reserve. **CONSERVATION** No issues.

Orange-bellied Flowerpecker
■ *Dicaeum trigonostigma* 橙腹啄花鸟 Sepah Puteri Dada Oren 9cm

DESCRIPTION ssp. *trigonostigma*. A petite blue and orange flowerpecker. Male (shown) has bright orange mantle, back and upper breast, grading to orange-yellow on vent and

uppertail coverts; head and wings slaty-blue. Female is plain olive on upperparts; throat and upper breast grey, with belly and vent washed yellow. **DISTRIBUTION** NE India, S Bangladesh, Myanmar, Thai–Malay Peninsula, Greater Sundas, Philippines. **HABITS AND HABITATS** Common resident of primary and secondary forests, and adjacent scrub and parkland, the dominant flowerpecker in the forest. Feeds on small fleshy fruits including mistletoes; also often seen descending to eat fruits of *Melastoma* and *Clidemia* shrubs. Seen singly or in pairs. Song is a rapid squeaky ascending 'si-si-si-si-si'. Breeds June–August. Builds a small pendant nest; usually with clutch of 2. **SITES** Bukit Batok Nature Park, Central Catchment and Bukit Timah nature reserves. **CONSERVATION** Forest dependent.

Scarlet-backed Flowerpecker
■ *Dicaeum cruentatum* 朱背啄花鸟 Sepah Puteri Belakang Merah 9cm

DESCRIPTION ssp. *cruentatum*. The familiar flowerpecker of urban areas. Male has a bright red crown, mantle and back, contrasting with blackish face, neck sides, wings and tail. Underparts white with grey wash on breast and flanks. Female is olive-grey above, with white underparts and bright red rump. **DISTRIBUTION** Himalayan foothills, NE India, SE China, mainland Southeast Asia, Thai–Malay Peninsula, Sumatra, Borneo. **HABITS AND HABITATS** The commonest flowerpecker in Singapore. Occurs from secondary forest, old

plantations and mangroves to parkland and urban green spaces, including wooded road dividers. Nest is small and globular, with side entrance and suspended from a branch a few metres above ground. Nesting recorded

almost throughout the year. Sings a thin, high-pitched 'tis-sit tissit tissit', also calls a metallic 'tick'. **SITES** Suitable habitat throughout Singapore. **CONSERVATION** No issues.

ABOVE: *Male*. RIGHT: *Female*

Brown-throated Sunbird
■ *Anthreptes malacensis* 褐喉花蜜鸟 Kelicap Mayang Kelapa 14cm

DESCRIPTION ssp. *malacensis*. Male is yellow on breast and belly with iridescent pinkish-brown throat. Upperparts glossy green and purple. Wings brown with a purple patch at shoulder. Female is olive-green on upperparts and yellowish on underparts, with diagnostic broken yellow eye-ring. **DISTRIBUTION** Mainland Southeast Asia, Thai–Malay Peninsula, Greater and Lesser Sundas, Philippines. **HABITS AND HABITATS** Very common resident of secondary forests, mangroves, old plantations, scrub and parkland, including urban green spaces. Second commonest sunbird, after Olive-backed Sunbird. Forages mostly in the

canopy and notably fond of coconut flowers and Heliconia. Seen singly or in pairs. Call is a monotonous, disyllabic 'peet-chew'. Breeds March–September. Builds a pendant nest; usually with a clutch of 2. **SITES** Suitable habitat throughout Singapore. **CONSERVATION** Has adapted well to parkland habitat.

LEFT: *Female*. RIGHT: *Male*

Van Hasselt's Sunbird ■ *Leptocoma brasiliana* 紫喉花蜜鸟
Kelicap Belacan 10cm

DESCRIPTION ssp. *brasiliana*. A small colourful sunbird of the forest canopy. Male appears dark, with shiny green crown, iridescent purplish throat, red breast and belly, and dark vent and undertail coverts. Female is olive-brown on upperparts and washed yellow on underparts. **DISTRIBUTION** NE India, much of mainland Southeast Asia, Thai–Malay Peninsula, Greater Sundas. **HABITS AND HABITATS** Common resident of primary and secondary forests, old plantations and occasionally scrub, mangroves and parkland. Usually forages in the canopy but occasionally descends to feed on flowers, especially those of *Saraca* trees. Suspected to undergo some post-breeding dispersal, as

evident from the scarcity of records after breeding season in May–August. Builds a pendant nest with clutch of 2. Song is a long series of metallic chirping and whistles. **SITES** Suitable habitat throughout Singapore (e.g. Central Catchment Nature Reserve, Bukit Batok Nature Park). **CONSERVATION** No issues.

RIGHT: *Male*. ABOVE: *Female*

Copper-throated Sunbird ■ *Leptocoma calcostetha*
铜喉花蜜鸟 Kelicap Bakau 14cm

DESCRIPTION Large sunbird of mangroves, with relatively long tail. Male appears dark with shiny green crown and shoulder patch, iridescent coppery-red throat and upper breast. Female is dark olive on upperparts and yellow on underparts, with greyish head and throat. Note also incomplete white eye-ring, unlike yellow of female Brown-throated Sunbird (see p.149). **DISTRIBUTION** Coastal Thai–Malay Peninsula and parts of mainland Southeast Asia, Greater Sundas, Palawan. **HABITS AND HABITATS** Uncommon resident of mangroves and coastal scrub, usually seen alone or in pairs. Appears to favour the large flowers of *Bruguiera* mangroves, which it is often seen probing for nectar. Nests

February–May and August–December, building a low pendant nest with clutch of 2. Call is a high-pitched series of 'tsii' notes and twittering. **SITES** Sungei Buloh Wetland Reserve, Mandai Mangroves, Pulau Ubin. **CONSERVATION** Extensive loss of mangroves has greatly reduced suitable habitat.

LEFT: *Male*. RIGHT: *Female*

Olive-backed Sunbird ■ *Cinnyris jugularis* 黄腹花蜜鸟 Kelicap Biasa 11cm

DESCRIPTION ssp. *ornatus*. A familiar sunbird of parkland and urban areas. Upperparts olive-green with white tail tip. Bill thin and decurved. Male has iridescent bluish-black forehead, throat and upper breast, contrasting with bright yellow underparts. Orange

pectoral tufts usually not visible, and erected during courtship display. Female is olive-green on upperparts with thin yellow brow; underparts yellow. **DISTRIBUTION** Widespread across Southeast Asia and Australasia, from S China and mainland Southeast Asia east to Maluku, New Guinea and N Australia. **HABITS AND HABITATS** The commonest sunbird in Singapore, found in diverse habitats from secondary forests to urban parkland. Very adaptable, and has been found nesting in potted plants in high-rise apartments. A generalist feeder, taking nectar and small insects. Nests January–July, with typical clutch 2. Call is a high-pitched, metallic chirping. **SITES** Suitable habitat throughout Singapore. **CONSERVATION** No issues.

LEFT: *Male*. RIGHT: *Female*

Crimson Sunbird ▪ *Aethopyga siparaja* 黄腰太阳鸟 Kelicap Sepah Raja 12cm

DESCRIPTION ssp. *siparaja*. A bright red, long-tailed sunbird. Male is unmistakable with combination of crimson head, mantle, throat and upper breast, dark blue forehead and moustache. Rump yellowish with rest of underparts dark greyish. Tail dark violet. Female is dull olive on upperparts and pale yellowish on underparts. **DISTRIBUTION** Himalayan foothills, E India, S China, much of mainland Southeast Asia, Thai–Malay Peninsula, Greater Sundas, and Sulawesi. **HABITS AND HABITATS** Common resident of primary and secondary forests, scrub, old plantations and occasionally parklands. One of the commonest birds in secondary forests. Forages at all levels of the forest, often descending low to feed at gingers and other low flowering shrubs. Feeds mostly on nectar and small invertebrates. Call is a distinctive 'chit-chit-chit-chew', noticeably higher-pitched than other sunbirds. **SITES** Central Catchment and Bukit Timah nature reserves, Bukit Batok Nature Park. **CONSERVATION** Unofficial national bird of Singapore.

LEFT: *Female.* ABOVE: *Male*

Little Spiderhunter
▪ *Arachnothera longirostra* 长嘴捕蛛鸟 Kelicap-Jantung Kecil 16cm

DESCRIPTION ssp. *cinireicollis*. The smallest spiderhunter. Long decurved bill, greyish sides of face with thin blackish moustachial stripe and incomplete thick white eye-ring. Crown olive-green with fine black scaling. Upperparts olive-green and throat white; rest of underparts yellow. **DISTRIBUTION** Himalayan foothills, SW and NE India, SW China, mainland Southeast Asia, Thai–Malay Peninsula, Greater Sundas. **HABITS AND HABITATS** Common resident occurring in the understorey of primary and secondary forests, forest edge, occasionally in scrub and parkland. Frequents areas in the forest with an abundance of large-flowered shrubs such as torch gingers (*Etlingera* sp.) and wild bananas. Takes mostly nectar and arthropods. Nest is a structure of plant fibres and dried leaves sewn onto undersides of broad leaves, with clutch of 2. Shy and usually seen flying through the forest understorey with a sharp 'chit'; song is a monotonous, rapid 'wit-wit-wit…'. **SITES** Bukit Timah and Central Catchment nature reserves, Bukit Batok Nature Park. **CONSERVATION** No Issues.

Thick-billed Spiderhunter

■ *Arachnothera crassirostris* 厚嘴捕蛛鸟
Kelicap-Jantung Paruh Tebal 17cm

DESCRIPTION A small, nondescript, yellow-olive spiderhunter. Similar to Little Spiderhunter (see p.151) but has thicker bill (difficult to see in the field), broken yellow eye-ring and greyish-olive throat and breast. Rest of underparts yellowish. Upperparts mostly olive-brown. **DISTRIBUTION** Thai–Malay Peninsula, Sumatra, Borneo. **HABITS AND HABITATS** Very rare resident, confined to primary and secondary forest in the Central Catchment Nature Reserve; interestingly there is one historical record of a bird in mangroves in the 1920s at Jurong. Easy to overlook, given its habit of foraging in canopy and middle storey, especially at flowering *Syzygium* trees; rarely descending to feed in low shrubs, unlike other spiderhunters. Call is a series of monotonous 'wit' notes, and a loud, grating 'chit'. **SITES** Central Catchment Nature Reserve. **CONSERVATION** Nationally critically endangered.

Yellow-eared Spiderhunter

■ *Arachnothera chrysogenys* 小黄耳捕蛛鸟 Kelicap-Jantung Telinga Kuning 18cm

DESCRIPTION ssp. *chrysogenys*. A medium-sized spiderhunter with thin, incomplete yellow eye-ring, and diagnostic bright yellow patch on cheeks and ear coverts. Throat

greyish-olive. Breast and rest of underparts yellow. Upperparts mostly olive-green. **DISTRIBUTION** Thai–Malay Peninsula, Sumatra, Borneo, Java. **HABITS AND HABITATS** A very rare resident, now confined to primary and secondary forests in the Central Catchment Nature Reserve, although there was a record of 1 bird at Pulau Ubin in 1998, possibly dispersed from Malaysia. Usually forages in the forest canopy but regularly descends to feed on nectar at ginger flowers. Also known to take insects. Territorial and defends regular foraging areas (e.g. flower clumps) from conspecifics aggressively. Nest is a basket-like structure of plant matter built beneath a large palm frond, with clutch of 2. Call is a rapid series of 2 or 3 harsh 'chik' notes. **SITES** Central Catchment Nature Reserve. **CONSERVATION** Nationally critically endangered.

House Sparrow ■ *Passer domesticus* 家麻雀 Ciak Rumah 15cm

DESCRIPTION ssp. *indicus*. Adult male (shown) distinguished from Eurasian Tree Sparrow by grey, not chestnut, cap, with hindcrown and neck chestnut. Also note white cheek and headsides, and large, diffused black bib. Female is drab, mostly pale brown with buffy brow and underparts, with dark streaking on mantle and shoulders. **DISTRIBUTION** Widespread across Eurasia, through much of Europe, North Africa, Middle East and Indian sub-continent, east to NE China and parts of Southeast Asia. Widely introduced worldwide. **HABITS AND HABITATS**

Introduced and known from two urban sites in Singapore, both near the port. Likely to have arrived by hitchhiking on ships. A strict commensal of man, foraging mostly on discarded food and refuse. Nests in eaves and cavities of buildings; builds an untidy ball-shaped nest with side entrance. **SITES** Pasir Panjang Wholesale Centre, Jurong Island. **CONSERVATION** No issues.

Eurasian Tree Sparrow ■ *Passer montanus* 麻雀 Ciak Eurasia 14cm

DESCRIPTION ssp. *malaccensis*. The familiar sparrow of urban areas. Combination of chestnut cap contrasting with pale head sides, black ear covert and throat patch diagnostic. Upperparts brown with black streaks on mantle and back, while underparts dull greyish. Sexes alike. Young birds are less strongly marked and lack the ear patch. **DISTRIBUTION** Widespread across Eurasia, from Europe and Middle East to parts of Indian sub-continent, East and Southeast Asia. Introduced to North America, Pacific Islands and Australia.

HABITS AND HABITATS A strict commensal of man, occurring mostly in the vicinity of human habitation and occasionally in parkland and scrub. Can be easily seen at hawker centres where small groups forage on leftovers and refuse. One of the commonest birds in Singapore, and believed to have been established here since the 19th century with human assistance. Nests in eaves and roof cavities of buildings, and tree-holes; with clutches of 4–5. **SITES** Suitable habitat throughout Singapore. **CONSERVATION** No issues. One of 6 species not protected by law in Singapore.

Baya Weaver ■ *Ploceus philippinus* 黄胸织雀 Tempua Raya 15cm

DESCRIPTION ssp. *infortunatus*. Breeding male has bright yellow crown and nape, dark face and pale buffish-brown underparts. Female and non-breeding male are mostly buffish-brown, with streaking on crown, nape and back, and light mottling on breast. Both sexes of introduced, now rare, Streaked Weaver *P. manyar* can be distinguished from this species by heavily streaked breast and flanks. **DISTRIBUTION** Indian sub-continent, SW China, much of mainland Southeast Asia, Sumatra, Java, Bali. **HABITS AND HABITATS** Common resident of grasslands, secondary woodland and old plantations. Gregarious, usually nesting colonially. Nests are globular and suspended from branches, at least 3m above ground. Used to regularly build nests on

Coconut trees, but *Acacia* is nowadays preferred, probably because of its abundance. Breeds March–August. Males attending to nests call a series of chattering notes, ending with a wheezy rattle. **SITES** Lorong Halus wetlands, Kranji Marsh, Sungei Buloh Wetland Reserve. **CONSERVATION** May face competition from various introduced African weavers and waxbills, which are increasingly common.

LEFT: *Male*. RIGHT: *Female*

White-rumped Munia ■ *Lonchura striata* 白腰文鸟 Pipit Tuli 11cm

DESCRIPTION ssp. *subsquamicollis*. A dark brown munia with diagnostic contrasting white rump. Upperparts, throat and breast mostly dark brown and finely streaked white, belly dirty white. **DISTRIBUTION** SW and E India, central and S China, Taiwan,

mainland Southeast Asia, Thai–Malay Peninsula, Sumatra. **HABITS AND HABITATS** Rare resident of secondary forests, forest edges, old plantations and scrub. The population of this bird has declined rapidly in the past two decades, and Pulau Ubin appears to be the last stronghold. Birds occasionally reported on Singapore mainland are likely recently released birds. Usually seen feeding in small groups in dense grassy areas by the forest edge. Nest is a ball-like structure made from grasses and leaves; clutch 5. **SITES** Pulau Ubin. **CONSERVATION** Nationally critically endangered.

Javan Munia ■ *Lonchura leucogastroides* 爪哇文鸟 Pipit Jawa 11.5cm

DESCRIPTION A dark, white-bellied munia. Similar to White-rumped Munia (see p.154), but lacks white rump and fine white streakings of upperparts, while face and breast are black. Upperparts dark brown with white belly and flanks. **DISTRIBUTION** South Sumatra, Java, Bali, Lombok. Introduced to Singapore. **HABITS AND HABITATS** Uncommon resident of grasslands, secondary scrub, parkland and golf courses. Introduced in Singapore in the 1920s and subsequently established. Populations have declined rapidly since the 1990s and now birds regularly found at few sites. Gregarious, often foraging in small parties with other munias. Breeds March–October. Nest is a ball-like structure of plant fibres, like other munias. Has recently colonised S Johor, Malaysia, and birds there may have Singapore origins. **SITES** Sungei Buloh Wetland Reserve, Kranji Marshes. **CONSERVATION** No issues.

Scaly-breasted Munia
■ *Lonchura punctulata* 斑文鸟 Pipit Pinang 12cm

DESCRIPTION ssp. *fretensis*. Whitish underparts with dark brown scaling from breast and flanks to belly distinguishes from other munias. Upperparts of adults (shown) dark brown, with rump and tail brownish grey. Young birds nondescript, with brown upperparts and dull buffish underparts. **DISTRIBUTION** Himalayan foothills and much of Indian sub-continent, S China, mainland Southeast Asia, Thai–Malay Peninsula, Greater and Lesser Sundas, Philippines. Widely introduced worldwide. **HABITS AND HABITATS** Most abundant munia, occurring in grasslands, old plantations, secondary scrub, parkland and even golf courses, where it feeds on grass seeds. Breeds March–October. Nest is ball-like structure made from plant fibres, with clutches of 4–5. Gregarious, roosting communally and forming flocks of over 100 birds when foraging, often with other munias. Birds just about to fly off signal to conspecifics by flicking their tails. Call is a soft, piping 'kii'. **SITES** Suitable habitat throughout Singapore. **CONSERVATION** No issues.

Chestnut Munia ▪ *Lonchura atricapilla* 黑头文鸟 Pipit Rawa 11cm

DESCRIPTION ssp. *sinensis*. A smart-looking, black-headed munia. Entire head and throat black, rest of body rich chestnut, with darker lower belly and vent. Bill pale greyish blue.

Young birds are nondescript pale brown, with buff underparts. **DISTRIBUTION** E India, S China, mainland Southeast Asia, east to Philippines, Sulawesi and Maluku. **HABITS AND HABITATS** Increasingly uncommon resident, having declined in recent years. Occurs in grassland, freshwater marshes and secondary scrub, especially in areas of rank grass; preferring wetter areas than other munias. Breeds March–June. Calls a soft 'preep', rather similar to White-headed Munia. **SITES** Lorong Halus wetlands, Kranji Marshes, Gardens-by-the-Bay, Tuas. **CONSERVATION** Loss of grasslands has greatly reduced suitable habitat.

White-headed Munia ▪ *Lonchura maja* 白头文鸟 Pipit Uban 11.5cm

DESCRIPTION A distinctive munia with a white head, aptly named the 'cigar bird'. Head, throat and upper breast white, rest of body chestnut brown. Centre of belly and undertail

coverts black. Rump and uppertail coverts maroon-chestnut. Bill pale grey-blue. Feet dull grey. **DISTRIBUTION** South Vietnam, Thai–Malay Peninsula, Sumatra, Java. **HABITS AND HABITATS** Uncommon resident of grassland, secondary scrub, parkland and golf courses, often colonizes scrubby vegetation on recently reclaimed land. Gregarious, often foraging in small parties with other munias, occasionally forming large mixed flocks of a few hundred birds. Breeds July–September. Nest is a ball-like structure with slightly spouted side entrance with a clutch size of 4-6. **SITES** Lorong Halus Wetlands, Gardens-by-the-Bay, Tuas, Pulau Ubin. **CONSERVATION** Loss of wet grasslands has greatly reduced suitable habitat.

Forest Wagtail ▪ *Dendronanthus indicus* 林鹡鸰 Pipit-Kedidi Hutan 18cm

DESCRIPTION An unmistakable wagtail of wooded areas. Crown and upperparts brownish-olive. Underparts whitish with two black breast bands, the lower one incomplete. Two broad white wing bars on blackish wings. **DISTRIBUTION** Breeds in E and NE China, Russian Far East, Korea and Japan. Winters in NE and SW Indiaeastward to Thai–Malay Peninsula and Greater Sundas.

HABITS AND HABITATS Fairly common migrant to primary and secondary forests, old plantations, mangroves and scrub. Forages by walking on the ground; when flushed, flies a few metres ahead or up to low perches. Unlike other wagtails, has unique habit of wagging its body from side to side. Birds mostly arrive in September–October, and depart by April. Call is a soft 'pink', especially when flushed. **SITES** Central Catchment and Bukit Timah nature reserves, Sungei Buloh Wetland Reserve. **CONSERVATION** Largely dependent on forests in wintering grounds.

Eastern Yellow Wagtail ▪ *Motacilla tschutschensis* 黄鹡鸰 Pipit-Kedidi Kuning 18cm

DESCRIPTION Breeding male is olive-green on mantle, back and rump, with bright yellow underparts and blackish wings with white fringe to coverts. Ssp. *macronyx* shows dark greyish crown and nape, while ssp. *taivana* has olive-green crown with long yellow brow. First-winter bird has greyish upperparts and white underparts, with varying amount of yellow on throat and belly. **DISTRIBUTION** Breeds across C and E Siberia, Mongolia, NE China, Japan to W Alaska. Winters in S China, Taiwan and much of Southeast Asia, east to New Guinea and Australia. **HABITS AND HABITATS** Common migrant to open habitats, including wet grasslands, golf courses, playing fields and bare ground, usually near water. Gregarious, typically seen foraging on the ground in small groups. When flushed, calls a high-pitched disyllabic 'twee-yip'. Begins to arrive in September, and the latest departure recorded is in May. **SITES** Lorong Halus wetlands. **CONSERVATION** No issues.

LEFT: ssp. *taivana*, RIGHT: ssp: *macronyx*

Grey Wagtail ■ *Motacilla cinerea* 灰鹡鸰 Pipit-Kedidi Kelabu 19cm

DESCRIPTION ssp. *cinerea*. A greyish wagtail of streams and canals. Similar to Eastern Yellow Wagtail (see p.157) but has grey (not olive-green) crown, nape and back. Underparts whitish, with breast, vent, rump and tail coverts washed yellow. Breeding males have black

throat and white malar stripe. **DISTRIBUTION** Widespread across Eurasia, breeds discontinuously from W Europe through much of Russia, NE China, Korea, Japan and Himalayas. Northern populations migrate to winter in Africa, Middle East and Indian sub-continent, east to S China, Southeast Asia and New Guinea. **HABITS AND HABITATS** Uncommon migrant, occurring along streams in the forests, forest edge, scrub and plantations, occasionally in urban canals. Solitary, usually seen foraging along streams and canals with flowing water. Birds mostly arrive in September–October, departing by March. When flushed, flies off with a sharp, repeated 'cheet'. **SITES** Central Catchment Nature Reserve. **CONSERVATION** No issues.

White Wagtail ■ *Motacilla alba* 白鹡鸰 Pipit-Kedidi Murai 19cm

DESCRIPTION Contrasting black and white plumage distinguishes this from all other wagtails. Forecrown, face and neck sides, most of wing and underparts white, with black patch on upper breast variable, depending on race. At least two subspecies known to occur, *ocularis* and the commoner *leucopsis*. Ssp. *leucopsis* can be distinguished from *ocularis* by absence of black eye-stripe. **DISTRIBUTION** Breeds across Eurasia, from W Europe across much of Central Asia and Russia to Himalayas, much of E Asia and Alaska. Winters in Africa, Middle East and Indian sub-continent, east to much of mainland Southeast Asia and Philippines. **HABITS AND HABITATS** Uncommon migrant to open scrubby

areas, usually near water, including well-vegetated ditches and canals, where it forages for small insects. Migrants arrive mostly in October, staying no

later than April. When flushed, calls a ringing, disyllabic 'chwee-tzit' as it flies off. **SITES** Lorong Halus wetlands. **CONSERVATION** No issues.

LEFT: ssp. *ocularis*. RIGHT: ssp: *leucopsis*

Paddyfield Pipit ■ *Anthus rufulus* 东方田鹨 Ciak Padang 16cm

DESCRIPTION ssp. *malayensis*. Most common pipit in Singapore. A drab brown bird of grassy fields. Upperparts tawny-brown with bold brown streaking on crown and mantle. Underparts pale buff with finer streaking on breast and neck sides. On face, note white brow, brownish ear coverts and white submoustachial stripe. Similar-looking Richard's Pipit A. *richardi*, which is very rare, is larger and shows more extensive dark streaking on breast. **DISTRIBUTION** Afghanistan and much of Indian sub-continent, SW China and mainland Southeast Asia, east to Philippines and Lesser Sundas. **HABITS AND HABITATS** Abundant resident of grassland, open scrub, playing fields, golf courses and barren ground on cleared or reclaimed land, where this is one of the first few colonising species. Usually seen singly or in pairs. Forages by running on ground, stopping regularly to pick up insect prey. Breeds March–June. Builds a small cup on ground by tufts of grass, containing 2 eggs. Call is a dry 'chew-wee', usually uttered in flight when flushed. **SITES** Suitable habitat throughout Singapore. **CONSERVATION** No issues.

Red-throated Pipit ■ *Anthus cervinus* 红喉鹨 Ciak Leher Merah 15cm

DESCRIPTION A small, well-marked pipit. Distinguished from Paddyfield Pipit (above) by smaller size, stockier build, and more extensive bold streaking across mantle and underparts. Underparts whitish, with bold dark streaking from breast to flanks and belly. Breeding birds (shown) show pinkish-orange throat and upper breast. **DISTRIBUTION** Breeds across much of northern Eurasia, from Scandinavia to E Siberia and Kamchatka. Winters in Sub-Saharan Africa and Indian sub-continent, east to S China and much of Southeast Asia. **HABITS AND HABITATS** Uncommon migrant to wet grassland, open scrub and damp patches in semi-barren fields, including on reclaimed land. Usually seen foraging alone or in small groups, usually in company of Eastern Yellow Wagtail. Birds mostly arrive from mid-November, departing by April. Call is a thin 'tsip', usually uttered in flight. **SITES** Tuas west. **CONSERVATION** No issues.

Sequence, nomenclature and taxonomy follow Gill, F. & Donsker, D. (Eds). 2017. *IOC World Bird List* (v 7.2). Accessed at http://www.worldbirdnames.org

Status

R Resident: species known to occur all year round and with recent evidence of breeding

I Introduced resident: non native species, but known to occur regularly and with recent evidence of breeding

M Migrant: species known to occur during the migration period, as a winter visitor and/ or passage migrant

P Passage migrant: species known to occur only during the passage migration months (Aug-Nov, Mar-May)

N Non-breeding visitor: species known to occur in the region and likely to disperse widely, but with no evidence of breeding in Singapore

V Vagrant: species outside of regular distribution, but occuring in an apparently wild state in Singapore

E? Possibly extinct: species with no confirmed records for over 10 years

Abundance/Sighting Frequency

5 Very common: occurs very frequently in preferred habitat (>75%); regularly seen in large numbers

4 Common: occurs frequently in preferred habitat (50–75%)

3 Uncommon: occurs infrequently in preferred habitat (10–50%); more than 5 records annually

2 Rare: occurs very infrequently, even in preferred habitat (<10%); 1-5 records annually

1 Very rare: unlikely to occur, even in apparently suitable habitat; less than 5 records in past 20 years

? Indeterminate: abundance currently uncertain due to difficulties in field identification

IUCN 2016 Red List Status

LC Least Concern
NT Near Threatened
VU Vulnerable
EN Endangered
CR Critically Endangered

Common name	Scientific name	Status	Abundance	IUCN Red List Status
Anatidae (Ducks, Geese) - 10 species				
Wandering Whistling Duck	*Dendrocygna arcuata*	I	3	LC
Lesser Whistling Duck	*Dendrocygna javanica*	R	3	LC
Cotton Pygmy Goose	*Nettapus coromandelicus*	R	2	LC
Eurasian Wigeon	*Anas penelope*	V	1	LC
Gadwall	*Anas strepera*	V	1	LC
Eurasian Teal	*Anas crecca*	V	1	LC
Northern Pintail	*Anas acuta*	M	1	LC
Garganey	*Anas querquedula*	M	1	LC

Common name	Scientific name	Status	Abundance	IUCN Red List Status
Northern Shoveler	Anas clypeata	M	2	LC
Tufted Duck	Aythya fuligula	V	1	LC
Phasianidae (Pheasants, Partridges And Francolins) - 2 Species				
King Quail	Excalfactoria chinensis	R	3	LC
Red Junglefowl	Gallus gallus	R	3	LC
Hydrobatidae (Northern Storm Petrels) - 1 species				
Swinhoe's Storm Petrel	Oceanodroma monorhis	P	3	NT
Procellariidae (Petrels, Shearwaters) - 2 species				
Wedge-tailed Shearwater	Ardenna pacifica	V	1	LC
Short-tailed Shearwater	Ardenna tenuirostris	P	3	LC
Podicipedidae (Grebes) - 1 species				
Little Grebe	Tachybaptus ruficollis	R	3	LC
Phaethontidae (Tropicbirds) - 1 species				
White-tailed Tropicbird	Phaethon lepturus	N	1	LC
Ciconiidae (Storks) - 2 species				
Asian Openbill	Anastomus oscitans	N	1	LC
Lesser Adjutant	Leptoptilos javanicus	N	2	VU
Threskiornithidae (Ibises) - 1 species				
Glossy Ibis	Plegadis falcinellus	V	1	LC
Ardeidae (Herons, Bitterns) - 19 species				
Yellow Bittern	Ixobrychus sinensis	R/M	4	LC
Von Schrenck's Bittern	Ixobrychus eurhythmus	M	3	LC
Cinnamon Bittern	Ixobrychus cinnamomeus	R/M	3	LC
Black Bittern	Dupetor flavicollis	M	3	LC
Malayan Night Heron	Gorsachius melanolophus	M	2	LC
Black-crowned Night Heron	Nycticorax nycticorax	R	3	LC
Striated Heron	Butorides striata	R/M	5	LC
Chinese Pond Heron	Ardeola bacchus	M	4	LC
Javan Pond Heron	Ardeola speciosa	N	3	LC
Indian Pond Heron	Ardeola grayii	V	1	LC
Eastern Cattle Egret	Bubulcus coromandus	I/M	4	LC
Grey Heron	Ardea cinerea	R/M?	4	LC
Great-billed Heron	Ardea sumatrana	R	3	LC
Purple Heron	Ardea purpurea	R	3	LC
Great Egret	Ardea alba	M	4	LC
Intermediate Egret	Ardea intermedia	M	3	LC
Little Egret	Egretta garzetta	M/N	5	LC
Pacific Reef Heron	Egretta sacra	R	4	LC
Chinese Egret	Egretta eulophotes	M	2	VU
Fregatidae (Frigatebirds) - 2 species				
Lesser Frigatebird	Fregata ariel	N	2	LC
Christmas Frigatebird	Fregata andrewsi	N	1	CR
Sulidae (Gannets, Boobies) - 2 species				
Red-footed Booby	Sula sula	N	1	LC
Brown Booby	Sula leucogaster	N	1	LC
Anhingidae (Darters) - 2 species				
Oriental Darter	Anhinga melanogaster	N	2	NT

Common name	Scientific name	Status	Abundance	IUCN Red List Status
Pandionidae (Ospreys) - 1 species				
Western Osprey	Pandion haliaeetus	M/N?	3	LC
Accipitridae (Kites, Hawks and Eagles) - 30 species				
Black-winged Kite	Elanus caeruleus	R	4	LC
Crested Honey Buzzard	Pernis ptilorhynchus	M/N	4	LC
Jerdon's Baza	Aviceda jerdoni	M	3	LC
Black Baza	Aviceda leuphotes	M	4	LC
Himalayan Vulture	Gyps himalayensis	N	2	NT
Crested Serpent Eagle	Spilornis cheela	R/N	3	LC
Short-toed Snake Eagle	Circaetus gallicus	M	2	LC
Bat Hawk	Macheiramphus alcinus	N	1	LC
Changeable Hawk-Eagle	Nisaetus cirrhatus	R	4	LC
Blyth's Hawk-Eagle	Nisaetus alboniger	N	1	LC
Rufous-bellied Eagle	Lophotriorchis kienerii	M/N?	3	LC
Greater Spotted Eagle	Clanga clanga	M	2	VU
Booted Eagle	Hieraaetus pennatus	M	3	LC
Steppe Eagle	Aquila nipalensis	M	1	EN
Eastern Imperial Eagle	Aquila heliaca	V	1	VU
Crested Goshawk	Accipiter trivirgatus	R	3	LC
Chinese Sparrowhawk	Accipiter soloensis	M	3	LC
Japanese Sparrowhawk	Accipiter gularis	M	4	LC
Besra	Accipiter virgatus	M	2	LC
Eurasian Sparrowhawk	Accipiter nisus	V	1	LC
Eastern Marsh Harrier	Circus spilonotus	M	3	LC
Hen Harrier	Circus cyaneus	V	1	LC
Pied Harrier	Circus melanoleucos	M	2	LC
Black Kite	Milvus migrans	M	2	LC
Brahminy Kite	Haliastur indus	R	4	LC
White-bellied Sea Eagle	Haliaeetus leucogaster	R	4	LC
Grey-headed Fish Eagle	Haliaeetus ichthyaetus	R	4	NT
Grey-faced Buzzard	Butastur indicus	M	2	LC
Eastern Buzzard	Buteo japonicus	M	3?	LC
Common Buzzard	Buteo buteo	M	?	LC
Heliornithidae (Finfoots) - 1 species				
Masked Finfoot	Heliopais personatus	M	1	EN
Rallidae (Rails, Crakes and Coots) - 12 species				
Red-legged Crake	Rallina fasciata	R/M	3	LC
Slaty-legged Crake	Rallina eurizonoides	M	1	LC
Slaty-breasted Rail	Gallirallus striatus	R	3	LC
White-breasted Waterhen	Amaurornis phoenicurus	R/M	5	LC
Baillon's Crake	Porzana pusilla	M	3	LC
Ruddy-breasted Crake	Porzana fusca	R	3	LC
Band-bellied Crake	Porzana paykulli	M	1	NT
White-browed Crake	Porzana cinerea	R	3	LC
Watercock	Gallicrex cinerea	M	3	LC
Black-backed Swamphen	Porphyrio indicus	R	3	LC

Common name	Scientific name	Status	Abundance	IUCN Red List Status
Common Moorhen	*Gallinula chloropus*	R	3	LC
Eurasian Coot	*Fulica atra*	V	1	LC
Turnicidae (Buttonquails) - 1 species				
Barred Buttonquail	*Turnix suscitator*	R	3	LC
Recurvirostridae (Stilts, Avocets) - 1 species				
Black-winged Stilt	*Himantopus himantopus*	M	2	LC
Charadriidae (Plovers, Lapwings) - 11 species				
Pacific Golden Plover	*Pluvialis fulva*	M	5	LC
Grey Plover	*Pluvialis squatarola*	M	3	LC
Common Ringed Plover	*Charadrius hiaticula*	M	1	LC
Little Ringed Plover	*Charadrius dubius*	M	4	LC
Kentish Plover	*Charadrius alexandrinus*	M	3	LC
Malaysian Plover	*Charadrius peronii*	R	3	NT
Lesser Sand Plover	*Charadrius mongolus*	M	5	LC
Greater Sand Plover	*Charadrius leschenaultii*	M	3	LC
Oriental Plover	*Charadrius veredus*	P	2	LC
Grey-headed Lapwing	*Vanellus cinereus*	V	1	LC
Red-wattled Lapwing	*Vanellus indicus*	R	4	LC
Rostratulidae (Painted-snipes) - 1 species				
Greater Painted-snipe	*Rostratula benghalensis*	R	3	LC
Jacanidae (Jacanas) - 1 species				
Pheasant-tailed Jacana	*Hydrophasianus chirurgus*	M	2	LC
Scolopacidae (Sandpipers, Snipes) - 36 species				
Eurasian Woodcock	*Scolopax rusticola*	V	1	LC
Pin-tailed Snipe	*Gallinago stenura*	M	?	LC
Swinhoe's Snipe	*Gallinago megala*	M	?	LC
Common Snipe	*Gallinago gallinago*	M	3	LC
Asian Dowitcher	*Limnodramus semipalmatus*	P	2	NT
Black-tailed Godwit	*Limosa limosa*	M	3	NT
Bar-tailed Godwit	*Limosa lapponica*	M	2	NT
Little Curlew	*Numenius minutus*	P	1	LC
Whimbrel	*Numenius phaeopus*	M	5	LC
Eurasian Curlew	*Numenius arquata*	M	2	NT
Far Eastern Curlew	*Numenius madagascariensis*	P	1	EN
Spotted Redshank	*Tringa erythropus*	V	1	LC
Common Redshank	*Tringa totanus*	M	5	LC
Marsh Sandpiper	*Tringa stagnatilis*	M	5	LC
Common Greenshank	*Tringa nebularia*	M	5	LC
Nordmann's Greenshank	*Tringa guttifer*	M	1	EN
Green Sandpiper	*Tringa ochropus*	M	1	LC
Wood Sandpiper	*Tringa glareola*	M	4	LC
Grey-tailed Tattler	*Tringa brevipes*	M	2	NT
Terek Sandpiper	*Xenus cinereus*	M	4	LC
Common Sandpiper	*Actitis hypoleucos*	M	5	LC
Ruddy Turnstone	*Arenaria interpres*	M	3	LC
Great Knot	*Calidris tenuirostris*	M	2	EN

Common name	Scientific name	Status	Abundance	IUCN Red List Status
Red Knot	*Calidris canutus*	P	1	NT
Ruff	*Calidris pugnax*	M	1	LC
Broad-billed Sandpiper	*Calidris falcinellus*	M	3	LC
Sharp-tailed Sandpiper	*Calidris acuminata*	P	1	LC
Curlew Sandpiper	*Calidris ferruginea*	M	4	NT
Temminck's Stint	*Calidris temminckii*	V	1	LC
Long-toed Stint	*Calidris subminuta*	M	3	LC
Spoon-billed Sandpiper	*Calidris pygmaea*	M	1	CR
Red-necked Stint	*Calidris ruficollis*	M	3	NT
Sanderling	*Calidris alba*	M	3	LC
Dunlin	*Calidris alpina*	V	1	LC
Pectoral Sandpiper	*Calidris melanotos*	V	1	LC
Red-necked Phalarope	*Phalaropus lobatus*	M	1	LC
Glareolidae (Pratincoles) - 2 species				
Oriental Pratincole	*Glareola maldivarum*	P	3	LC
Small Pratincole	*Glareola lactea*	V	1	LC
Laridae (Gulls, Terns and Skimmers) - 15 species				
Brown-headed Gull	*Chroicocephalus brunnicephalus*	V	1	LC
Black-headed Gull	*Chroicocephalus ridibundus*	M	2	LC
Lesser Black-backed Gull	*Larus fuscus*	V	1	LC
Gull-billed Tern	*Gelochelidon nilotica*	M	3	LC
Caspian Tern	*Hydroprogne caspia*	M	1	LC
Greater Crested Tern	*Thalasseus bergii*	M/N	4	LC
Lesser Crested Tern	*Thalasseus bengalensis*	M/N	4	LC
Little Tern	*Sternula albifrons*	R/M	4	LC
Aleutian Tern	*Onychoprion aleuticus*	M	3	LC
Bridled Tern	*Onychoprion anaethetus*	R	3	LC
Roseate Tern	*Sterna dougallii*	M	1	LC
Black-naped Tern	*Sterna sumatrana*	R	3	LC
Common Tern	*Sterna hirundo*	M	3	LC
Whiskered Tern	*Chlidonias hybrida*	M	2	LC
White-winged Tern	*Chlidonias leucopterus*	M	4	LC
Stercorariidae (Skuas) - 3 species				
Parasitic Jaeger	*Stercorarius parasiticus*	M	3	LC
Pomarine Jaeger	*Stercorarius pomarinus*	M	2	LC
Long-tailed Jaeger	*Stercorarius longicaudus*	M	2	LC
Columbidae (Pigeons, Doves) - 13 species				
Rock Dove	*Columba livia*	I	5	LC
Red Turtle Dove	*Streptopelia tranquebarica*	I	3	LC
Spotted Dove	*Spilopelia chinensis*	R	5	LC
Common Emerald Dove	*Chalcophaps indica*	R	4	LC
Zebra Dove	*Geopelia striata*	R	5	LC
Cinnamon-headed Green Pigeon	*Treron fulvicollis*	R/N?	2	NT
Little Green Pigeon	*Treron olax*	R/N?	2	LC
Pink-necked Green Pigeon	*Treron vernans*	R	5	LC
Thick-billed Green Pigeon	*Treron curvirostra*	R	3	LC

Common name	Scientific name	Status	Abundance	IUCN Red List Status
Jambu Fruit Dove	*Ptilinopus jambu*	R/N?	3	NT
Green Imperial Pigeon	*Ducula aenea*	R	3	LC
Pied Imperial Pigeon	*Ducula bicolor*	I/N	3	LC
Mountain Imperial Pigeon	*Ducula badia*	N	1	LC
Cuculidae (Coucals, Cuckoos and Malkohas) - 19 species				
Greater Coucal	*Centropus sinensis*	R	3	LC
Lesser Coucal	*Centropus bengalensis*	R	4	LC
Chestnut-bellied Malkoha	*Phaenicophaeus sumatranus*	R	3	NT
Chestnut-winged Cuckoo	*Clamator coromandus*	M	3	LC
Jacobin Cuckoo	*Clamator jacobinus*	V	1	LC
Asian Koel	*Eudynamys scolopaceus*	R/M?	5	LC
Asian Emerald Cuckoo	*Chrysococcyx maculatus*	N	1	LC
Violet Cuckoo	*Chrysococcyx xanthorhynchus*	R	3	LC
Horsfield's Bronze Cuckoo	*Chrysococcyx basalis*	M	2	LC
Little Bronze Cuckoo	*Chrysococcyx malayanus*	R	4	LC
Banded Bay Cuckoo	*Cacomantis sonneratii*	R	3	LC
Plaintive Cuckoo	*Cacomantis merulinus*	R	3	LC
Rusty-breasted Cuckoo	*Cacomantis sepulcralis*	R	3	LC
Asian Drongo Cuckoo	*Surniculus lugubris*	R/M	3	LC
Large Hawk-Cuckoo	*Hierococcyx sparverioides*	M	2	LC
Malaysian Hawk-Cuckoo	*Hierococcyx fugax*	N	2	LC
Hodgson's Hawk-Cuckoo	*Hierococcyx nisicolor*	M	3	LC
Indian Cuckoo	*Cuculus micropterus*	M	4	LC
Himalayan Cuckoo	*Cuculus saturatus*	M	2	LC
Tytonidae (Barn Owls) - 1 species				
Eastern Barn Owl	*Tyto javanica*	R	3	LC
Strigidae (Owls) - 9 species				
Sunda Scops Owl	*Otus lempiji*	R	4	LC
Oriental Scops Owl	*Otus sunia*	M	2	LC
Barred Eagle-Owl	*Bubo sumatranus*	R	2	LC
Buffy Fish Owl	*Ketupa ketupu*	R	3	LC
Spotted Wood Owl	*Strix seloputo*	R	3	LC
Brown Wood Owl	*Strix leucogrammica*	R	2	LC
Brown Hawk Owl	*Ninox scutulata*	R	4	LC
Northern Boobook	*Ninox japonica*	M	2	LC
Short-eared Owl	*Asio flammeus*	M	1	LC
Caprimulgidae (Nightjars) - 4 species				
Malaysian Eared Nightjar	*Lyncornis temminckii*	R	2	LC
Grey Nightjar	*Caprimulgus jotaka*	M	3	LC
Large-tailed Nightjar	*Caprimulgus macrurus*	R	4	LC
Savanna Nightjar	*Caprimulgus affinis*	R	4	LC
Hemiprocnidae (Treeswifts) - 2 species				
Grey-rumped Treeswift	*Hemiprocne longipennis*	R	4	LC
Whiskered Treeswift	*Hemiprocne comata*	N	1	LC
Apodidae (Swifts) - 10 species				
Plume-toed Swiftlet	*Collocalia affinis*	R	3	LC

Common name	Scientific name	Status	Abundance	IUCN Red List Status
Black-nest Swiftlet	Aerodramus maximus	R	3	LC
Germain's Swiftlet	Aerodramus germani	R	5	LC
Silver-rumped Spinetail	Rhaphidura leucopygialis	N	1	LC
White-throated Needletail	Hirundapus caudacutus	V	1	LC
Silver-backed Needletail	Hirundapus cochinchinensis	M	2	LC
Brown-backed Needletail	Hirundapus giganteus	M/N	3	LC
Asian Palm Swift	Cypsiurus balasiensis	R	3	LC
Pacific Swift	Apus pacificus	M	3	LC
House Swift	Apus nipalensis	R	3	LC
Coraciidae (Rollers) - 1 species				
Oriental Dollarbird	Eurystomus orientalis	R/M	4	LC
Alcedinidae (Kingfishers) - 1 species				
Stork-billed Kingfisher	Pelargopsis capensis	R	3	LC
Ruddy Kingfisher	Halcyon coromanda	M/R?	3	LC
White-throated Kingfisher	Halcyon smyrnensis	R	4	LC
Black-capped Kingfisher	Halcyon pileata	M	3	LC
Collared Kingfisher	Todiramphus chloris	R	5	LC
Blue-eared Kingfisher	Alcedo meninting	R	3	LC
Common Kingfisher	Alcedo atthis	M	4	LC
Oriental Dwarf Kingfisher	Ceyx erithaca	M	3	LC
Meropidae (Bee-eaters) - 2 species				
Blue-tailed Bee-eater	Merops philippinus	M	4	LC
Blue-throated Bee-eater	Merops viridis	R/M	4	LC
Bucerotidae (Hornbills) - 2 species				
Oriental Pied Hornbill	Anthracoceros albirostris	R	3	LC
Black Hornbill	Anthracoceros malayanus	N	2	NT
Megalaimidae (Asian Barbets) - 3 species				
Lineated Barbet	Psilopogon lineatus	I	4	LC
Red-crowned Barbet	Psilopogon rafflesii	R	3	NT
Coppersmith Barbet	Psilopogon haemacephalus	R	4	LC
Picidae (Woodpeckers) - 7 species				
Sunda Pygmy Woodpecker	Dendrocopos moluccensis	R	5	LC
White-bellied Woodpecker	Dryocopus javensis	R/E?	1	LC
Banded Woodpecker	Chrysophlegma miniaceum	R	4	LC
Laced Woodpecker	Picus vittatus	R	4	LC
Common Flameback	Dinopium javanense	R	4	LC
Rufous Woodpecker	Micropternus brachyurus	R	3	LC
Buff-rumped Woodpecker	Meiglyptes tristis	R/N?	1	LC
Falconidae (Falcons) - 7 species				
Black-thighed Falconet	Microhierax fringillarius	R/E?	1	LC
Lesser Kestrel	Falco naumanni	V	1	LC
Common Kestrel	Falco tinnunculus	M	2	LC
Amur Falcon	Falco amurensis	V	1	LC
Eurasian Hobby	Falco subbuteo	M	1	LC
Oriental Hobby	Falco severus	N	1	LC
Peregrine Falcon	Falco peregrinus	M/N	3	LC

Common name	Scientific name	Status	Abundance	IUCN Red List Status
Cacatuidae (Cockatoos) - 2 species				
Tanimbar Corella	Cacatua goffiniana	I	4	NT
Yellow-crested Cockatoo	Cacatua sulphurea	I	3	CR
Psittacidae (Parrots) - 7 species				
Blue-crowned Hanging Parrot	Loriculus galgulus	R	4	LC
Red Lory	Eos bornea	I	3	LC
Coconut Lorikeet	Trichoglossus haematodus	I	3	LC
Blue-rumped Parrot	Psittinus cyanurus	R	3	NT
Rose-ringed Parakeet	Psittacula krameri	I	3	LC
Red-breasted Parakeet	Psittacula alexandri	I	4	NT
Long-tailed Parakeet	Psittacula longicauda	R	4	NT
Eurylaimidae (Broadbills) - 2 species				
Green Broadbill	Calyptomena viridis	N	1	NT
Black-and-red Broadbill	Cymbirhynchus macrorhynchos	N	1	LC
Pittidae (Pittas) - 3 species				
Hooded Pitta	Pitta sordida	M	3	LC
Blue-winged Pitta	Pitta moluccensis	R/M	3	LC
Mangrove Pitta	Pitta megarhyncha	R	3	NT
Acanthizidae (Australasian Warblers) - 1 species				
Golden-bellied Gerygone	Gerygone sulphurea	R	4	LC
Tephrodornithidae (Woodshrikes and allies) - 1 species				
Black-winged Flycatcher-shrike	Hemipus hirundinaceus	N?	2	LC
Aegithinidae (Ioras) - 1 species				
Common Iora	Aegithina tiphia	R	5	LC
Campephagidae (Cuckooshrikes) - 4 species				
Lesser Cuckooshrike	Coracina fimbriata	R?	1	NT
Pied Triller	Lalage nigra	R	4	LC
Ashy Minivet	Pericrocotus divaricatus	M	4	LC
Scarlet Minivet	Pericrocotus speciosus	R	1	LC
Pachycephalidae (Whistlers and allies) - 1 species				
Mangrove Whistler	Pachycephala cinerea	R	3	LC
Laniidae (Shrikes) - 3 species				
Tiger Shrike	Lanius tigrinus	M	4	LC
Brown Shrike	Lanius cristatus	M	4	LC
Long-tailed Shrike	Lanius schach	R	3	LC
Oriolidae (Orioles) - 1 species				
Black-naped Oriole	Oriolus chinensis	R/M	5	LC
Dicruridae (Drongos) - 4 species				
Black Drongo	Dicrutus macrocercus	M	3	LC
Ashy Drongo	Dicrurus leucophaeus	M	2	LC
Crow-billed Drongo	Dicrurus annectans	M	3	LC
Greater Racket-tailed Drongo	Dicrurus paradiseus	R	4	LC
Rhipiduridae (Fantails) - 1 species				
Malaysian Pied Fantail	Rhipidura javanica	R	4	LC
Monarchidae (Monarchs) - 4 species				
Black-naped Monarch	Hypothymis azurea	R	3	LC

Common name	Scientific name	Status	Abundance	IUCN Red List Status
Blyth's Paradise Flycatcher	*Terpsiphone affinis*	M	4	LC
Amur Paradise Flycatcher	*Terpsiphone incei*	M	3	LC
Japanese Paradise Flycatcher	*Terpsiphone atrocaudata*	M	2	NT
Corvidae (Crows, Jays) - 2 species				
House Crow	*Corvus splendens*	I	5	LC
Large-billed Crow	*Corvus macrorhynchos*	R	4	LC
Pycnonotidae (Bulbuls) - 13 species				
Straw-headed Bulbul	*Pycnonotus zeylanicus*	R	4	EN
Black-and-white Bulbul	*Pycnonotus melanoleucos*	N	1	NT
Black-headed Bulbul	*Pycnonotus atriceps*	R	2	LC
Black-crested Bulbul	*Pycnonotus flaviventris*	I	3	LC
Red-whiskered Bulbul	*Pycnonotus jocosus*	I	3	LC
Sooty-headed Bulbul	*Pycnonotus aurigaster*	I	3	LC
Yellow-vented Bulbul	*Pycnonotus goiavier*	R	5	LC
Olive-winged Bulbul	*Pycnonotus plumosus*	R	4	LC
Cream-vented Bulbul	*Pycnonotus simplex*	R	3	LC
Asian Red-eyed Bulbul	*Pycnonotus brunneus*	R	3	LC
Buff-vented Bulbul	*Iole crypta*	N	1	NT
Streaked Bulbul	*Ixos malaccensis*	R/N?	2	NT
Cinereous Bulbul	*Hemixos cinereus*	N	3	LC
Hirundinidae (Swallows, Martins) - 5 species				
Sand Martin	*Riparia riparia*	M	3	LC
Barn Swallow	*Hirundo rustica*	M	5	LC
Pacific Swallow	*Hirundo tahitica*	R	5	LC
Asian House Martin	*Delichon dasypus*	M	2	LC
Red-rumped Swallow	*Cecropis daurica*	M	4	LC
Phylloscopidae (Leaf Warblers and allies) - 5 species				
Dusky Warbler	*Phylloscopus fuscatus*	M	1	LC
Arctic Warbler	*Phylloscopus borealis*	M	5	LC
Yellow-browed Warbler	*Phylloscopus inornatus*	M	2	LC
Sakhalin Leaf Warbler	*Phylloscopus borealoides*	M	2	LC
Eastern Crowned Warbler	*Phylloscopus coronatus*	M	3	LC
Acrocephalidae (Reed Warblers and allies) - 2 species				
Oriental Reed Warbler	*Acrocephalus orientalis*	M	4	LC
Black-browed Reed Warbler	*Acrocephalus bistrigiceps*	M	3	LC
Locustellidae (Grassbirds and allies) - 2 species				
Lanceolated Warbler	*Locustella lanceolata*	M	3	LC
Pallas's Grasshopper Warbler	*Locustella certhiola*	M	3	LC
Cisticolidae (Cisticolas and allies) - 6 species				
Zitting Cisticola	*Cisticola juncidis*	R	4	LC
Yellow-bellied Prinia	*Prinia flaviventris*	R	4	LC
Common Tailorbird	*Orthotomus sutorius*	R	4	LC
Dark-necked Tailorbird	*Orthotomus atrogularis*	R	4	LC
Rufous-tailed Tailorbird	*Orthotomus sericeus*	R	3	LC
Ashy Tailorbird	*Orthotomus ruficeps*	R	4	LC
Timaliidae (Babblers) - 2 species				
Chestnut-winged Babbler	*Stachyris erythroptera*	R	3	LC

Common name	Scientific name	Status	Abundance	IUCN Red List Status
Pin-striped Tit-Babbler	Macronus gularis	R	5	LC
Pellorneidae (Fulvettas, Ground babblers) - 3 species				
Abbott's Babbler	Malacocincla abbotti	R	3	LC
Short-tailed Babbler	Malacocincla malaccensis	R	4	NT
White-chested Babbler	Trichastoma rostratum	R	2	NT
Leiothrichidae (Laughingthrushes) - 2 species				
Chinese Hwamei	Garrulax canorus	I	3	LC
White-crested Laughingthrush	Garrulax leucolophus	I	4	LC
Zosteropidae (White-eyes) - 1 species				
Oriental White-eye	Zosterops palpebrosus	R/I?	4	LC
Irenidae (Fairy-bluebirds) - 1 species				
Asian Fairy-bluebird	Irena puella	R	4	LC
Sturnidae (Starlings) - 10 species				
Asian Glossy Starling	Aplonis panayensis	R	5	LC
Common Hill Myna	Gracula religiosa	R	4	LC
Crested Myna	Acridotheres cristatellus	I	1	LC
Javan Myna	Acridotheres javanicus	I	5	VU
Common Myna	Acridotheres tristis	R	4	LC
Red-billed Starling	Spodiopsar sericeus	V	1	LC
Daurian Starling	Agropsar sturninus	M	4	LC
Chestnut-cheeked Starling	Agropsar philippensis	V	1	LC
White-shouldered Starling	Sturnia sinensis	M	3	LC
Rosy Starling	Pastor roseus	V	2	LC
Turdidae (Thrushes) - 3 species				
Orange-headed Thrush	Geokichla citrina	M	3	LC
Siberian Thrush	Geokichla sibirica	M	2	LC
Eyebrowed Thrush	Turdus obscurus	M	3	LC
Muscicapidae (Chats, Old World flycatchers) - 20 species				
Oriental Magpie-Robin	Copsychus saularis	R	4	LC
White-rumped Shama	Copsychus malabaricus	R	3	LC
Grey-streaked Flycatcher	Muscicapa griseisticta	V	1	LC
Dark-sided Flycatcher	Muscicapa sibirica	M	3	LC
Asian Brown Flycatcher	Muscicapa dauurica	M	5	LC
Brown-streaked Flycatcher	Muscicapa williamsoni	N	3	LC
Ferruginous Flycatcher	Muscicapa ferruginea	M	3	LC
Chinese Blue Flycatcher	Cyornis glaucicomans	M	1	LC
Mangrove Blue Flycatcher	Cyornis rufigastra	R	2	LC
Brown-chested Jungle Flycatcher	Cyornis brunneatus	M	3	VU
Zappey's Flycatcher	Cyanoptila cumatilis	M	?	NT
Blue-and-white Flycatcher	Cyanoptila cyanomelana	M	?	LC
Siberian Blue Robin	Larvivora cyane	M	4	LC
Yellow-rumped Flycatcher	Ficedula zanthopygia	M	4	LC
Narcissus Flycatcher	Ficedula narcissina	M	1	LC
Green-backed Flycatcher	Ficedula elisae	M	2	NT
Mugimaki Flycatcher	Ficedula mugimaki	M	3	LC
Blue Rock Thrush	Monticola solitarius	M	2	LC
White-throated Rock Thrush	Monticola gularis	M	2	LC

Common name	Scientific name	Status	Abundance	IUCN Red List Status
Stejneger's Stonechat	Saxicola stejnegeri	M	2	LC
Chloropseidae (Leafbirds) - 3 species				
Greater Green Leafbird	Chloropsis sonnerati	R	3	VU
Lesser Green Leafbird	Chloropsis cyanopogon	R	2	NT
Blue-winged Leafbird	Chloropsis cochinchinensis	R	4	LC
Dicaeidae (Flowerpeckers) - 5 species				
Scarlet-breasted Flowerpecker	Prionochilus thoracicus	N	1	NT
Thick-billed Flowerpecker	Dicaeum agile	N/R?	2	LC
Yellow-vented Flowerpecker	Dicaeum chysorrheum	N/R?	2	LC
Orange-bellied Flowerpecker	Dicaeum trigonostigma	R	4	LC
Scarlet-backed Flowerpecker	Dicaeum cruentatum	R	4	LC
Nectariniidae (Sunbirds, Spiderhunters) - 9 species				
Plain Sunbird	Anthreptes simplex	R	1	LC
Brown-throated Sunbird	Anthreptes malacensis	R	5	LC
Van Hasselt's Sunbird	Leptocoma brasiliana	R/N	4	LC
Copper-throated Sunbird	Leptocoma calcostetha	R	4	LC
Olive-backed Sunbird	Cinnyris jugularis	R	5	LC
Crimson Sunbird	Aethopyga siparaja	R	4	LC
Little Spiderhunter	Arachnothera longirostra	R	4	LC
Thick-billed Spiderhunter	Arachnothera crassirostris	R	2	LC
Yellow-eared Spiderhunter	Arachnothera chrysogenys	R	2	LC
Passeridae (Old World Sparrows) - 2 species				
House Sparrow	Passer domesticus	I	3	LC
Eurasian Tree Sparrow	Passer montanus	R	5	LC
Ploceidae (Weavers) - 2 species				
Streaked Weaver	Ploceus manyar	I	2	LC
Baya Weaver	Ploceus philippinus	R	4	LC
Estrildidae (Waxbills, Munias and allies) - 5 species				
White-rumped Munia	Lonchura striata	R	2	LC
Javan Munia	Lonchura leucogastroides	I	3	LC
Scaly-breasted Munia	Lonchura punctulata	R	4	LC
Chestnut Munia	Lonchura atricapilla	R	4	LC
White-headed Munia	Lonchura maja	R	3	LC
Motacillidae (Wagtails, Pipits) - 9 species				
Forest Wagtail	Dendronanthus indicus	M	4	LC
Eastern Yellow Wagtail	Motacilla tschutschensis	M	4	LC
Citrine Wagtail	Motacilla citreola	V	1	LC
Grey Wagtail	Motacilla cinerea	M	3	LC
White Wagtail	Motacilla alba	M	3	LC
Richard's Pipit	Anthus richardi	M	1	LC
Paddyfield Pipit	Anthus rufulus	R	5	LC
Olive-backed Pipit	Anthus hodgsoni	M	1	LC
Red-throated Pipit	Anthus cervinus	M	2	LC
Emberizidae (Buntings) - 1 species				
Yellow-breasted Bunting	Emberiza aureola	V	1	EN

FURTHER INFORMATION

Websites and E-groups
The growing interest in birdwatching and nature photography in recent years has spawned numerous online groups and websites where information on identification and latest sightings are being disseminated.

Nature Society (Singapore) Bird Group
singaporebirdgroup.wordpress.com; facebook.com/groups/singaporebirdgroup/ – The blog provides regular updates on sightings, plus regular articles on ornithology in Singapore. The facebook group is a regular platform for sharing sightings.

Nature Photographic Society (NPSS)
npss.org.sg – another excellent source of information on recent sightings, and a platform where bird photographs are shared.

Singapore Bird Project
singaporebirds.com - a large collection of photographs and notes on birds in Singapore.

Cloudbirders.com cloudbirders.com – A vast repository of birdwatching reports from around the world. Useful for planning trips.

Xeno-canto xeno-canto.org – a vast online repository of bird sounds covering most of the world's birds, and a good starting point to familiarise oneself with bird calls.

Oriental Bird Images
orientalbirdimages.org – a large online repository of bird photographs with an emphasis on the Oriental region; a useful resource for bird identication.

eBird ebird.org – a global online platform for birdwatchers to share sight records and checklists.

Organisations
Nature Society (Singapore) 510 Geylang Road #02-05, The Sunflower, Singapore 389466. nss.org.sg
The Nature Society (Singapore) conducts regular birdwatching walks to many of the sites described in this book, and also organises talks, surveys and other activities relevant to birdwatching and conservation.

National Parks Board 1 Cluny Road, Singapore 259569. nparks.gov.sg
The National Parks Board website is an excellent resource for information on all public parks and nature reserves in Singapore, and provides details on access. Regular nature walks are also conducted by its volunteers.

Lee Kong Chian Natural History Museum National University of Singapore, 6 Science Drive 2, Blk S6, #03-01, Singapore 117546. lkcnhm.nus.edu.sg
The Lee Kong Chian Natural History Museum houses a large collection of Southeast Asian animal and plant specimens. Its staff and volunteer guides organise regular workshops, outreach events and nature walks. The museum also publishes a variety of nature-based mobile apps, natural history books and two online journals: *Raffles Bulletin of Zoology* and *Nature in Singapore*.

South-east Asian Biodiversity Society
504 Choa Chu Kang Street 51, #01-173, Singapore 680504.
Email: tropicalbiologist@gmail.com
The South-east Asian Biodiversity Society holds a repository of information on conservation sites throughout Singapore and is a good resource centre for those interested in birds, biodiversity and conservation.

Suggested Reading
Books
Brazil, M. (2009). *Birds of East Asia.* Christopher Helm.

Davison, G.W.H., Ng, P.K.L. and Ho, H.C. eds. (2008). *The Singapore Red Data Book*. Nature Society (Singapore).

Eaton, J., van Balen, B., Brickle, N.W. and Rheindt, F.E. (2016). *Birds of the Indonesian Archipelago*. Lynx Edicions.

Gan, J., Tan, M. and Li, D. (2012). *Migratory Birds of Sungei Buloh Wetland Reserve*, 2nd edn. National Parks Board.

Jeyarajasingam, A. and Pearson, A. (2012). *A Field Guide to the Birds of Peninsular Malaysia and Singapore*, 2nd edn. Oxford University Press.

Lim, K.C., Lim, K.S., Low, B.W., Yong, D.L. and Goh, Y.Y., eds. (2010). *Birds in a Garden City*. Photographic Society of Singapore (with photographs by Lee Tiah Khee).

Lim, K.S. and Gardner, D. (1997). *An Illustrated Field Guide to the Birds of Singapore*. Suntree Publishing.

Lim, K.S. (2009). *The Avifauna of Singapore*. Nature Society (Singapore).

Lim, K.S. and Lim, K.C., eds. (2009). *State of Singapore's Wild Birds and Bird Habitats: Results of the Annual Bird Census 1996–2005*. Nature Society (Singapore).

McClure, H.E. (1998) *Migration and Survival of the Birds of Asia*. White Lotus Press.

Robson, C. (2009). *A Field Guide to the Birds of Southeast Asia*. New Holland.

Wells, D.R. (1997). *The Birds of the Thai–Malay Peninsula, Volume 1: Non-Passerines*. Academic Press.

Wells, D.R. (2007). *The Birds of the Thai–Malay Peninsula, Volume 2: Passerines*. Christopher Helm.

Academic Papers and Articles

Castelletta, M., Sodhi, N.S. and Subaraj, R. (2000). Heavy extinctions of forest avifauna in Singapore: lessons for biodiversity conservation in Southeast Asia. *Conservation Biology* 14, 1870–80.

Harris, J.B.C., Yong, D.L., Sodhi, N.S., Subaraj, R., Fordham, D.A., & Brook, B.W. (2013). Changes in autumn arrival of long-distance migratory birds in Southeast Asia. *Climate Research* 57, 133-141.

Sadanandan, K. & Rheindt, F. E. (2015). Genetic diversity of a tropical rainforest understory bird in an urban fragmented landscape. *The Condor* 117, 447-459.

Yong, D.L. (2009). Persistence of Babbler (Timaliidae) communities in Singapore forests. *Nature in Singapore* 2, 365–71.

Yong, D.L. (2011). The White-bellied Woodpecker in Singapore. *Nature Watch* 19(1), 18–24.

Yong, D.L. (2011). Eating aliens: the diet of the grey-headed fish-eagle *Ichthyophaga ichthyaetus* in Singapore. *Forktail* 27, 97–9.

Yong, D.L., Lim, K.S., Lim, K.C., Tan, T., Teo, S. and Ho, H.C. (2017). Significance of the globally threatened Straw-headed Bulbul *Pycnonotus zeylanicus* populations in Singapore: a last straw for the species? *Bird Conservation International*. In press.

ACKNOWLEDGEMENTS

We are grateful to a number of individuals who helped us tremendously during the preparation of this book. Alfred Chia, Bert Harris, Geoffrey Davison, Lim Kim Seng, Richard Carden, and James Eaton provided many useful comments on the initial manuscript. Liu Yang helped with the Chinese names while Tou Jingyi helped with the Malay names. Many photographers responded quickly to our requests with their excellent images, especially Con Foley, Lim Kim Seng, Francis Yap, Cheng Heng Yee, Frankie Cheong, Ronald Orenstein, Alan OwYong, Quek Oon Hong, Shahril Ahmad, Andrew Tan, John and Jemi Holmes, Michelle and Peter Wong, Myron Tay, Raphaël Jordan, Seetoh Yew Wai, Syahputra, and Mohamad Zahidi. We thank John Beaufoy for conceiving the book, and for his constant encouragement, and our editorial team (Rosemary Wilkinson, Hugh Brazier, Bikram Grewal and Alpana Khare) for their immense support. Lastly, we thank our families for putting up with the many late hours spent working on the manuscript.